Wobbles:
an Olympic Story

Nadine Neumann

Glass House Books
Brisbane

Glass House Books
an imprint of Interactive Publications
Treetop Studio • 9 Kuhler Court
Carindale, Queensland, Australia 4152
sales@ipoz.biz
ipoz.biz/GHB/GHB.htm

First published by Interactive Publications, 2009
© Nadine Neumann

All rights reserved. Without limiting the rights under copyright reserved above, no part of this publication may be reproduced, stored in or introduced into a retrieval system, or transmitted, in any form or by any means (electronic, mechanical, photocopying, recording or otherwise), without the prior written permission of the copyright owner and the publisher of this book.

Printed in 11 pt Book Antiqua on 16 pt Book Antiqua by Konway Printhouse, Malaysia.

National Library of Australia Cataloguing-in-Publication entry:

Author:	Neumann, Nadine.
Title:	Wobbles : an Olympic story / Nadine Neumann.
ISBN:	9781921479298 (pbk.).
Subjects:	Neumann, Nadine. Swimmers--Australia--Biography. Women swimmers--Australia--Biography.

Dewey Number: 797.21092

for you, my reader

Acknowledgments

Cover Images: *Khonji, iStockphoto (front); Reece Scannell (back)*

Jacket Design: *David Reiter*

Author Photos: *Michael Dyer*

"If we shadows have offended,
Think but this, and all is mended,
That you have but slumber'd here
While these visions did appear…"
   – William Shakespeare, A Midsummer Night's Dream

I would like to warmly thank all those who appear in these pages by name or otherwise. Without you, I would not be me. It is no easy task to write about others from an honest-to-goodness-point-of-view-at-the-time, and while some of you may feel as though you have been hard done by in this story, I hope you can find it in your hearts to forgive my short-sighted attitudes of the past and, rather, take the hand of friendship and gratitude I offer to you now. In Puck's immortal words:

"Gentles, do not reprehend:
if you pardon, we will mend…
Give me your hands, if we be friends,
And Robin shall restore amends."

Thank you to those wonderful people who have encouraged, cheered and cajoled me along these many years: Rose Moxham, for telling me I should write in the first place; Geoff McGeachin and Wilma Schinella, for convincing me I had something worth publishing; John Konrads, for your Foreword and your inspiration when I was small; Catherine Hammond, Helen Turner, Geoff Armstrong and Mark Evans for your insightful, honest and invaluable feedback. My fabulous editor, Lauren Daniels, thank you for your expert eye when I thought I was done! To my family, for your part in this story and the project; your unfaltering faith in me has been the driving force when I doubted it was possible.

My husband, Michael – you keep me sane, honest and real. And to my publisher, IP, thank you for taking a chance on me.

Thanks to Visva-Bharati University for permission to use 'Fruit Gathering' from the **Collected Poems and Plays** *of Rabindranath Tagore.*

Glass House Books
Wobbles: an Olympic Story

Nadine began swimming when she was seven years old and by the time she was eight, she knew she wanted to be an Olympian. She overcame Chronic Fatigue Syndrome at the age of 15, only to have her dream of an Olympic berth in Barcelona shattered by a broken neck. Nadine fought back to achieve her goal, swimming at the 1996 Atlanta Olympic Games in the 200m Breaststroke where she came 6th in the final in a personal best time. She went on to captain the Australian Swimming Team at the 1998 Commonwealth Games and 1999 Pan Pacific Championships.

On retiring from competitive swimming, Nadine had to completely redefine her life. She struggled with depression for five years while studying for dual teaching qualifications (Primary and Secondary English) and working in PR & Marketing. In 2004 she began teaching English at high school and it was then that she began seriously shaping the memoir she had started in 1999 as part of her university degree.

Since Nadine's story captured the attention of the media in 1996 she has enjoyed success as a motivational speaker on both the corporate and schools circuits. She says that one of her greatest joys is "connecting with an audience and feeling that my experiences, in some small way, might help inspire them."

Nadine lives in Newcastle, NSW with her husband and one-year-old son. She spends her days cleaning up after her little boy and trying to find time to work on her next writing projects: a historical novel based on the lives of her grandparents (French/Jewish and German) and a picture book that uses the Humpty Dumpty nursery rhyme as a basis for an exploration of bullying. She has plans for four more novels beyond this.

Glass House Books
Brisbane

Contents

Foreword	ix
Take Your Marks	1
One	7
Two	53
Three	141
Go	233
Beyond	239

Photo by Reece Scannell

Foreword

A continual reward for Olympic champions is the fantastic sense of gratification that comes from inspiring young athletes. Sports history testifies to this phenomenon, particularly when you look at the medals Australians have won at the Olympic Games in the men's 1500m Freestyle – Andrew 'Boy' Charlton in 1924 and 1928 gave rise to John Marshall in 1948 who handed over to Murray Rose in 1956, inspiring me in 1960, then Bobby Windle in 1964, Greg Brough in 1968, Stephen Holland in 1976, Max Metzker in 1980, who later inspired the next generation with Glen Housman in 1992 and Kieran Perkins in 1992 and 1996 and finally Grant Hackett in 2000, 2004 and 2008. Who is being inspired by Grant Hackett as they're doing the miles now? Watch this space for 2012!

In 1972, 15-year-old Shane Gould swam faster over 1500m than my world record of 1960, transcending any gender gap that may have been perceived (although nobody dared to speak about this in the old days of amateurism!). Shane was coached by the great Forbes Carlile and while my coach, Don Talbot, may have produced more world record holders and Olympic medallists, Don took us to Forbes for testing of blood, cardiograms, etc., during the dawning era of worldwide sports science. Swimming, like all sports, is a team sport, and this sharing of knowledge and encouragement has been part of the swimming culture since the beginning. Coach, club, physio, team mates and family all play a role, but in the end Nadine has to touch first, just as David Beckham has to net the ball passed to him.

Artist Margaret Olley once said, 'Giving is like a permanent receiving', and this is true of all kinds of giving, whether you are aware of it or not. I didn't know that a very determined young girl was inspired by my picture on the wall of her swimming pool. At the time, I was engrossed in my corporate career with a young family in Melbourne and hardly ever went to a swim meet. I only vaguely knew of Nadine through the press.

What a thrill, then, to read Nadine's manuscript, to realise that she had been speaking with me all along:

"I wondered if John Konrads ever did the open 800m Freestyle at the Castlereagh District Championships, at the Auburn Swimming Centre. I wondered if he would laugh knowingly at how cold and windy the nights could be, and how it always threatened to rain while you waited without shelter behind the starting blocks… I imagined how impressed with my dedication he would be and how he would wish me good luck."

As an old champion, that's about as good as it gets!

Nadine's story is unique in that it says what she thought as a young girl, warts and all. In my opinion, too many sports biographies glorify the athlete's success and pain with the glossy view of hindsight, but they leave out the real, deep down thoughts which Nadine unflinchingly reveals. I think it's an absolute must for any parent of an ambitious youngster to have a glimpse of what may lie ahead. It's not as pretty as the TV makes it out to be.

There certainly is a generation gap and I've got three children to prove it. What I thought and how I articulated those feelings may have been different from the kids of today, but despite this, there are some aspects of the human experience that are the same for every generation. The road to elite sporting success is one of those common experiences and a parent may not be able to imagine that their 12-year-old might want to scream "Fuck!" when the road gets hard, but I think it is crucial for our children's sense of acceptance, support and love that we don't hide under a blanket of our own inhibitions. They must feel able to talk to us in any way that works best for them, otherwise, like Nadine did, they may get lost along the way.

For all its brutal honesty, in the end this is an uplifting story; one of the satisfaction, the triumph and the sheer fun of going after a dream, of overcoming phenomenal odds and learning about yourself along the way. I'm sure you'll be as touched and inspired as I was.

Thank you, Nadine, for telling it as it really is!

– John Konrads

Take Your Marks

There will be storms, child
There will be storms
And with each tempest
You will seem to stand alone
Against cruel winds
But with time, the rage and fury
Shall subside
And when the sky clears
You will find yourself
Clinging to someone
You would have never known
But for storms.

– *Storms,* Margie De Merrell

1.

"Will you make it in the end, through all the twists and bends?"

– *"Weir"*, Killing Heidi

May 2000.
    Homebush, Sydney.
    Australian Championships and Selection Trials.
    The dream – the Olympic Games in my home town, in my home pool this September.
    It's the 200m Breaststroke for me, and to be selected I have to touch the wall first or second ahead of the toughest world-class field in any country on the planet. My mind is tight with voices, full of ideas too fluid to grasp and too heavy to probe. I'm nervous again and, as always, I'm categorising the mental static: good – bad; useful – destructive; true – false; keep – discard.
    Two months ago a few of my training partners came down with an ugly flu. I was stronger. I kept it at bay and continued training. Two weeks ago more of the girls succumbed, but I held it off. Two days before the 200m Breaststroke and my body betrayed me. Again. It has happened before, at other crucial times, but this race means much, much more…

It is the night before my final and I am so sick I can't stop shaking. It's devouring all my energy just to stay positive; just positive enough to produce the winning swim – a perfect symphony of mind, technique, stamina and spirit – against the odds. Again. I've done it before, at other crucial times, but this race means much, much more.
    Tonight I dream of floating in slow motion music. I am safe, embraced by a hum of distant voices that echo like thoughts through water. My heart dances to the rhythm. I am the water and I am the song until morning brings birth and I suddenly burn in competition's fluorescent lights.

The heat swim passed without a murmur yesterday. Each competitor plays their cards close. I am in the final and that is all that matters. Today I will find my place in folklore. Nobody needs to know the rest.

But I am sick. Denial won't fix it. It is not a psychosomatic self-sabotage, like it seems to have been every other time. It's a simple, scorching flu that everyone else has had, so I strut with a confident smile and say, "I've swum with a sniff and a cough before at other crucial times and I can do it again, because this race means much, much more."

Pool deck in the buzz of warm-up time. The hundreds of hopefuls jostling for their patch of limited lane space to hone, perfect and make final contact with the water before their moment in the spotlight. My coach, Glenn, looks at his stopwatch. "Thirty-five point six. Do you want to do another one?"

I was swimming 34.5 easily for my 50m Breaststroke pace checks only days ago. On a regular day I would do another couple to make sure my synapses realise they are about to race, go fast, wake up! But I'm heavy, my bones ache, my limbs are petulant.

"Think I need to save what I have left for the real thing."

He understands as a coach does, and attempts a mask of cheer. I am buoyant in return. I will not falter. I've worked too damned hard for too long to just let go and it's my turn to sing the song of the triumphant!

As the evening deepens and my 200m Breaststroke final approaches, I ponder the words for just a moment – evening, final – and categorise them as bad, destructive, false, discard. Today will be the day of miracles, again, like it has been before, at other crucial times.

My turn. The announcer calls my name and lists my achievements like a catalogue. I am a hero in his words. My body responds with a tremor. Good. Each cell sparks as I stand to face the watching world and the crowd bellows support.

"Go, Nads!"

Crude, but warming. It doesn't seem so long ago that they

called me 'Wobbles' – 'Wobbs', 'Wob-dan', 'Wobber'. They tried 'Earth Shaker' for a short time, but nicknames need to be discernable over the clamour of swimming crowds and concentration's barrier. Wobbles made everyone take note, so that was the one that stuck. It was aptly chosen at the time and now I think I hear them chanting 'Wo-bbles – Wo-bbles…' from somewhere far away.

Colette, my sister, whistles; I know it's her. I feel more like Wobbles than Nads today and she's trying to turn the tide for me. I think I see the water ripple as she pierces through the roar and I hold onto that sound. It bounces and fills the stadium like the music from my dream and I feel it shimmer through my core – clarity, strength, precision – I am almost ready to race.

A TV camera is thrust in my face to show Australia what lies beneath the brief CV of a local – so much, too much to share it in a single gesture, but I need to be free of it all to race. My body has been trained to move to an ancient rhythm, but I have to give the conductor space. I know what happens when my mind muddles the flow, when I try too hard, and today of all days I cannot allow it to come between me and that song I know is mine.

I blow a kiss into the lens and watch as all my neatly categorised thoughts, my light and my dark float from my palm into the eye of the nation. I am free and ready.

I kneel reverently at the water's edge, blocking out the rest of the introductions, swirling with my hands, acquainting my skin to the liquid silkiness. I thank the Universe for this moment and surrender to Fate. I cup the water in my hands and focus:

Three quick, violent splashes to the face – mind be still.
Two slower bursts of water to the chest – heart be strong.
Two, more deliberate, over the head – body be powerful.
One final explosion of water to the face – spirit shine.

I cannot remember when this routine started; it has been part of me for eons. My cool, blue element trickles over skin. Body and water become one. The starter's whistle is shrill and sets eight in motion. We climb the blocks – three steps. It seems higher than normal, or perhaps today I am further away.

"Take your marks."

Four laps as fast, as fierce, as flawless as I can.

I draw three deep lung-fulls from the silent atmosphere. Always the number three. Conductor taps. I am poised. The world holds its breath.

And in the pause, as I teeter towards the blue, I see it all played out before me like a film – every laughing, screaming, singing moment that has brought me here, to the Olympic Swimming Trials, Sydney, 2000.

One

When you are inspired by some great
purpose, some extraordinary project,
all your thoughts break their bonds;
Your mind transcends limitations,
your consciousness expands in every direction,
and you find yourself in a new, great
and wonderful world.
Dormant force, faculties and talents
become alive, and you discover yourself
to be a greater person by far
than you ever dreamed
yourself to be.

Patanjali

2.

"From little things big things grow"

– Paul Kelly

"Her respiratory system's just weak. Something like swimming will help strengthen her lungs and, well, overall make her a bit sturdier. Hey, Nadine? How would you like to swim?"

I thought maybe Dr Fisher was really a fish in disguise. Maybe I was a fish in disguise too and maybe that's why I had trouble breathing on land.

"Mummy says it sounds like I'm trying to breathe underwater all the time, snorting and gurgling."

Adults always think children are being funny when they're not.

On the way home from Dr Fisher's, Mummy bought some strawberries just like the ones I had in the hospital when Dr Fisher said we should try an operation to take out my adenoids. At six, 'adenoids' sounded like something from outer space, so I agreed it would be a good idea to get rid of them. I didn't want to be a home for aliens, even ones tiny enough to fit in my nose.

I was nervous at the hospital, and they wouldn't even let me wear my new pyjamas for the operation. I was upset about the back-to-front gown they gave me until a kind doctor wearing a white dress and baker's hat arrived in the room. He looked funnier than I did, so I figured it was just the uniform. He put a mask over my face and I was glad he had brought something to catch the nasty adenoids as they tried to escape out of my nose.

"What does it smell like, pet?" the doctor asked. "Patients tell me it smells like something different every day, so what is it today?"

I wondered how many people were running around with aliens living in their noses if he was doing this kind of thing every day. The mask smelled like one of those soft jellies I used to get in ten cent bags of mixed lollies – not the strawberries and cream, they were my favourites, but the ones I didn't like.

"Pineapp..."

When I woke up after the operation my body was still fast asleep. I could hear everything, but my eyes wouldn't open. The doctors were talking about me and I wanted to laugh because I felt funny, but I couldn't. I wondered how much power those adenoids had.

Later, Mummy sat next to me with a 'Get Well Soon' balloon.

"You are such a brave mouse. Are you hungry?" she asked as Papa and Colette came with strawberries and a *Sesame Street* colouring book all for me. It felt like I hadn't eaten for centuries! They were the tastiest strawberries ever, so I ate them all in one go. In minutes, they came back up – all over my new colouring book.

Those adenoids weren't the problem after all and that's why we went back to Dr Fisher. He must have figured out my secret identity when I was asleep in the hospital and I guess that's why he asked me if I wanted to swim to strengthen my lungs. I thought I had hidden my fishiness quite well up until then.

I remember the first time I thought I was a fish was when I was six, before I knew I had adenoids, when I tried gymnastics. I had a new leotard to make me feel good on my first day. It had red and white stripes with long sleeves and it looked very smart, like a Christmas candy cane. But my hand was sweating in Mummy's because secretly, I was terrified.

The teacher was a square lady with a huge, booming voice that echoed around the whole hall. She sounded like I imagined God would sound when He's angry. She took me to the biggest trampoline I had ever seen – much bigger than the one my friend Katie had at her house. Mummy sat near the door, smiling. I think the square lady scared her, too. The other children were so good at tumbling and bouncing and swinging. Mummy said I looked 'utterly intimidated'. I didn't feel as clever as the other boys and girls.

When it was my turn in the middle of the 'tramp' (I tried to use the right words so the others wouldn't know that I was new), my knees shook. I had to concentrate not to pee into my shiny new leotard, but I could feel a sneeze coming on. All the chalk dust in the hall made my nose tickle so much that I didn't hear the teacher shouting at me to start jumping.

I bounced as high as I dared and it felt like I was almost at the moon. "Sit!" came the order from the angry God. I knew what that meant because I had watched the others obey the same orders, so I stuck my legs out in front and hoped that bouncing on my bottom wouldn't make my bladder burst. I nearly flew sideways over the edge and I wanted to get down, but my turn wasn't over yet – back to the middle and bounce again!

"Front!" boomed Mrs Square-Angry-God-Teacher. This meant going face-first towards the trampoline and I could feel the water from my bladder move up to my eyes because it knew what was coming. I stuck my legs out behind me, shut my eyes tight, folded my hands under my chin, and landed, first on my legs, then I hit my head into my hands... knees, face, knees, face... I felt like a poor little sardine flopping on the sand while the children watched me slowly drown in all the oxygen. I knew then that I did not belong on land, playing land-children's games, but how do you tell your friends you're a fish?

So, after a giant-sized headache, a sore neck and going home in tears, I was a little bit scared of Katie's trampoline, even if it was smaller. I sometimes pretended to have a sore leg so I could sit and watch while Katie flew in the air like an angel.

Katie used to go swimming every Saturday at a proper swimming club, so Mummy and Papa knew where to start asking when Dr Fisher made the swimming suggestion for my gurgling lungs.

"We go to club every Saturday," Katie's dad said. "You should come along."

"That sounds perfect, hey, Nadine? Katie and John swim in the races. Do you want to give that a go?"

I was all dressed up like a ballerina, but have you ever seen a fish move like a ballerina? Katie was the one who could really dance. She looked like a fairy queen and when she spun around and around her blonde curly hair bounced like a golden sun. We were putting on a concert for the grown-ups and I was the fairy queen's helper. Colette was in it too, even though she was really too little to be anything more than a nuisance. I would never admit that she was a better dancer than me, especially since she was only 3½. Grown-ups always smile at the cute ones and the talented ones, never at the fish.

"They have diving boards and everything," Katie said, with a wave of her wand.

"Yeah! That'd be fun. We could play Marco Polo! Do they have a slippery slide, too?"

"Nah, just different pools like little ones for babies and an inside one that's really warm."

It sounded good. While Katie made up the dances we were to perform in our concert, I let my mind wander. Mostly, I was less-than-gifted when it came to sport, but I was glad at the idea that Colette would have a separate baby-pool to go to where the adults could smile at her in her floaties without me having to watch. I had already graduated from swimming lessons at Forbes and Ursula Carlile's pool at Cross Street in Ryde, so I could swim and she couldn't. I had a head start – and I was a fish.

One of my teachers at Cross Street was Paul. He signed my 'Nadine Neumann has successfully completed 12½m Backstroke' certificate. It was a winter afternoon when Paul said I should try the 12½m clothed swim. If I did it, I could start doing lessons at the big pool at Ryde. I only had my tracksuit and sneakers that I had worn to my lesson, but Papa said I could have a go. It was like I had jelly in my tummy, but I wasn't scared. It was the longest, hardest, hottest swim of my life! I swallowed litres of steamy chlorine water. I tried to splash my feet but they dragged to the bottom in my heavy sneakers; I lifted my arms, but my tracksuit tangled around me and I thought my chest was going to burst. I was that shiny, suffering little sardine again, but this time I was caught in a net and I wriggled and squirmed to try and get free. And I did it! Paul cheered and Papa smiled so big that I could hardly see his eyes. I got two jelly babies and two jelly beans, and I was allowed to choose the colours. Also, I got a cold from my wet clothes.

I don't really know why we never went to lessons at the Ryde pool. Maybe Mummy and Papa knew that I would have more fun if we could go with Katie. I secretly hoped I would be the one who swam the best, because I had never been the best before, and the dance that Katie designed for our concert made her and Collie look beautiful.

* * *

"Six and under 25m Freestyle to the marshalling area please. Six and under 25m Freestyle."

"Colette, that's your race," Mummy called from the side of the pool.

"I know!" Collie said as she swung upside down from the hand railing. I couldn't swing like that anymore because, at eight, my head nearly hit the ground. I could do summersaults around the rail if I spun really quickly, though, and sometimes Collie tried to do it, too. She was always copying me. Collie thought she was all grown up because she was swimming in the six and under age group even though she was only 4½, but I found ways of reminding her that she was really still just little.

It was cold and a bit rainy that day at club races. Katie didn't come to club anymore, but I had other friends, so it didn't matter. The boys played handball between their races and I liked to join in even though I was not very good at it. They were nice and never told me to get lost; at least not to my face. But sometimes they would already have a full court with people waiting, so I would just watch and wish I was like my Papa – he was great at ball games. When he was young, he was captain of his Rugby Union team in Paris, and his father, my Pépé, introduced the game of handball to France from Hungary. Papa never got to like swimming and I felt sorry for him for that. Growing up in a place that gets so cold in the winter and where they don't have beaches like we do must be really hard. Papa always said, 'It is beyond me why you would get cold and uncomfortable for any reason other than washing', and I wondered if he had cold showers even though the hot tap always worked well at home. Maybe he liked the water being uncomfortable, like an old habit. Anyway, when we were at club races, he did time-keeping and he remembered all of my best times, which was lucky, because I could never remember what to write on my entry cards.

Mummy did time-keeping too, and on that particular cold and rainy Saturday she was taking the times for Lane 5. She sometimes swam in the races as well and I was teaching her how to do Butterfly. She was a good swimmer, but she grew up in East Germany and when she was going to start training, her family had to escape from the government before they closed the gate in the big wall in Berlin and trapped the whole family inside. They had to catch a train in the middle of the night, leaving all their things behind; ever their swimsuits. I felt sorry for her too, because they were really poor, so she couldn't get another swimsuit to swim at a proper club. Mummy was like the opposite of Papa – she couldn't catch or throw (just like me) and she couldn't remember my times, but she could tell exactly what was wrong with my stroke and she always tried to help me fix it. Sometimes I wished she wouldn't.

As I watched Colette swim her 25m Freestyle race on that cold and rainy Saturday, she looked like a miniature mermaid and when she got to the end rope she bobbed like a little cork in the waves. She was so clever. She taught herself all four strokes without having any lessons! I thought it was lucky that we raced in different age groups because I would have hated for her to beat me. Mummy and Papa said that it was okay to have a little bit of 'sibling rivalry' because it made us work hard, as long as we loved each other and didn't fight. But sometimes it was hard not to get angry that she was so clever.

"Eight years 50m Freestyle to the marshalling area. Eight years 50m Freestyle."

I was cold and thinking about clever Collie. She was like Mummy and Papa combined into one person. She was born when I was 3½ and she could instantly do everything. Everyone adored her. She was cute when I was ugly because I lost my teeth. I learned to knit at school, and she copied me! All my parents' adult friends said 'at the age of three she should not possess the fine motor skills to knit so proficiently', but she could still do it. And now she could swim like a dolphin.

"Nadine, did you hear that?" Mummy called from time-keeping in Lane 5. "Your race has been marshalled. Are you warm enough?"

"Yeah."

Mummy was always checking on us.

I was a bit nervous about racing my 50m Freestyle on that grey Saturday because I was close to swimming the qualifying time for a competition where the really good swimmers went – Castlereagh District. If I didn't swim fast enough at club that day, we would have to go to competitions at other pools around Sydney until I did make it. Mummy would pack food – bean salad, marinated chicken legs (my favourite) or chicken schnitzel, rockmelon, pasta – that we'd carry in plastic containers to Auburn, Blacktown, Warringah, Sun Valley, Galston, Gosford, Hornsby, Killarney Heights, Epping, wherever the races were. All the swimming families did the same thing. Some meets lasted for one afternoon and others, like Castlereagh, went on for a whole weekend or two. If I made it to Castlereagh, I'd try to do the qualifying times for the Metropolitan Championships, then State, then Nationals. I didn't know what happened after that.

"Take your marks…"

I wondered what it would be like to swim at the Olympics.

"BANG!"

My goggles slipped halfway down my face and squashed my nose. The googly bits caught the water and spilled it into my mouth whenever I turned my head to breathe. I was sure fish didn't feel this uncomfortable when they got water in their mouths. I wished for gills, but they didn't come. Maybe Dr Fisher was wrong and I wasn't really a fish after all. I stroked and stroked and kicked my hardest. But I wasn't very fast.

Puffing, I walked over to Papa. I had scratchy bits in my throat and a stitch from all the water I had swallowed.

"Oh well, maybe next weekend," he said with his ever-friendly face.

He was watching Megan power down his lane towards the wall. She was in the ten years age group and she was the best swimmer in the whole world. She was so strong and tanned and good at netball too, and everyone liked her. I wondered if she knew what happened after you got to Nationals. I secretly copied everything Megan did.

She had a long, relaxed Freestyle with a slow 'two-beat' kick and she only breathed on the left side. She just glided into the wall like she was riding a wave at the beach. Papa wrote down her time, but I was too short to see it. I knew it was fast from the look on his face. She just jumped right out of the pool and I couldn't wait until I was big enough to do that.

It was still raining and freezing cold, but I'd been jumping off the diving boards anyway. It had been a long morning at club and my stroke correction class was about to start when the announcer called for attention. We all gathered around the starting end of the pool to listen to the results of the Shell Age Championships the weekend before; Megan's results.

"Wow, the best ten-year-old in New South Wales," I thought as Megan stood up on the block where everyone could see her. "I want to be like that."

A man near me said, "She's going to break the drought, that one."

"Four years' time, d'ya think?" said another dad. "She'd only be 14."

"Maybe eight years."

"It'd be fantastic – back to the glory days of Ryde, our swimmers up there in lights again. Olympic champions. It's been a long time."

I thought about the black and white pictures of all the Ryde swimmers who had gone to the Olympics hanging on the entrance wall at the pool. People like Shane Gould, Karen Moras, John Konrads... he was handsome and he looked a bit German, so I just knew we would be friends if we met. There hadn't been any new pictures put up there for a long time and a lot of people thought Megan's was going to be the next one. I wondered if it would be in black and white so it would look like part of the same family, or if they would use a colour picture because it was not the olden days anymore.

When I had first started swimming at the Ryde club with Katie, when I was seven, I used to be like all the other boys and girls speed-walking past those photos with my cap and goggles already on. It's sometimes hard to put your cap and goggles on yourself, but after watching Megan, I figured out that real swimmers didn't rush to training and they didn't need their parents to help them put on their cap and goggles. So I walked slower and, because I didn't have my goggles on, I could see the photos every day.

At that moment, standing there, looking at Megan on the block with everyone in the club saying how good she was, thinking about the Olympians in the entranceway, something burst in my brain like a bubble blown from the bottom of the deep end popping on the surface. It was like the boom when you hit the water from the top of the ten metre diving tower!

I was eight and I knew the answer to the question grown-ups always ask you when you're eight: 'What do you want to be when you grow up?' I used to want to be a princess called Sylvia with a pony, but everyone laughed when I said that. I was so childish. Now I really knew! It was like I had grown up in an instant! I had to tell Mummy!

I looked for her at Lane 5, but she wasn't there. I looked for her in the officials' room, but she wasn't there. I ran to the change rooms (even though you're not allowed to run), but she wasn't there, and on the way out I looked at the photos in the entranceway. I could hear John Konrads saying, "So, Nadine, when are you going to join us up here?" And there I was, in black and white, smiling with my cap and goggles in my hand, like a real professional.

I finally found her at the announcer's desk.

"Mummy! I have a secret to tell you!" And I whispered in her ear so no one else could hear.

She smiled and didn't say anything for a while. She patted me on the head and laughed with a song in her voice, "That's great. Why not?"

I was so glad Mummy was happy. She would be so proud of me. So would Papa.

My future was planned.

But I didn't quite know what to do then – what do future Olympians do? How do they act? I guessed Megan was the best person to follow, because she was going to break the drought in four or eight years' time, so I went to my stroke correction lesson and tried to swim like her. I knew I would need a lot of stroke correction if I was going to have my photo on the wall with hers one day. And I would definitely have to qualify for Castlereagh District!

3.

"Living two lives is a little weird"
  – *"Best of Both Worlds"*, Hannah Montana

WE HAD TO WRITE A STORY FOR MISS MASON, but I needed help and she just didn't understand why it was so hard for me. Adults and 11-year-olds speak entirely different languages – they just sound the same. And it didn't help that my school, Glenaeon, was a bit different to most other schools. It was a Waldorf school and everything was done differently to how it was done at normal schools. Competition was considered bad, so when it came to my swimming, I had to be pretty careful about what I said.

"I don't know," I tried to explain. "Hobbies are like the things people do on the weekend for fun, but swimming is different. It's something I want to do for the rest of my life. It's not the same as going to the movies or riding my bike or reading books, which is what everyone else is writing about. So I don't know what to write."

"Well, what other things do you do outside of school?" Miss Mason asked.

"That's the problem. Nothing."

"You just swim? You don't like reading or going to the beach?"

"I *like* those things but I don't have time outside of swimming to do them much, especially with homework." I thought I'd get that one in, but it passed her by without a flicker of recognition and I wondered if she was even listening.

Miss Mason raised her eyebrows the same way I always did when I thought Colette was being dumb. I could tell – she thought I was crazy, just like everyone else at my school.

"Well, just write about swimming then. Tell me why you like it so much and why it's the only thing you want to do." She went back to her marking.

I was pretty sure Miss Mason didn't like me much. She had bright red hair and she played the part of Satan in the teachers' Christmas play. I thought it suited her, mainly because her hair was like fire, but her temper could be like fire too, especially when she kept telling me to stop talking in class. She always had lipstick on her teeth and she was an awful speller, so whenever I got into trouble for talking, I quietly said to myself, "I talk too much and you're a bad speller, so we both do some things wrong." Mostly, she was nice, even though she wanted me to write my story about swimming.

I didn't want to write about swimming because of what happened one morning when I was in Class 3 and it was my turn to get up and tell the class my 'news'. I had brought my ribbons and medals that I won at a weekend competition to talk about. Bad idea. No one else really cared about my wins. I was just really excited and I wanted people to think I was good, not that I was a bragger, but a few days later I didn't have anyone to play with anymore. After finishing our lunch, we were allowed to go and play, but I stayed on the big rock. Miss Mason saw me crying and said, "Come on, Nadine, what's the matter now?" I'm sure her eyes rolled a bit, as though she was thinking, 'Oh man, sooky pants...'

"I have no friends. Nobody likes me. They won't play with me." I was sobbing like a lost little kid.

"Well, if you weren't so selfish and grumpy all the time, then maybe people would like you more. So, off your bottom! Go and be nice and find someone to play with."

I don't think that was the most helpful thing she could have said, but she must have been having a bad day. It did make me realise that I had no friends because of the whole swimming thing, though. I was grumpy because no one understood what I was on about when I talked about the fire spirit of the Olympic Games and I was selfish because I really wanted people to listen to what I was doing at swimming, so I just kept talking about it.

That day I promised myself I'd be a perfect friend to anyone who needed it (well, maybe except for Eggy Ellen because she was really bad for popularity), and I promised that I'd stop trying to make people understand me and my Olympic Dream. So that's when my double life started. By the time I got to Class 6, I was living the life of a superhero – by day: student; by night: super-fish. But superheroes never reveal their true identity, so Miss Mason telling me I had to write about swimming was against the rules. Unfortunately, 11-year-olds don't make the rules.

I looked around the quiet classroom, at all the other boys and girls writing and I tried, 'My hobby is swimming and I like it because I am good at it and I love to win races…' but I couldn't say that in a story for Miss Mason. She always encouraged us to work hard on the things that we were less-than-capable at, like spelling and fractions for me, and she never made a big fuss about our 'talents' because that was the school philosophy.

At Glenaeon, they didn't make a big deal about sport. It annoyed me sometimes because I wanted my chance to shine, but when we played ball-games like captain-ball or basketball or Kanga Cricket, I was glad that being competitive was not something the school emphasised. I was pretty bad at those. Some of my swimming friends got certificates and ribbons at their school carnivals, but we never even had a school carnival. Rudolf Steiner, the man who started Waldorf Schools like mine, believed that competing was harmful because it could make people feel like they were better than others and he thought people shouldn't feel like winning was the most important thing. I could understand where he was coming from, because sometimes I felt bad for the people that I beat in swimming, especially if it upset them to come second or third, and I certainly knew how it felt to come last in a running race. Those were the times when I really liked Miss Mason, because she said that if I tried my best then that was all that mattered and if I kept trying my best I'd keep getting better. So competition wasn't always good. But secretly, I still liked winning races.

That wasn't the only way that my school was different to the regular ones my swimming friends went to. Glenaeon was in the bush and all the buildings were beautiful with stained glass windows and round staircases and nice wooden desks with flip-top lids. Some of the kids called it a 'herbal school'. We didn't do subjects in the same way as other schools and we didn't use blue, black and red biros – we used coloured pencils and if our writing was really neat we could graduate to use a fountain pen. Miss Mason drew an amazing picture on the chalkboard every week and our classroom was filled with our water colour paintings, beeswax models and woollen handcrafts. We did heaps of things that needed imagination and artistic skills, like decorating every page so our teacher could see that we had respect for the work we did. We'd say a prayer in the morning to welcome the sun and a prayer in the afternoon to welcome the moon and we learned about all the different myths and legends and religions from all around the world. I secretly thought it was really cool. We still did English and maths and science and languages, but it was all more creative and, well, fun. Mum always said it was 'an holistic approach to education'. I never bothered to ask what she meant by that.

When I was in the lower classes, I used to be a long way behind what other kids at other schools were doing, and I think that made Mummy and Papa a bit worried. My cousin Natalie could read and write whole stories before I even knew how to sound out words. But when I got to Class 6, that all changed. It was like I had caught up without any real effort, and at the same time, I could imagine strange and different worlds and I could do art and crafts and music and tell stories from ancient times… all sorts of things that other kids didn't know about. Mum said that Waldorf schools don't push children to learn things that they are not ready for, and I reckoned that was true, because even though some subjects were hard, learning them was always fun. I never hated any subject. It was also nice to be in a small school with the same teacher right from Class 1 to the end of Class 8. It made school feel like a kind of family; a family that didn't know my secret identity, that is.

"Nadine, stop daydreaming and get to work," Miss Mason whispered.

I hated it when she snuck up on me like that.

Rudolf Steiner may have believed in teaching only what children were 'ready for', but he certainly never told his teachers to just let the kids do whatever they felt like. Miss Mason was always watching, so I picked up my fountain pen and wrote, 'Swimming is my hobby and I love it because I have the spirit of the Olympics living inside me, like a candle light in my heart'.

Corny.

'My hobby is reading and I love it because…' I wondered if John Konrads ever had to protect his secret identity like I did.

***

"…and then we had to do the whole lot of chapter four just because Chloe was talking. And I hate percentages!" Jess said. "What did you do at school?"

It was fun to sit on the big green hill by the outdoor pool and chat with my friends before training. I could look through Jess' magazines – magazines that Mum would never buy me! I wouldn't really know what to ask for anyway. We didn't watch much TV at home either, but I didn't mind about that because I never really had much time. I preferred reading my *Lord of the Rings* books anyway. The music magazines were cool, though, and I had so much to learn about being cool. Some of the girls at Glenaeon would sneak magazines to school, but if Miss Mason found them, they got into big trouble. 'Trashy media' wasn't something that Glenaeon approved of, probably because they thought it was all about sex and the coolest clothes and rebel rock bands, really the opposite to what we were being taught at school. I didn't really care about the sex stuff, but I loved the music magazines, even though I didn't know any of the songs in *Smash Hits*.

I didn't want to answer Jess' question about what I did at school, because when I was at swimming, my school life was my secret identity and I wanted my swimming friends to think

I was like them. I was pretty sure they all thought I was a bit weird anyway, so sharing that Miss Mason told us an Indian myth called the *Ramayana*, or that we made swings over the creek out of bamboo, or that my five-minute landscape picture that I did in art was put up on the wall, would just add to how weird I seemed. Jess was my best friend, but some things just can't be shared. Sometimes I didn't feel like I fitted into either of my worlds properly.

"Oh, nothing much," I said as I studied a picture of Jon Bon Jovi. He was so hot.

"Well, after maths we had language and German is so boring..." Jess continued, unfussed.

"I'm going to Germany soon," I said without looking up.

"Really? When?" She was impressed. Jess was really pretty and popular and she knew everything that cool 12-year-olds have to know, so it felt good to impress her. I couldn't wait to turn 12 at the end of the year.

"In July. For six months. It'll be cool." I tried to sound casual.

"Wow! Are you gonna swim over there?"

"Oh yeah!" I said with a smile. "I reckon they'll be really fast."

4.

"Why'd you have to go and make things so complicated?"
 – *"Complicated"*, Avril Lavigne

IT WAS COLLIE'S EIGHTH BIRTHDAY and she was bursting with the excitement of a puppy. Going on an aeroplane was her best present ever. Going to Germany on an aeroplane was almost too much to bear. I'd already been to Germany, when I was seven, so it was not such a big deal for me. Not really. Well, I *was* nervous. I *did* have that wobbly feeling in my stomach like I always got before a race and I wondered why.

"I'm going to eat everything they give us!" Colette said with her eyes opening so wide they looked like Herbie the Love Bug's headlights. She was looking at the menu she had found in the seat pocket in front of her and she was reading the hard words a lot better than I could when I was just eight. Damn that was annoying! She was good at everything. We used to go to ballet once a week and I was told that I had nice hands but Colette won a scholarship. I did a bit of jazz dancing but before long Colette was put into my class and she got to demonstrate all the moves. On performance night I was in the middle of the group and Papa found it hard to video me because he couldn't see where I was, but Collie was front row centre and even had a special solo part in the adults' dance. She got a trophy that night and Mum and Papa gave me a medal that they had bought at the shops; a medal for effort. I often thought Colette had a secret identity too – a witch who could cast spells and magically do anything she wanted to; not a wicked witch, but a tricky sprite who could weave mischievous magic.

It occurred to me that maybe that was why I was scared of going to Germany – because we were going for so long and she was the only person I would know and what if she adapted to our new school better than I did? Six months is a long, long time to be on your own with a little sister who is better at everything than you are. We were going for six months because Papa had sabbatical to do some research in Paris. He was a French lecturer at Macquarie University in Sydney and he did lots of research about French writers. A man he wrote a book about, Claude Simon, ended up getting a Nobel Prize for literature so Papa became the world expert. That's why he had to spend so long overseas, why we were spending so long overseas. At least Collie and I and Mum would be in Germany with my grandma, Mutti.

"Nad, are they going to give us colouring in books?" Colette was always butting into my daydreams.

"I don't know. Ask the hostess," I said, taking the wrapper off a mint lolly.

"How come you've got Minties?" Collie whined.

"So I can chew on them when the plane takes off."

"Why?"

"To stop my ears from popping."

She didn't know anything about flying.

"Can I have one?" Collie asked with hand outstretched. Always wanting what I had.

Maybe I was nervous about going away because Collie was annoying me with her copying. How was I meant to cope with her being the only person to talk to in English? You can't discuss anything important with an eight-year-old.

Then again, maybe it was the whole language problem that made me nervous. We were going to go to school and it was all going to be in German. Even though I could speak enough to get by, my writing was pretty awful sometimes and, in German, the tiniest mistake, like putting the 'i' and the 'e' in the wrong order, could change the meaning of a word from 'shoot' to 'shit'. That was exactly what I did in a German assignment at Glenaeon. Mutti thought it was really funny that, writing about playing space invaders, I said I was going to shit the baddies dead.

The language was a potential problem at the pool as well, not to mention the fact that they swam on the wrong side of the lane! I didn't know any of the jargon. In English, Fly, Back, Breast, Free, drill, scull, paddles, pull buoy, chicken-wing... they all made sense, but I had no idea what they were in German!

"Please ensure that your tray tables are secure and your seats are in the upright position."

"Is mine in the upright position?" Colette asked anyone who would listen. "Eeeee! We're moving!" she squealed and bounced in the seat like she wanted to lift off right then and there.

I had to smile. She was kind of cute and it was going to be an adventure, and even though my stomach was shaking, it was not all bad.

The last little while in my life had felt very complicated, as though I'd been living four lives instead of just two – my family life at home (one) and my herbal life at school (two) was my world 'Away from Swimming', and my fish life in the pool (three) and my social life outside of the pool (four) were the world 'At Swimming'. It was pretty tiring keeping up with it all, especially when my fish life and my 'social' life were so hard to keep sorted.

I was looking forward to getting away from all the heartache that came with Sean too, which seemed crazy, because he was my boyfriend.

I was pretty popular with the boys. Not romantically, but just as friends. Probably because I went to a co-ed school, I didn't really think boys were anything special. Most of the other girls at Ryde went to girls' schools and they got weird and giggly around the boys, but I liked to muck around with them and make bets and race them and stuff like that. Some people at the pool thought I was 'boy crazy'. Sure, I used to sometimes get 'crazy' about a boy, but it only depended on who liked me at the time. It was all just the junk we talked about in training. But with Sean it was different.

Just because I was 11, people thought it was puppy-love or some silly crush that little kids have, but it wasn't. I would choke up in my chest when I thought about him, and anyone who has ever been in love will know what I mean. It was all-consuming. Whenever I had a fight with him I'd get a burning feeling in my throat. The only other person who could make me swim slow when we had a fight was my best friend, Jess.

I was sure that was why Mummy and Papa didn't like Sean much, so I didn't talk about him at home, even though he had been my boyfriend for nearly half a year, with a few breaks in-between.

Sean was a good swimmer. Sometimes he would dump me because he wanted to be Jess' boyfriend, but Jess and I would never let that get in the way of us being friends – we were more mature than that! At those times I didn't enjoy swimming much because it made me sad to see them having fun without me. I felt so left out, but when he broke up with me because he wanted to hang around with Megan more, I always seemed to swim fast. Maybe it was because I hoped that by swimming faster, like Megan, he would come back to me. And most of the time he did. I was sure Megan and I were going to go to the Olympics together one day and I only hoped that we could be friends, but I could never think of what to say to her without sounding desperate.

Sean broke up with me just before we left for Germany. He said we needed a break, but I thought it was because Megan had swum really well at Nationals and success is a big drawcard. I hadn't even qualified for Nationals yet, so there was no doubt that was it. I cried a bit, I missed him instantly, but the whole on-again, off-again thing was getting hard, so the fact that I was going away for six months made me kind of glad. Jess promised she'd write and tell me all the gossip, especially if Sean was missing me, too. She was sure he would and I hoped she was right. Love can be so complicated.

"Hey, Nad, when we've taken off, do you want to play cards?" Collie was so excited.

"Yeah, okay." I figured I might as well do the big sister thing. After all, it was going to be a long flight and if I played it right, six months in Germany with my white-witch sister surely couldn't be that bad.

5.

"There once was a child with a dream in his mind and a thousand things to learn"
  – *"Theatre of Fate"*, Viper

EVEN THOUGH IT WAS SMALL, Mutti's place just oozed warmth like the sticky, sweet molasses Mummy let us eat a spoon-full of every morning. As soon as you walked through the little red door baking would hit your nose, make your mouth water and tummy grumble. Her tiny kitchen was always abuzz, and, with her big bottom, it was impossible to fit more than one pair of helping hands in! In summer and autumn she would bake, preserve and jam the cherries, plums, mirabelles, apricots and peaches that came from her backyard (well, the ones that Collie, Papa and I didn't eat straight off the trees) and, in winter or spring, her cellar would burst with what the autumn visitors couldn't finish. Papa had to build shelves to fit it all in and our suitcases were full of illegal imports on the way home from that German paradise.

"Why don't we call her 'Grandma' or *Oma* or something like that?" Collie asked one warm afternoon as she sucked the insides out of a gooseberry from the bush at the far end of the garden. She wasn't annoying me as much as I had expected. In fact, I think we had become good friends. She seemed smarter than the average eight-year-old, so it was actually possible to share secrets with her. She was funny, too.

"I don't know," I replied, surprised at the depth of contemplation that her question implied. "Mutti's too energetic and fun to call her *Oma*."

"Yeah, that sounds like little old ladies in rocking chairs with blankets on their laps!" That was more like an eight-year-old.

"I don't think she'd fit into a rocking chair!" I laughed at the thought as I bit a gooseberry in half and turned it inside out on my thumb. Colette watched me with no attempt to hide.

"Mutti said that she swims every day because '*Ich liebe das Essen!*'" Collie giggled and quickly caught her breath – "Tss-ahh!" – as she sucked at the little spot of blood that the thorny bush had left on her middle finger.

"Careful."

She nodded.

"Well who doesn't love eating at Mutti's house?!" I brushed a tickling ant off my leg.

"Remember when she nearly drowned at Currumbin?" Collie mused.

"Mmm hmm."

"Did she really want Papa to let her go?" She bit into her yellow, veiny fruit and turned it inside out on her thumb.

"Mmm hmm. So scary."

"Is that why she calls him her handsome lifesaver?" She glanced at me and started to scrape the insides with her teeth like I was. For some reason, the copying didn't bother me so much anymore. She was kind of cute.

"I think she's teasing him a bit when she says that. He's a bit short and hairy for a lifesaver!" I said.

"Hehe! Yeah... Hey Nad, do you get nervous before going training? Here, I mean?"

"I kind of did, but not as much now. Why? Do you?"

"Yeah. I don't think my coach likes me." Collie looked so sad as she popped a whole berry in her mouth as though she wanted to push whatever was welling up back down again.

"Why?"

"He kind of picks on me."

I bit through another bursting gooseberry and turned it inside out in my mouth with my tongue. At the 'Schwimmgemeinschaft (SG) Frankfurt' club, Collie and I were by far the best swimmers. It was weird – I thought Germany was a really strong swimming nation because they had people like Michael Gross, but they didn't even have proper races for age group swimmers, only relays. Colette, especially, was a freak, but I already knew that. She had a good 50m Butterfly and that was not entirely unusual in Australia, but in Frankfurt there was not a single person younger than about 14 who could do more than 25m of the stroke. It didn't make sense that her coach wouldn't like her. She was gold.

"Maybe he's just having a bad time at the moment," I offered, aware of how lame my attempt at comfort was. "I mean, he smokes and drinks and never seems to be without a pretzel in his mouth. He can't be a happy man."

She chuckled and reached for another gooseberry. "Yeah. He mustn't have a gooseberry bush at home to make him happy." She brightened a little and I hoped that her fantastic performances in the club relays would bring her coach around.

* * *

That year, 1987, The SG Frankfurt club made it to the State Championships in two relays – with Collie's team and mine. Collie and I were both doing the Butterfly legs of our relays. At the State, Colette's team was running last until she hit the water and passed everyone. The girl who was swimming last got so nervous when she realised they were winning that she false-started. Their team was disqualified and Collie was devastated. Her coach was silent.

My relay team won and qualified for the National Championships for the first time ever. My coach was thrilled and I was an instant hero amongst the 16-20 year-olds in my squad, even though I had only just turned 12. I was it – for the first time in my life I was the best at something, the centre of the universe and it felt fantastic! The adults actually looked at me and smiled! Even the fastest swimmer in the club (prior to my arrival) congratulated me. I was an equal and I felt so grown up!

But Colette's coach was getting weirder. I didn't think much of him as a coach. He would sneak out the glass door that connected the pool with the canteen to have a cigarette, and he would sit there having coffee and pretzels while his squads were doing lap after lap after lap, and starving – you always get ravenous when you swim. I thought that was pretty slack. None of my coaches back home would have done that. He was always a bit grumpy and he reminded me of those two cranky men from *The Muppets* – the ones who sit in the box and heckle the Muppets on stage, especially Fozzie. He really was picking on Collie in training, she wasn't just being sensitive, and he had started making things hard for my coach, Stefan, too.

Stefan told my parents that it was because of Tanja. She was the best swimmer in the club until we arrived and Tanja used to do the Butterfly in the senior relay but they never made Nationals, not like they did when I swam. And Tanja was 16. And Tanja was the cranky Muppet's daughter. That's why he didn't much like our presence and why he couldn't find a way to hide it.

Mummy and Papa said it was just 'politics' that we shouldn't worry about, but it was hard not to see it. Besides Colette's challenges, a whole lot of people who liked us when we first arrived and who were happy for us to swim for the club, suddenly decided that we weren't really part of the club and we shouldn't be allowed to swim at the Club Championships. It was the only chance we had to swim normal races instead of just relays! Stefan explained that Tanja had won the overall point score trophy in those Championships for the last two years, and she had to win a third consecutive year to keep the trophy forever. But if anyone was going to beat Tanja, it was me.

Luckily the cranky Muppet was outvoted when the decision was put before the club's managing committee. The majority decided we were allowed to race.

It was like a movie script on the night of the Club Championships. Tanja won one race, I'd win the next. The whole club was split – one group cheering for her and one for me. We were neck and neck in the point score through the whole competition and going into the last race we were on equal points. It was the 200m Individual Medley. Tanja's dad actually put out his cigarette and came inside to watch his daughter race from the pool-side of the glass.

It was about 30°C in the 25m indoor pool. Germans like it warm, especially when it's freezing cold winter outside. I figured they came to the pool when they didn't want to spend money on heating their own houses. I was used to swimming outdoors and sometimes in our winter the water got well below 20°C at Ryde, making your lungs freeze and your nose bleed. The stuffy atmosphere made me feel sick. My stomach was wobbling like jelly all over the place! I had never been so nervous. I reckoned that was what the professional swimmers called getting 'pumped' because it wasn't the bad nervous you get when you're in trouble.

Tanja and I were just as fast as each other in the Butterfly, but she was a better Backstroker and took the lead. My Breaststroke was better than hers, so we touched together and turned for the last 50m Freestyle. I powered away and, like in a movie, I won and set a new club record, too! She leaned over the lane rope and shook my hand. The cranky Muppet went back to his cigarettes.

* * *

In the end, despite the heady glory of being a star, I was glad to leave the mean eyes of the SG Frankfurt club, and I knew Mummy and Papa were, too. I wore my German medals around my neck through the airport because they didn't fit in the suitcases and the airline wanted to charge us a fortune for excess baggage – full of illegal jams and jellies, remember! I walked through the metal detector after check-in and the alarms screamed, heads all turned and the whole German national security force surrounded me in seconds, machine guns ready to fire. And I thought showing my ribbons at school was embarrassing! I was definitely not going to tell my friends at Ryde about that final, noisy exit from stardom!

It was so good to be going back home, to a country where people understood that being competitive in sport doesn't mean hating each other outside of sport. Tanja knew, but her dad didn't. Stefan couldn't stop smiling after that Club Championship night and when we left Germany, he said, "*Nadine, mach was*" meaning 'become something special'. I was sure he meant that I should get my black and white photo on the wall next to John Konrads – he understood the whole swimming-obsession thing.

I just wanted to get back to my two lives where 'Away from Swimming' meant being creative and learning interesting stuff and 'At Swimming' meant racing for the wall with someone and then going off the diving boards together, still friends.

6.

"They love to tell you 'stay inside the lines'"
 – *"No Such Thing"*, John Mayer

1988.

The first time that I'd ever missed a Ryde Club Championships.

And it sucked.

They wouldn't let us swim because we only raced in seven Saturday mornings instead of eight.

"But one of those Saturdays was the Swimathon," Papa had said to the president.

"The rules are clear," was the cold reply.

"Surely the girls swimming and raising money for the club on a Saturday counts as 'taking part in club swimming over eight Saturdays'. They were here, swimming, doing something good for the club."

"It's the rule," the president said.

"Well, make an exception," Papa pleaded.

"The committee will discuss it," the president said, but he really meant 'No'.

I loved doing the Swimathon because Collie and I always got a lot of money for it. We had to swim for 60 minutes and most of my sponsors would give me 'donation' amounts instead of putting down for ten cents a lap, or whatever they could afford. That was because Mummy and Papa always talked about how our swimming was going with the people at their work and some of them no longer believed me when I'd say that I was going to try to do 50 laps. They'd been burned once before – the time when I said I was going to try and do 20 laps but ended up doing 44. In the 1988 Swimathon, I think I did 65 laps. Megan did 100 – she was so fast.

By the time Club Champs came around, a few of the girls at swimming weren't talking to me much anymore. I didn't really know why, but Mummy said they probably felt threatened because I did such fast times when I was in Germany. I was pretty sure she was wrong. That sort of stuff didn't happen in Australia. But my fish life was not as fun as it used to be and that annoyed me. At least the boys were still talking to me, especially the older ones. I felt more like one of the older people anyway because they reminded me of the squad in Germany.

Jess was still my best friend, but since we came back from Germany, training at Ryde was getting boring. Ursula was my coach in the top squad, but her sessions were always the same and the only thing that made training interesting was 'shredding' the program when she wasn't watching – we'd skip a few repetitions here and there, cut corners, jump off the bottom of the pool in the middle of a lap, pull on the lane rope, and all that stuff that everyone did, but no one talked about. I was pretty sure Ursula knew we did it and that she hated it, but I was also pretty sure that she couldn't be bothered shouting at us all the time. When something really bad came onto the program, like 16 x 50 Butterfly, we would suddenly 'desperately need to go to the toilet!' and that would usually last about ten minutes. Sometimes we'd stash 20c pieces in our cossies for a hot shower when we went on our quick toilet break, or we'd just splash ourselves with hot water from the hand-basin until some public swimmer would dob us in.

Training... it was a drag, but I had to keep going because I'd finally made it to Nationals, well, Age Nationals. At the time, it seemed like forever since I had first heard the black and white photos call me to the Olympics, but four years is not such a long time in sport. I'd swum at District, I'd swum at Metropolitan, I'd swum at State, and every year I had come closer to the big time: Age Nationals as a 12-year-old!

* * *

I was more nervous than I had been at SG Frankfurt's Club Championships. I didn't know if I wanted to stand up or sit down, smile or cry. I had to remind myself to breathe! The night before my first Nationals race was like torture!

"Nadine, how would you like to shave your legs for the big race?" Mummy asked from the door of my room. She could tell I was nervous.

"Shave down, like … the big … like Olympic swimmers?"

"Mmm hmm, this is Nationals. I think you should prepare for your race like a National swimmer."

"Okay! But…" I wasn't sure how to go about it, and the thought of cutting myself scared me.

"I'll help, ja?" Mum knew.

"Yeah."

I raced in the 100m and 200m Breaststroke in the 13 and under age group at the Brisbane National Age Championships. As I swam my shiny, smooth legs felt tingly, as though the jelly in my wobbling stomach had slid down into them. I felt fast. I did my best times in both races and came about 35th. Sean asked me to be his girlfriend again. He said that he missed me, but I think he liked my shiny legs. I was getting fast, too. I had broken Megan's 100m Butterfly District record and I had also won my first State medals.

My secret identities were still safe, and nobody at Glenaeon really knew that my star was rising, that I was getting closer to the Olympics, and it made me feel kind of special to have such a huge secret. I was just 'the girl with short hair who always smells like chlorine' to them. For all they knew, I could have been washing myself in bleach… except that Miss Mason asked me to demonstrate tumble turns when our class went to swimming lessons for sport. I wondered what they would think if they knew I was competing almost every weekend.

I watched the 1988 Seoul Olympics on TV and a guy called Duncan Armstrong won a gold medal and broke the world record when no one thought he had a chance. It was like another Australian in the Olympics before, in Los Angeles, Jon Sieben, who also won a gold medal when no one thought he had a chance. Even though they were boys, I thought they were inspiring because no one was talking about me breaking the Ryde Olympic drought. Most people didn't even know that that was what I was aiming to do! So I knew that, in four years' time, when I was 16 with my black and white photo up on the wall with John Konrads', everyone would be surprised, just like they were about Duncan and Jon. And in the photo I'd be biting into my gold medal just like they did. And Megan would be my friend because she'd win a medal, too. And Sean would love me forever.

Yep, that's how it would be.

7.

"You can push me out the window; I'll just get back up"
— *"Can't Keep Me Down"*, Pink

SUNSETS OVER THE SEA ARE BAD LUCK. They are so beautiful – rainbow-coloured sparks jump off the water and dive into your eyes, imprinting the image so brightly that you cannot forget the moment. But all those little sunset sparkles started off sunsets all over my life, and before I knew it, those flying embers had turned to raging fires that burned everything in my world to dust.

In April 1989, at the Perth National Age Championships, holding Sean's hand as we walked along the powdery white Scarborough Beach sand, watching the sun turn the ocean to gold, everything began to burn. We kissed – real kisses like in the movies. I was a goddess at the top of the world; a teenage goddess oblivious to the spot fires brewing.

The first one started with Sean. He kissed me, then dumped me. Burn! He liked Megan more than me again and I wondered if it had anything to do with my kissing. Was it possible that she was better at that too? I was getting to the point where I liked her more than me as well. Actually, I liked everything about her life more than mine, especially on the last night of Nationals, when she got to go to the swimmers' disco. It was at Scarborough surf-club and my parents wouldn't let me go and celebrate with every other age-group swimmer in the country… but Megan could… and Sean could… and Jess could…

I got to stay back and find my own fun at the crappy hotel where all the Ryde Swimming Club families had spent the last week eating, sleeping, relaxing between race days. Lucky me. The hotel was like an echo chamber with a small rockery, a wading pool and miniature waterslide in the middle of a courtyard surrounded by three floors of rooms. I wasn't the only one who didn't go to the disco, but all the cool people went, and I wanted to be with them.

Even most of the parents went to the pub for their version of a party after the week-long competition, but not mine. God, I was so embarrassed that they couldn't even make an effort to mingle with the right people. Parents never understand how painful it is when yours are the parents who 'don't drink' and are the ones who hang around to 'keep an eye on the kids'.

So, I couldn't even run amok at the hotel because I was scared of getting busted. Try being bad without being really bad – we sniffed pepper, I don't know why exactly, but at the time it seemed wild and reckless, but all it achieved were fiery, weeping eyes, a nose in fits and a throat that scolded. Most of my evening was spent with my head upside-down under a tap to wash the pepper out and wishing Sean was there; then at least I'd have a chance of convincing him to kiss me again.

When the cool kids eventually did come back to the hotel with all the gossip, I tried not to look jealous and made out as though the few nerds who had stayed behind had had an awesome time. When the popular parents got back from their night out, they were suitably jolly and I thought that was so cool… at first, anyway. It wasn't long before the second sunset spot fire ignited though.

The tipsy mums squealed a shrill echo that spun around and around the concrete walls, woke everyone up and brought an audience to the balconies for a real show. The drunken dads decided to go play in the courtyard splash-pool, and watching them dance around in the water, Megan's dad included, was like watching a car accident. Somewhere in my mind I was embarrassed for Megan and that bad-luck sunset burned my desire to have her life. Un-drunk parents weren't so bad after all.

What a way to end the Perth Age Nationals.

* * *

Since the bad luck sunsets had started and I no longer had a boyfriend or an idol, I found myself despising my double life. I was no superhero. I just wanted to have one life, like a normal teenager. I was tired of not being quite 'right' with my school friends and not quite 'right' with my swimming friends.

One Saturday night one of the girls from school was having a party, but again, I wasn't there. I never was. Everyone else from school was, dressed in fashionable jeans and tops, the girls all wearing makeup and dancing, having fun. I was damp, shivering and waiting for the marshals to finally call my 800m Freestyle. I didn't even own cool jeans or tops anyway, and I wouldn't have been allowed to wear makeup, but it never stopped me daydreaming.

That night, I didn't even really know why I was doing the 800m. Megan was in it, and ten foot tall, red-headed and smiley Elli Overton. I was a baby compared to them and I wondered if John Konrads ever did the open 800m Freestyle at the Castlereagh District Championships, at the Auburn Swimming Centre. I wondered if he would laugh knowingly at how cold and windy the nights could be, and how it always threatened to rain while you waited without shelter behind the starting blocks. I could imagine him there, with his arms wrapped tight around his black and white body saying, "I'm tired... really tired... and hungry... and cold... and I could be at a party like a normal person... God! Why do we wait around until 9pm just to dive into freezing water and pound up and down forever, when no one's here watching anyway?"

I would say, "Well you ought to know. You've been to the Olympics."

And he'd say, "That's true. All those parties you can't go to and all those friends who don't get it, and nights like this. They really are all worth it in the end. Nothing comes close to the special club you're headed for; that club for the best in the world where everyone understands what it takes to make it."

Then he'd ask, "But why are you doing the 800m Freestyle? I thought you were a Breaststroker."

And I'd tell him about how I'd had pretty awful trouble with my knees and how I went to a sports physio for a fix and came out with bruises from kneecaps to hips. And how they said it was hyper-mobile patellas that caused me excruciating pain in Breaststroke and often made walking around hard. So I'd tell him how I went for bruise treatment a few times, got a whole lot of exercises and stretches that I never remembered to do and how I learned to strap my knees. I'd tell him how they'd been sticky and hairless ever since and how I didn't do any more Breaststroke kick in training, only pull, so I had to make up for it with a lot of Medley, Butterfly and distance Freestyle training to stay sane.

I imagined how impressed with my dedication he would be and how he would wish me good luck.

But no daydreaming could change the fact that I was tired and that I would have preferred to be at Eloise's party.

As the gun blasted through that quiet night and the freezing water shocked the breath out of me, my nervous stomach wobbles took control of my body and turned my heavy arms over as fast as they would go. My mind drifted elsewhere again, hypnotised by the rhythm of my arms – splish-splotch, splish-splotch, splish-splotch – and the soothing rumble of my breath in the water. I'd often had times in training when I'd fallen asleep as my body went through the motions, up and down and up and down and up and down and… not surprising I guess. But I really should have been counting my laps – it was a race, after all!

After an age, the whistle called me back. Megan and Elli were coming up behind me, FAST! I was cranky at being roused from my sleep, cranky at the night air, cranky at the rain that had started spitting on us and I was damned if they were going to have the satisfaction of lapping me. It would be too humiliating at that time of night.

The tiny group of parents who had waited so patiently for us to act out our strange obsession was going wild. I was sure Megan and Elli had broken the record. Always that step ahead of me.

I sprinted the last 100m with everything I had. I wanted to make the State qualifying time so I could say to Mum and Dad that the hanging around was worthwhile. I wanted to vent my frustration. I started to wheeze and burn all over and with my insides turning out I hit the wall, looked up to the time-keeper whose grinning face turned my frustration to hope. Elli was smiling too, with an outstretched hand, but Megan had her back to me. I guessed Elli had won.

"Did you get the record?" I asked, puffing.

"No. You did two laps extra you idiot!" Elli said. There was no movement from Megan.

"Huh?" My mind took its time. "I won?"

It was the first time I'd stood on a podium higher than the girl I had so desperately wanted to be, and I didn't quite know what to do.

Neither did she.

John Konrads' black and white photo smiled at me in my mind.

The local paper said I was a 'Rising Star'.

But rising stars only come out after sunsets.

* * *

I was targeted as part of the youth squad, 'Barcelona Bound'. It meant that the people in Australian Swimming would be watching me and giving me all kinds of opportunities to help my chances of getting to the Barcelona Olympics in two years' time. But I was confused. I didn't know what kind of life I wanted. Did I really want to be the swimming-obsessed freak I sometimes felt like or an average Nadine who went to parties and watched TV? The black and white picture of John Konrads still called to me every day.

I was invited to a 'Barcelona Bound' training camp at the Australian Institute of Sport (AIS) for biomechanics testing and profiling. It was the first time science ever played a role in my swimming, but I didn't go on camp with everyone else like I was supposed to. My family had a trip to Palo Alto in California planned at the exact time when the rest of the squad was going to the institute, so I went down there on my own. It was meant to be inspirational, I'm sure, and I'm sure the others made friends and felt like real professionals, but Canberra was the loneliest week of my life.

I hated the AIS. It was a prison. Everywhere I turned I saw visions of sporting perfection but they planted black demons of doubt in my soul rather than inspiring me with their example. A place of silent isolation and stupefying boredom, it reminded me, every hollow second, that I still had such a long, long way to go. And the institute made me afraid I might never get there.

Between testing sessions I spent a lot of time in the dining hall (the apple crumble with hot custard was divine!) but it made me feel pathetic as I watched sporting constellations gossip about last night's events. They didn't notice the frightened little girl at the corner table who was too immature to know exactly what they meant by fellatio anyway. Even the miniature gymnasts who looked as grey as I felt had friends to share their lettuce-leaf rations with.

At the pool, I didn't recognise any famous faces. They were beautiful to watch, their technique perfect and smooth like a ballet, but I felt as though we had nothing in common. They didn't even see me. I had hoped to find an idol, someone to replace Megan, but each day I left the pool more lost than I'd arrived.

Each day I'd drag my little heart back to my hole in the wall and stare at the lamp on my desk. I tried listening to music, but it felt wrong to play music in such silence, so I checked the clock every 47 seconds to make sure I didn't miss the laundromat kiosk opening. I could buy myself a packet of Fruit Tingles, smell that powdery warmth of clothes drying and feel just a little further away from home. At least it was something to do and someone to talk to:

"Hello…" I'd say shyly.

"Hello luv, what'll it be?" The lady was round and nice.

"Um. Just these thanks…"

"Eighty cents, thanks… Ta."

"Thank you." I'd stall.

"See ya later."

"Um," I'd search for something to say, "do you know where there's a payphone?"

I already knew where the phone was. And the lady knew that I knew.

Coming home after that week I should have been fired up, but I was still confused. I still didn't know what I really wanted. Sean loved me again because I was swimming fast and because I'd been to the Australian Institute of Sport. Jess was still my best friend and I could tell that she didn't really care how fast I swam, and that was a comfort. I did love saying good morning to my black and white friends smiling from the wall. I loved that they looked over me like guardian angels. I loved the sound of the water. I loved the feeling of the cold as the water prickled up my skin. I loved the challenge of swimming as fast as the boys, even beating them sometimes. But I wanted what everyone else had, too – a life with parties and boys and stories about what happened at the movies on Friday night. I felt so left out. I had nothing to say to people at school and they had nothing to say to me. I wanted to be surrounded by people who didn't frown whenever I talked about competing, people who understood that wanting to win doesn't make you a bad person with a sick obsession. People like the squad I trained with for a month in America. Actually, I wanted a life like I had had for those four short weeks in America.

It was magic with my Aunt Marianne – training in a wintry outdoor pool with frozen puddles on the concourse, steam rising off the water so thick that you felt like you were in the clouds and the only way to see the end of the pool was to dunk under the water; my mum and her sister, kindred souls, one minute talking like they were going for the *Guinness Book of Records*, and the next minute doubled over in hysterics until they both turned purple and threatened to pop; rugged-up strolls down 'Christmas Tree Lane' where the mansions of rich people were decorated with squillions of fairy lights, just like in the movies; neighbours singing carols for neighbours and being greeted with hot cinnamon cider; windy walks under the very red Golden Gate Bridge.

I wondered, was it possible to have my picture on that wall along side my guardian angels without feeling so alone everywhere outside the water? I was 'Barcelona Bound' but it was frightening.

* * *

At the end of Class 8, the end of our eight years with the same teacher, Miss Mason played Satan for the last time and she cried when we gave her an encore. I think the principal was disturbed that we were calling for more of Satan – forget the Baby Jesus! But I didn't cry when I left Glenaeon. I was glad to be stopping that stupid double life crap; I was glad that the school fees got too much for my parents to pay. I couldn't wait to start in a real school with hundreds of students and a canteen and school swimming carnivals and exercise books where you write in blue and red and black biro and you don't have to draw pictures on every second page.

I was glad for a new start. Finally, a sunrise!

Mum tried to get me into one of the top local girls' schools, but Cheltenham rejected me with 'we have girls coming out of our ears'. So I ended up going to Jess' school. I could catch the bus to training in the afternoon, like a real teenager, and I had almost an hour before training started to hang out with Sean. Mum and Dad hated Sean. He was a distraction or something, and they couldn't understand that he was part of the reason I kept going every day. I was beginning to feel alive and I was beginning to hope that the sense of loneliness would soon be gone for good. I was entering the 'real' world.

The canteen at school was a novelty for me and I copied everything that Jess did: I got chicken'n'corn rolls and Cheezels, hot cheese rolls and bubbleberry Billabongs... but that was about the only thing that turned out to be good about the 'real' world. I had managed to be at the centre of a bitch fight before I even arrived at the school and I didn't even know it was happening. I guess I was foolish to think that I was the only one with two separate lives – Jess' best friend at school didn't like the presence of a best friend from swimming, and it all blew up.

I just wanted people to like me, so when three of the 'rough pigs' cornered me in the toilets in my first week there, I was determined to say all the right things.

"So, Jess reckons you've got a boyfriend," one of them said.

"Yeah. He's pretty cool." I thought they were being friendly.

"So do you 'do it'?"

"Um..." I didn't know what to say. I was so embarrassed.

"Oh my God! She fucks him! That's so cool. How many guys have you done it with?"

I guess my silence had given them all the answer they wanted. No one had ever called me cool before, and I didn't want them to think I was soft. I'd been warned about how nasty the rough ones could be, so I said, "Oh, only three," hoping that it was enough for them to still think I was cool but not so much that it made me sound like I was lying. Three for a 14-year-old seemed reasonable at the time.

But the impact was instant. I was either a slut or a liar, depending on who you talked to.

Jess didn't want anything to do with me anymore. I was bad for her reputation, or something, and it didn't help that I broke 12 school records at the swimming carnival; records that she always used to break. So I broke 'her' records again at zone and district to rub it in, and I couldn't wait for the Combined High Schools (CHS) meet where all the top school-swimmers from each district in the state were to race. The PE teachers thought I was a hero. Shame about my 'best' friend.

I won three medals at the CHS, and my hero status was confirmed, but that day was not over and it was all about to turn ugly.

I was racing in the 50m Breaststroke at the Open State at the Warringah Aquatic Centre that very night. It was the first event on the program, but the traffic from North Sydney to Frenchs Forest was working against us. Mum was already waiting at Warringah with Collie, while Dad was sighing at every red light, his stress levels rapidly rising. He's so cute when he gets frustrated. I was trying to relax, maybe even catch a few minutes' sleep between competitions because I knew I wouldn't have much time to think once we got there.

When Dad finally pulled up out the front of Warringah Aquatic Centre, screeching to halt, I flew out of the car and straight to the marshalling area, shouting an explanation over my shoulder to the poor lady at the entrance. The marshal was waving my entry card and the first heat of my event was already in the water. Forty-five seconds – grab my card, run to the blocks, undress, put on cap and goggles, GO!

I was left on the block at the gun. In a 50m sprint, that's all it takes. I touched third. By the time I reached the stands and my mum and dad held out my towel with faces that mingled understanding, warmth and disappointment, I was pissed off.

"That was the most fucked up start ever!" I exploded.

And the silence that descended that very moment was filled with gleeful gasps from many of my Ryde Swimming Club peers.

Sore loser.

* * *

They talked about me. I could feel it. It bristled and stabbed at my spine and sometimes I felt like the only ones I could trust were those black and white faces on the wall. No shadows there to hide what they really thought. They were honest and their smiles came from their eyes, not just from lips that curled back in a sneer. Not like my 'friends' at the swimming club.

I heard John Konrads. 'It's okay, Nadine. Every champion has to face those who are bitter. Every champion has to face those who feel threatened. Just be yourself.'

But I could hear them, the people who were once my friends, and I pretended that I didn't know what they were saying; I pretended that nothing had changed. But I could hear them:

"You know she told some of the girls at school that she'd

done it with three guys."

"And I heard she said that she did it with Sean, but he said there was no way he'd do it with her."

"Well, it wouldn't surprise me if she had. Not with Sean, but you know what she's like with all the older guys and, I mean, you've heard the way she talks."

"She swears more than anyone."

"And Dad reckons even Ursula says she's boy-crazy."

I cried sometimes, and Mum and Dad were getting tired of the back-biting. It can be really hard to know who your friends are on a good day when you're 14 – this was making me sea-sick. Dad resolved to clear the air at the Ryde Club Annual General Meeting, after the Melbourne National Age Championships. I thought it was brave of him, although it made me nervous. No teenager wants their parents getting involved in their stuff.

It wasn't the same at training anymore and it made me mad. I'd done nothing wrong. I'd done nothing to hurt them, but they'd turned, so I was determined to get them the only way I knew how. I'd swim – FAST.

* * *

It was a shock to see I was ranked Number 1 at the Melbourne Age Nationals in my 100m and 200m Breaststroke, and I was in the top five in the 200m and 400m Individual Medley; a satisfying shock. I was even well placed in the 200m Butterfly. My wobbling gut started early that year. I had a reason beyond an Olympic ambition to swim fast; I wanted them all to see that they could criticise my language and my behaviour, they could spread stories about me and reject me, but they couldn't touch me when I raced.

I'd never been so close to the big time. In the 100m Breaststroke my main competition was a greyhound from Queensland called Julie Majer. She scared the guts out of me – tall, lean, bronzed, with a reputation for being amphibious.

I always swam my races the same way: I'd be a fair way behind at the beginning of the race (not out of choice but because my muscles wouldn't wake up), and then I'd fight back in the last half of the race (not out of choice but because of a mysterious endurance and because I loved a good challenge in a world where I felt capable). Mum and Dad said it made for an exciting race. Julie beat me by 0.11 seconds in the 100m. Collie screamed herself hoarse. And, despite coming second, I was thrilled.

The 200m Breaststroke was identical – Julie beat me by 0.21 seconds and my dad couldn't hold the video camera still. I'd done my best times in both races and it was somehow okay that Julie was the faster one, at least this time! It felt good to be really racing, exhilarating to do battle without all the stupid emotional baggage that came with the Ryde mob. It was like I wasn't afraid of winning or of losing. I just wanted to go fast. And I did.

The most important race for me, my big chance for a National gold medal and selection for the New South Wales Youth Team to compete in Darmstadt, Germany, was in the 400m Individual Medley, even though it was for swimmers 16 Years & Under and I was just 14. I knew I had to beat Megan to make that team. She knew she had to beat me. But the 400m Medley clashed with my age group's 200m Butterfly only fifteen minutes before it – two of the hardest races on the program. I asked Ursula if I could withdraw from the Butterfly.

She said, "No." No reasons, just 'No'.

My tolerance for her had already dwindled – she kept cheering for random yellow caps because I was sure she couldn't tell if they were Ryde swimmers or not; she had suggested that mega-doses of bi-carbonate of soda might thin the blood and help a person to swim faster (I shouldn't worry, the nausea and diarrhoea are only temporary); her sessions were mind-numbingly boring. But I was shocked and angry at her refusal to see the bigger picture in this case. It didn't cross my mind to withdraw anyway. In the swimming world, what coach says goes. I wanted to do the right thing and she was the boss, but I hated her for it.

I came fourth in the Fly and, completely stuffed, I struggled to seventh in the Medley. Elli Overton won and I was glad of that. Megan, second. Sometimes you just know what should have been. My chances for the Darmstadt team were buried and I was furious, embarrassed at my seventh place and betrayed by my coach. My dad came down to the pool's edge to console me and I lived up to the foul-mouthed reputation they'd given me: "I'm never training with that fucking bitch again."

Self-control was not something that came easily that night, but when I'd sucked the tears back sufficiently I emerged from the change room. Megan's father spoke to me for the first time in months.

"Y'can't winnem all, luv," he gloated.

Somehow I managed to purse my lips into something that resembled a smile and turned away, but inside I boiled.

My step-ladder to the Barcelona Mount Olympus was buried with my chances for the New South Wales Darmstadt team and I was lost. The next challenge was going to be sitting through the announcement of the New South Wales team without disgracing myself. But sit I would. John Konrads would have been gracious enough in defeat to do as much and I was determined they weren't going to have the satisfaction of seeing me run like a snivelling coward. I was a warrior, albeit a sore and sorry one.

I'd never go back to Ryde.

Never.

I'd carry those black and white images in my heart, but I'd never go back.

Two

Wherever you go, you'll top all the rest.
Except when you don't.
Because, sometimes, you won't.
 – *"Oh the Places You'll Go"*, Dr Seuss

8.

"Take away my pride, I will rise again"
 -*"Rise Again"*, DJ Sammy

GRACE AFTER LOSING IS NO MORE THAN the window dressing of disappointment. There is always a vow to get them next time. That's what I think. Megan was on the Darmstadt team. Ursula hadn't even nominated me.

I was suddenly very tired and I just wanted to go home. Melbourne was cold and raining for me that night and I needed to escape that suffocating, steamy indoor pool full of those suffocating, smiling faces so I could cry and blame my wet cheeks on the rain. But I couldn't move fast enough. I was in slow motion, just like Collie and I used to move when we played underwater tea parties – every moment floaty despite the rush to get arrival, tea, cake, animated conversation and departure done in one breath; every expression exaggerated like a clown so the message was clear without words; the rising panic that you were running out of air… But I wasn't underwater. Sadly, I was in the stands while the announcer droned on about other teams, some kind of Australian one, amid the boom of everything stiflingly aquatic.

"Julie Majer, Queensland…"

"Hmm… the greyhound…" I registered.

"Nadine Neumann, New South Wales…"

Dad jumped out of his seat and I had a vision of him in a line out on a Paris rugby oval. Why was he jumping? Still slow-motion.

"Elli Overton, New South Wales…"

Collie screamed. I thought she'd been bitten by something. But Mum's trembling tears beat the understanding into me, still in slow-motion.

"What?" I said, not sure whether it was a sick joke.

I didn't even know that the team existed – The Australian Youth Team. I went to jelly for a whole new reason – I was on an Australian team! I would contest a tri-series of meets in New Zealand. I was one step closer to a black and white photograph! Fast-forward took over.

John Konrads winked at me from somewhere distant and I laughed! Sometimes it pays to sit tight.

We did leave Ryde, as I'd eloquently vowed. My dad did have it out with the club president. And he was not re-elected. Sean loved Megan and Jess. And I was not sad to see it all go.

This new chapter began with roses and joy and anticipation. It also began with me, a 14-year-old, calling the shots. I decided where I would swim, with whom, and how often, and my parents turned themselves into pretzels to accommodate. Up at 4.15am; drive from Ryde to the other side of Sydney to train with the coach I had chosen at the Warringah Aquatic Centre; wait, bleary eyed in the grandstand to take Colette 45 minutes through peak-hour traffic to her school in Denistone while I walked across the road to my new, co-ed school in Frenchs Forest; work at Macquarie Uni in Ryde; collect Collie and make the peak-hour trip back across Sydney to the pool; wait for two hours before the night-time trek back across Sydney again. And do it all again the next day. And the next… I didn't see my home in daylight for months before we moved house in desperation.

For me, it was worth it simply because training was never boring. I loved my coach, 'Grub', a teddy bear of a man with an eye for Breaststroke I'd never come across. I felt sure any man who could smile so energetically at 5am was a man worth being around. But I did miss the Ryde outdoor pool.

My mum had loved her morning swims. She loved the smell of the air and the damp of the grass and the tingle of the sun being born, waking the birds and gently coaxing the world to life. My dad always said he did his best work at night when the silent hush stretches forever and there is nothing but a darkness he could carve with his thoughts. I liked crisp summer mornings at Ryde in the growing light, standing beside my mum as we waited for the pool gates to be opened, wondering at her discipline to come every morning for her forty laps. But I always did my best work in the evenings, just like my dad. And when the winter came, the mornings were a torture of icy rain drops that reminded me that Dad would also rather be warm and safe in bed.

Warringah was different. It was controlled, indoors, always the same yellow light and sticky musk air. It was never summer or winter and the only hint at time of day came from the absence of noise in the mornings and the aroma of hot vinegar chips in the evenings. My new life began each day with the excitement of slipping down the 4.15am rabbit hole, adventures in Wonderland that began and ended in the darkness of car rides north-east, west, north-east, west… But the schedule lost its sheen trip by trip, stale-aired morning followed by stale-aired night. The buzz of the new never lasts.

As it turned out, my new chapter wasn't a long one. History does, in fact, repeat itself – swimming club stars usually have club presidents as fathers; coaches usually bow to the pressure exerted by the club that employs them; and swimming fast tends to piss exactly the wrong people off. I did it again at the Warringah Aquatic club, pissed exactly the wrong people off, so I decided I would leave after my international debut in New Zealand. It would be easier to just go and try again elsewhere; see if I could finally get it right, socially. They say third time lucky, so I figured I was in with a chance.

*　*　*

Going to New Zealand with The Australian Youth Team made me feel invincible. My Uncle Toby's branded bag full of goodies was a sure sign that I was elite. I'd made the big time. At the airport I didn't say a proper goodbye to Mum and Colette because they were just too embarrassing; blubbering all over the place. No one else had to kiss and hug their family as much as I did. It was like my mum was trying to octopus herself to me and Colette had no sense of personal space either. Dad had his video camera glued to his face like he was filming a movie star for a story on *60 Minutes*, and why he had to do the whole mushy goodbye thing I'll never know, because he was coming with me! When I finally prized myself away, Colette ran after me with her arms outstretched like she was meeting some lost lover in a field of daisies. I just kept walking.

Even though I felt like a bit of a loser having my dad tag along with a professional swimming tour, it was kind of comforting. He was pretty good with a camera but more than that, he was a great person to have around at competition time – always calm and he always knew what to say, when to say it and when to just talk about something else.

The tour started in Christchurch and I felt good in the water: smooth and powerful, like a sailfish (they can swim faster than 110km/h, you know). It showed in every event. I was a champion. I rose to every challenge, was unafraid of the 'big meet stage' and I flew!

Before the 400m Individual Medley at the second meet of the tri-series in Wellington, I was pretty sore from all my other races over the past few days. When discussing my race plan, Dad said that I should go out hard but relaxed in the Butterfly and then just tough it out for the rest of the race because he knew that I had the endurance, even if four days of racing a full program had taken its toll on my muscles. I wasn't so sure. I felt good in the water, but the light and powerful Nadine had been sapped. He said to go out there and just have fun and that appealed to me. I *was* having fun, so expressing it in my race should be no problem all.

"You've got nothing to lose, and you know your Breaststroke is the best out there."

He was right. I had to try the 'out hard and hang on' race plan.

But after the Butterfly leg I knew I was going to die. The burn was everywhere, but my Backstroke was my weakness, so I had to keep pushing until my stomach felt like it was going to explode. When I turned for the Breaststroke, I couldn't see anyone behind me… only one splashing body a long, long way in front. For a moment I wondered if they'd all passed me, but I realised that the girl ahead was doing Backstroke, so the others must have all been behind... I was dizzy and strangely disassociated from my body, but thankfully not burning anymore, so I tried to catch her, the New Zealand cap in front of me... and I did... then I passed her and kept going. I'd never felt so euphoric!

As I approached the wall on my last lap, the rest of the team were on their feet, I could hear them and I skimmed the surface of the water like a speed boat, the spray from my own wash whipping my face on every breath. I was light and powerful again and I became the third 14-year-old Australian ever to break the five minute barrier! No one was more excited than my dad.

Nothing beats sharing a celebration with your family, no matter how daggy it is for a teenager to have a chaperone. But it was strange: I didn't feel judged by that group of elite swimmers. I could sit and chat with my dad, I could swim fast, I could be as gregarious or as focused as I liked and I didn't feel frowned upon. For the first time, on that Australian Youth Team, I felt like I had actually found friends who understood me and my swimming thing: Daniel Kowalski, Matthew Dunn, Elli, Jacqui, Simon, Jules... There was no bitching, no wicked eyes that pretended to embrace but really spat, not even bitter rivalry between us and our Kiwi competitors.

Well... the Kiwis did laugh at our pathetic team cheers, but who could blame them? "Lean to the left! Lean to the right! We all train on Vegemite!" was hardly goose-bump material. They took pity on us on our final bus trip together. We were heading through the countryside to the last of our competition venues in Auckland, Aussies on one side of the bus, Kiwis on the other. They tried to teach us the Haka, but when the boys stood up, started stamping their feet and beating their chests, the whole bus tipped on a deadly angle over the narrow bridge we were crossing. The rear-vision mirror smashed and the driver bellowed, pale faced and trembling! Haka lessons were over.

I swam fast again on the last night of competition in Auckland, as I had throughout the tri-series. The Australians smashed New Zealand in the point score and nobody seemed to care. It felt like I had reached a level beyond all petty concerns and was racing for nothing more than experience and fun. Okay, so maybe the team's head coach withdrew me without explanation from the 200m Individual Medley, my last event; and maybe that decision was made to make sure that one of the other Aussie girls won the 200m Medley instead of me; and perhaps that was to make sure she won the point score for the overall Swimmer of the Series award; and it's possible that her coach being mates with the team head coach helped influence the decision. It felt a bit like history repeating again, but I really didn't care. In New Zealand it had been about the swimming, about going fast and about being with people who did the same, who were made of the same stuff as me. I'd found my place. This was where I belonged.

* * *

Back in Australia and looking down the barrel of starting at a new club again, I was nervous, though I didn't know why. It was not as though I'd never changed clubs before, started with a new group of swimmers, new coach. In the past I had looked forward to it. "Looking in the mirror at 4.15am can be a rude shock to anyone's confidence," I told myself. "Just get going."

As Dad drove me to the pool, I tried to figure out why my stomach felt so damn wobbly. I guess I'd kind of ignored what happened to my body over in New Zealand and that would make anyone shaky. We had never finished racing until late at night over there, and over there everything shut at nanna-hours, so most of the time we got scraps of greasy chicken and meat with a few frozen veggies from restaurant owners who reluctantly reopened their doors for a few starving swimmers. Snacks of anything healthy had been hard to come by, but luckily we were sponsored by Uncle Toby's, so we'd had a permanent all-you-can-eat buffet of yoghurt-top muesli bars to stuff ourselves with. By the end of the nine-day tour, I had set a new 'world record': I was nine kilos heavier than on the day I'd left Australia. One kilo a day. And my dad had the video to prove it. My slow and steady expansion was clear, but I'd been blitzing the pool, so why should I care? It was about swimming fast, right?

I'd risen to new swimming heights. I needed a squad that was professional, elite; one with real Olympians and Commonwealth Games medallists; real stars to add to those whispered promises of my black and white John Konrads. The Carlile Club was the one I had chosen.

I slipped into the homogenous environment of the Warringah Aquatic centre, but instead of turning left to go to the deep end of the pool with Grub and his club; I turned right and headed for the shallow end where my new squad was gathering. It felt spooky, like I'd come full circle. Megan was there – she'd started training with the Carlile Club after the collapse of the old president's reign. And the head coach, my new coach, was a man named Paul. I wondered if he remembered how much I loved the jelly babies he used to give me if I did well in one of his lessons when I was just learning to float, bubble and splash my toes.

"Breathe," I told myself. "It is an elite squad. Exactly where I belong." But the butterflies in my gut wouldn't be silenced.

They say tornadoes start with the beating of butterfly wings, and I reckon they're right.

My first Australian Team.
Leaving for New Zealand as part of the Uncle Toby's Dolphins.

9.

"I'm not crazy; I'm just a little unwell"

-"*Unwell*", Matchbox 20

ONE TRUE LIFE, ONE PERSONALITY, ONE ME – as long as I was aquatic and terrestrial, it was never going to happen. My heart split again.

My parents thought I should be nice and polite and generous and kind and smart and mature and responsible, so that's what I tried to be. The guys at training thought I should be tough and smart and funny and cool and hot and naughty and one of the boys, so that's what I tried to be. And at school I tried to be whatever I should be to fit into the group I was hanging out with at the time, but I was always the outsider trying too hard to fit in. And I felt pathetic when I should have been happy. But why?

Maybe it was because my parents were stricter than most other parents I knew and I was too scared to disappoint them. Or maybe it was the guilt I felt for getting them into financial trouble all because, at 14, I had decided that we should move house for my swimming. The guilt made me try so hard to live up to what I thought they expected of me. Or maybe it was because I so desperately wanted the people at swimming to like me and respect me as one of them, so I tried too hard to be what I thought they wanted. Or maybe I was just naturally a liar and a fake. Whatever the reason, I had one identity for the water, another on land and I didn't much like it.

At home, in our new house in Narraweena on Sydney's Northern Beaches, I had the best bedroom in the world. My dad built it for me. The house was too small for us all – four humans, a large, hairy and very dopey dog and a budgie with a bigger personality than all of us put together – but in the rush to buy it, nobody noticed how small it was until we actually moved in. That's why Dad built out the garage with mezzanine level, skylight and double glass doors opening to the garden; built it especially for me. He was a frustrated carpenter and thanks to him I could pretend to study in peace. Even Buffy the dog wouldn't enter without an invitation. Piccolo the budgie did because, according to him, he owned the joint.

I should have been happy in my 'teenager's retreat', but the room became important to me because my world had begun to deteriorate. I didn't know what to do, how to handle it all, so I'd literally crawl into my cave and shut the door on everyone… except the bloody bird. In a way the escape was gold, especially in the short-term, but in the long-term it turned out to be brimstone.

The madness had all started in New Zealand without me noticing, but slowly other events added their punches to my spirit until I was knocked out flat.

First, it was the Carlile Club high performance squad. It was as tough to break into as my bedroom, and I certainly didn't have an invitation. They were real Olympians and Commonwealth Games medallists, and mainly teenage boys and I was out of my league. To be honest, I was more intimidated by the sprinkling of skinny, beach-bronzed, sun-blonde, wide-eyed, bikini-model-perfect-girls, than the boys. In comparison, I was the fat, ugly duckling who, on a whim and in a moment of complete insanity, thought she suited that kind of stage. My only hope of being respected was to be tougher than the rest. That's the kind of thing that gets people to raise their eyebrows and nod their head in the swimming world.

I'll never forget my first week. I nearly killed myself in the first session and session two had me in tears (take note – crying is a rather ineffective way of gaining respect in a male-dominated sporting arena). Crammed into a tiny 25m indoor tub at Narrabeen – five to a lane – I found myself in the same lane as Simon Upton. He was an endlessly tall man with an arm span that took up the entire lane width and then some, the perfect physique for a Backstroker. I was devastated to be in his lane – not only was I a Breaststroker (notoriously slow), but I was new and scared of him. About halfway through the session, my hand clipped Simon's as I swam past him on the other side of the lane and I thought I'd broken my wrist. I stopped in mid-stream, gasping, tears already flooding my goggles, and gingerly nursed my crimson hand. Simon towered and, obviously hurt as well, bellowed, "Who the hell do you think you are? You fucking idiot! What are you doing in my lane anyway? Shit! Bloody idiot..."

I stuttered some blithering comment and shut my eyes. Pathetic. He sped off in a rage. I churned and seethed for the rest of the session. Deep down, I was sick of running away from prima donnas who didn't like me crowding their spotlight. I may have been the round little new kid, but I was tired of feeling bad for things I shouldn't.

From that day, I got angry and got tough and matched it with the boys at every session. If they cursed at me, I trumped them. If they tried to shake me with their smut, I smiled and took their jokes to a new low. I swam tougher than them; I pushed harder than them; I was coarser and meaner and smarter than they were. And it really wasn't too difficult to pretend I was a boy. I found the swearing part came particularly naturally; after all, I did get some good training from the rough girls in the toilets early on in my schooling, and my first official English word, spoken with great conviction when I was just two, was actually 'fuck' – uttered in Mutti's lounge room when my block tower fell. I was a natural.

It can actually be quite satisfying to just let it all out sometimes, but rising to every one of the boys' physical challenges got harder and harder. It began to feel like round ten of a title fight. John Konrads' smiling black and white face was fading. His smile didn't look as encouraging anymore. Some days my shadowy memory of that photo made him sneer, superior that he made it while I was not tough enough to; other days he winced at my pain and his promises of Olympic glory that still pushed me. But most of the time I couldn't even remember what the picture looked like. I wanted to ask him if this was how it was meant to be, if this was really what it took…

The guys at training called me 'Wobbles' because my mountainous rear end would send shock waves up my back fat and down my thunder thighs whenever I limbered up for a race. They thought it was hilarious, so I went along as though it didn't upset me. I even joined in and called myself a 'pea-hearted porker'. They laughed, approval gained, but I cried a lot when I was alone in my cave. Their quips – "Whoa! Was that an earthquake? Oh, Wobbles, it's just you!"; "Tidal wave! Sound the alarm! Oh, it's just Wobbles diving in!"; "Quick, call Greenpeace! A whale is beaching itself!"; "Hey! Where did all the pool water go?" – weren't very original, but they cut.

I knew I'd put on weight in New Zealand, a lot of weight, but I had swum fast, so I hadn't thought about it. Until it became the only thing I thought about. So I stopped eating. Not completely, but almost. I had to lose the enormous Uncle Toby's yoghurt top muesli bar I had strapped on in New Zealand, but no matter what I did, the weight just kept piling on. I could sniff a celery stick and I'd get fatter. I'd have a Vegemite sandwich and an apple all day, no breakfast, half my dinner, but the weight wouldn't budge. Paul worked out with me in the gym for a while, but nothing changed. I was sure he thought I was a closet pig with chocolate stashed in my sock drawer.

I weighed in every morning, but that pressure did nothing for weight loss. We just watched it creep higher until I topped 76 kg (I was only 155cm tall), so Paul gave up watching. Scientists believe a reasonable skin-fold range for female athletes is between 50 and 70mm (a measurement of how much fat you're carrying over your muscle at various points on your body); I was well in the 100-club and not proud to be so. By the time I reached 127.8mm skin folds and 79kg, I wanted to die. You can't swim fast when you're dragging an extra 20 kilos of lard through the water. I was getting slower by the day, despite being a workhorse.

It was bad for a long time, but it really hit home how much trouble I was in when I couldn't concentrate in training. It took all my focus to count the four laps it took to swim 100m. One... Two... Three... It was primary school stuff and it was beyond me. I was swimming slow and sluggish for no reason and I was continually being lapped. A lot of the time I couldn't remember how often they'd passed me. It was as though my brain was dying. I couldn't read, couldn't even see properly a lot of the time. And I didn't care. Just wanted to swim. Make it to Barcelona. Photo on wall.

I became sensitive to the heat, and my skin itched and burned with a kind of heat rash a lot of the time at training. And the itching was usually accompanied by a troupe of drummers that pounded in my head. Sent me spinning. Every time, I panicked. I wheezed. I couldn't breathe. The roof closed in on me. I suffocated. My costume was too tight. My goggles and cap squeezed the brain that threatened to explode from my skull. I was in an oven. Needed to get out. Get out. Get out...

Other days I was cold. So cold that my insides shook uncontrollably and I'd sit under a scalding shower, huddled in a ball, rocking and shivering, praying for it to end. The earthquake in my bones made me clench my jaw so tight that the drummers returned to smash around in my head again. Sometimes the headaches got so bad that I was in a vice and my eyeballs were being scooped out with teaspoons. Someone was slowly grinding away the bones in my skull. I wanted out...

It was not surprising how my body ached, given the training, but there was never a moment of relief. I wondered if every Olympian felt that way. God, how did they do it? Every morning I woke to the alarm, feeling as though I hadn't slept in a century, as though I'd been stoned for a crime I couldn't remember committing, every muscle stripped from bones that groaned, brittle in the acid water. Everything creaked, everything screamed and the migraines had me quietly weeping in the corner of the training lane at almost every session. But I was always there. I trained on. I had to. I had nothing else.

I hated school. I didn't understand anything that the teachers said and no one really liked me and it was boring and because my brain didn't work, it was like I was not even there most of the time anyway. I was sick of my family. They just nagged and I had nothing to say to them because they wouldn't have understood and they were more focused on cute and perfect Colette anyway. I had no friends or interests outside of swimming or school. No time or energy for that anyway. No parties. No invitations anyway. No boyfriend. No interest anyway. Nothing except swimming.

Still, I figured this is what it took to make it to the top, and I was Barcelona bound, remember?! They said so. Though I didn't know how it was possible anymore. John Konrads had been replaced by images of Laurie Lawrence dragging his knuckles down a brick wall until they bled and then holding them up. "This is pain. Now get back in the water." He flashed through my delirious mind a lot. He was the whip with which I self-flagellated, diligently, twice a day, every day through sessions I never dreamed I could complete; six to seven kilometres each time; sessions that looked like:

1500m warm-up (skills, drills, short sprints to get the body going)

10x400m Individual Medley (each within ten seconds of your personal best time)

10x100m Main Stroke (one easy one maximum effort)

500m cool down

If you weren't vomiting, paralysed or unable to breathe after that, you were one of the lucky ones because you'd be less likely to die in the ripper of a session they had planned for the afternoon. I hoped I would die. Then at least the pain would stop and they'd never be able to say I didn't make it because I was too weak.

A good angel and a bad one were constantly doing battle in my head but I didn't know which was which. One voice said, 'This is not natural. If this is what it takes to be the best, then it's too hard. You can't keep this up.' When I heard that voice and considered stopping, the other voice would say, 'That's right, maybe this was never your destiny anyway. Maybe it is all just a silly childish fantasy that you're too stupid to realise is impossible ... for you anyway.'

It worked every time. The two voices, so similar, I'd get back in the water.

Paul was convinced I was just a moody teenager with boyfriend issues, girly issues or crap at home. Parents weren't allowed on pool deck, so they didn't see me hurt. A lot of coaches believe parents are a nuisance, and I agree, some of them are. They ask too many questions, make too many demands. Terrestrial life and aquatic life were perfectly separated by a wall of silence. Paul wanted me to swim fast, that was his job, and I was failing him. My parents were baffled that I was still getting up for training every morning despite looking like Death. They were confused by my outbursts of fury, and I couldn't blame them. They wondered who this monster that had taken Nadine's place was. I wondered the same thing. I could see that I was different, that I'd changed dramatically, but I couldn't stop it. All I knew about myself was that my name was Wobbles and I was 15. Everything else was a mystery to me.

Even though I was deadly tired, I couldn't sleep. Days and nights were exactly the same – a stream of drifting in and out of consciousness whether upright or horizontal, eyes open or closed, on land or in water. But I still swam.

It was like being possessed. Not in control, not able to make a decision and not able to articulate what was happening. My brain didn't have access to words. But I still swam.

I snapped like a rabid dog for no reason at almost everyone. I abhorred myself for my anger, my weakness, my eating, my fat, my misery, for everything, and I turned the smallest mistakes into powerful evidence to support my self-loathing. But I still swam.

* * *

My darkest point came on a sunny day. I sat alone in the concrete quadrangle at my average Sydney public school. I did so almost every lunch time. I couldn't be bothered making the effort to be friendly. The drab, grey, slightly scarred concrete surroundings reflected my mood perfectly.

"I'm fat, lonely, stupid. I can't do anything right. I'm a try-hard. I'm weak, I'm untalented. I'm a cranky bitch. I'm nothing," drifted through my mind.

My disgust circled in my head like a ring of bullies shoving a frightened little dweeb from sneer to sneer, taunting, pinching, terrorising.

I observed the other kids about their happy business of charming each other and I wondered, "If I didn't pretend to be something I'm not, then who would I be?" Simon Upton's furious question resurfaced, "Who *do* I think I am?"

"I am nothing," was the only reply and the bullies in my head started chanting, "Wobbles is nothing! Wobbles is nothing! Big, fat, nothing!"

A hole that I neither had the will nor the strength to climb out of entombed me, and all my dreams of Olympic glory evaporated. The only way out was to end it. All of it.

I wanted an eternal sleep that would drown the bullies in my head. I wanted to die.

When I got home, after training of course, I crawled into my bedroom-cave and wondered how I might do it.

I wondered the same thing every night for weeks.

But I still trained.

I trained to get away from my perfect sister: she looked like a nymph, she sang like a nightingale, she studied like a scholar, she did charitable work, she volunteered to make old people smile at a nursing home for Christ's sake! I hated her!

I went through the motions of every day just to keep my nagging mother off my back: "Are you okay? You look tired. What's wrong? How is training? Did you eat your lunch? Why aren't you hungry? Have you got homework?" She never stopped!

I hid my plummeting school results to avoid my father's disappointment: "Do you need help with your essay? What are you reading? How is training? How far did you go today? Are you sure you're keeping up with your school work? You look tired…"

"I am tired, so back off!" my mind screamed.

And all the time I wondered how I was going to opt out. The voices kept taunting, "You can't even get it together enough to top yourself. You really are pathetic. A total loser." They were relentless. And right. I couldn't muster the will or the focus to even make that decision.

I sat my half yearly Year 10 exams, and it was my geography test that eventually made my exit decision for me.

10.

"And so that I do remember to never go that far, could you leave me with a scar?"

– *"Scar"*, Missy Higgins

WATER IS DIVINE WHEN IT MOVES: it sings and burbles, brimming with life, power and exuberance. I was a stagnant pool that destroyed the very things that once gave me joy. Where I once was spurred on by the nobility of a dream, I was now only motivated by a desire to spit in the faces of all those who said I couldn't do it. Where I once was called by a love of the sport, I was now driven by a fear of life without it. Where I once was thrilled at the thought of being great, I was now plagued by the thought of being nothing.

And yet swimming, paradoxically, was keeping me alive only to slowly drain every sparkle of life from me.

I got 0/100 in that geography exam. My name said it was my paper but I hadn't even attempted the multiple choice section. I couldn't understand what the questions said, let alone what they were asking, and by the time I reached option D, I'd forgotten what A, B and C had been. When I got my result, dread emptied my stomach. It was only a matter of weeks before my report would squeal to my parents.

That afternoon, Mum picked me up from school. She was nice to me. I hated her. She asked questions and I grunted. She kept on once we were home and I snapped… properly.

I called her the name that no girl utters, "Fuck off, c…"

The glossy sheen of her skin became a lather and the flawless curve of her cheeks crumpled under the vice of her jaw. Her perfect button nose flattened and flared as her lips became a gash that made her eyes fill with blood. The veins in her neck pulsed to the surface, bringing with them fierce red blotches that spread until her head was a molten rock set to launch. I turned away, satisfied that she'd lay off now.

But she flew, enraged.

She swung.

She cracked me across my back with the full weight of her fury.

We stared, stunned.

She'd broken the barrier I had built.

My walls crumbled and we cried.

The truth of nine months in Hell spilled from every crack in my fragile being. Even my dad cried while Colette frantically, silently searched for a way to ease our pain. I told them everything. All of it.

I had no choice but to accept that I was sick.

I stopped training.

Paul was disgusted, but not surprised.

Wobbles was weak.

* * *

The search for answers began with Dr Fisher. I was afraid of him. He'd embarrassed me once when I'd stuffed my Blu-Tack ear plug too far into my ear and a piece got stuck. The next morning, Mum and I had sat in the silent waiting room flicking through magazines from the early '80s, pretending to read but really trying to guess what ghastly infection every other person in the room had. Our musings had been interrupted when the secretary decided to play back all her old answering machine messages and carefully erase them, one by one, making sure she had not missed any important details. My mother's voice came through the speakers like a voice from above:

"Uh, good morning Dr Fisher, it's Helma Neumann. You may think you're not hearing right, but Nadine has a piece of Blu-Tack stuck in her ear and we're a bit concerned. We can't get it out. We've tried all sorts of things, but she is totally deaf on one side, so it would be lovely if you could see us in the morning…"

Everyone had pretended that what they were reading was mildly amusing, but I saw their clumsy glances at the crimson girl who was well over the age of putting strange objects in her ears. I hated Dr Fisher for that.

But this time there was no public ridicule, just a stubborn refusal to believe that I could have glandular fever, and when the test came back negative I was sure I sensed his satisfaction.

"She's just a bit run down. Rest for a while, and have some fun. You know, if she had glandular fever, she wouldn't be able to train the way she has been. She'd be flat on her back."

Barcelona was only 18 months away.

I went to another doctor, had another blood test – negative to all anomalies.

Two more doctors, more tests – negative, negative, negative to everything.

"You're fit and healthy. There's nothing wrong with you." But the bass drum and axe in my head suggested otherwise. Perhaps I had a tumour.

"It's all in your mind. Maybe it's time you snapped out of it." But I knew how much I wanted out and clicking my ruby heels was not working.

"It's just teenage stuff, you know, puberty blues. Do you have a boyfriend?" No! Because I'm too damned fat and too damned angry!

"Maybe she needs to see a psychiatrist. She really could do with some help for her depression. There are drugs that could pep her up a bit." The doctors stopped speaking to me directly. I was incapable of comprehending their wisdom. Maybe they were right. All in my head – imagining exhaustion, pretending to ache, creating head spins, manufacturing migraines... Maybe I was completely mad.

But my parents wanted their daughter back.

New doctor. New tests. Positive to Epstein Barr Virus.

"Nadine, these tests tell us that you had glandular fever. Probably about nine months ago. That's why it's been so hard to detect. You don't have it now, but because you kept training when you were sick, your body has broken down completely. According to these tests your… liver doesn't work properly. Your metabolism is shot. And given the symptoms you've described I'd say you're suffering adrenal exhaustion. Do you find it hard to sleep?… mhmm… Your serotonin levels are probably, well, not good, which will throw your melatonin levels out, too. Your immune system is completely hypersensitive and hyperactive. It's attacking itself every time you're under any kind of stress and, well, basically it all adds up to Chronic Fatigue Syndrome." The doctor paused for a response.

Blank.

"It's otherwise known as ME."

Blank.

"Yuppie flu?" he tried.

"And the depression, the mood swings, the big fat air-head bitch that I am?" I finally asked.

"Is all part of it. You're not making it up. It's a very real condition, but it's relatively new on the scene so it's not really well understood."

The word 'chronic' in conjunction with 'fatigue' sounded like an accurate description of how I felt. I was strangely relieved. It was something physical, an actual disease.

"So it can be fixed, yes." I was seeing a glimmer of hope for the first time in ages.

"Well… we can try vitamins… ah… we can try some new, experimental treatments like Chelation Therapy – it's very good for the removal of heavy metals from the system and we've had some success with people suffering similar illnesses…" his voice trailed off and he started shuffling papers in my file.

"What do you mean?"

"Ah, what we really know about Chronic Fatigue is that you need a lot of rest. It's still not well understood, so…"

"Rest?"

"Yes. If you want to get some semblance of a normal life back, rest is crucial and it's important to learn how to manage your illness."

"What do you mean 'a normal life'? 'Manage my illness'?"

"Nadine, you won't be able to swim like you used to. It

would be unrealistic to think your body could cope with that, but you're pretty fit, so you might be one of the lucky ones. You might see some improvement in three, six months, but you know, most people struggle to get out of the worst of it for years. The research indicates that once you've got it, it's there for good, but people have found ways of managing it with things like meditation, vitamin treatments, you know?"

No. I didn't know. Too much talking. No swimming? No water? Struggle for years?

"We can help you with all of that, to try to get you back to school, able to concentrate for most of the day, get those mood swings under control. But it's going to take time. And loads of rest."

Time.

"We can help you with all that." He could see the glimmer of hope fading from my eyes.

I didn't want his fucking help! I either wanted my old life or no life at all!

* * *

I slept. I cried. I raged. I slept. I ached. I was tired of breathing – it was such an effort. I tried to will myself away, but I had no will. I didn't have the energy to fight with my parents when they took me to experimental treatment after experimental treatment – mega-doses of vitamin C that made my eyes puff up like a goldfish; Chelation Therapy that cost two arms and two legs and had me on a drip for hours at a time, three times a week; vitamin B12 injections.

Nothing made a scrap of difference.

I felt like I was on a Gravitron, spinning around and around so fast that I stuck to the wall as the floor dropped away from under me, fighting to suck in a breath, lift an arm, turn my head, formulate a coherent sentence that didn't contain some kind of fury-filled expletive. And no one knew where the stop button was.

Open Nationals arrived. The Carlile Club needed their Breaststroker for their Medley relay team. Mum and Dad said 'no'. The club heavies begged. I said 'yes' just to get away from the shot of guilt I got every time I looked at Mum and Dad's stress-worn faces. I thought maybe doing fun stuff with other teenagers might help me 'snap out of it'. We agreed, nothing more than the relay swim.

Mum wrote a long letter to Paul, explaining every nasty detail of my condition and I think she threatened castration should he break the pact. But Paul ignored the threat and without my parents in Melbourne to keep an eye on me, I found myself swimming every event. I couldn't say 'no' to coach. At the end of the meet, exhaustion and fury overcame weakness. Wobbles spat her anger to Paul's face.

I'll never forget his response: "It is my job to train you to be the best, so I'm going to flog you and if you survive and make it, that's great, and if you die in the process, that's just too bad."

There was nothing left to say.

Getting 'some semblance of a normal life' was the only thing left to do, but what for? Nothing about my life had ever felt normal anyway. And which life? The screwed up one in the water where I was just the resident fat joke, or the screwed up one on land where I was so awkward that I made myself cringe?

Frankly, I couldn't be fucked fighting for either.

11.

"Thank you India, thank you terror, thank you disillusionment"

– *"Thank U"*, Alanis Morissette

IF YOU'VE EVER HELD A LAMINGTON DRIVE, you'll know what it's like to be covered, ground to rafters, in chocolate and coconut. Mountains of boxes teeter – left side empties, right side fulls. Cream filled sponge and choc powder plumes choke the atmosphere where production lines of people dunk, drip, roll, pack, dunk, drip, roll, pack... By the end of the day every part of you is freckled with dark goo and the thought of cleaning those industrial-sized buckets of muck is enough to make your stomach flip.

And it was in our lounge room! Collie dunked and dripped, I rolled, Mum packed, Dad did whatever was needed after having constructed the trestle tables and drip trays, and the dog vacuumed coconut off plastic drop sheets on the floor.

We needed money.

Johanna Griggs trained with the Carlile squad. She was famous, and gorgeous – exactly the kind of glamour I was jealous of. She stopped coming to training one day and nothing was really said about it. I thought she might be having a well-earned break, but because she was a Commonwealth Games medallist, she had a write up in the paper. She was sick. Chronic Fatigue probably brought on by Glandular Fever. Same as me.

When Mum ran into her at my sister's school one afternoon, she was surprised to see Jo looking as radiant as she had always been. No sign of the cheesecake pallor that made my black eyes stand out like panda spots. Jo had heard I was struggling and I hoped she hadn't heard it in all its glory – I was still disgusted by my own frailty. But she knew what it was like and she put Mum onto a woman who sold herb-food that Jo thought may help. I was embarrassed that she was concerned for me, especially since no one else in the swimming world appeared to care.

You couldn't get the herb-food stuff in shops; it was still pretty new in Australia. It was sold through distributors, kind of like Amway, except there was no catalogue or 'Avon Calling'. It was much more like a secret drug deal. Under cover of night, we went to a stranger's house, she gave us the spiel, we had tea and watched a video about a 16-year-old middle distance runner who described my experience to the core, and then we had to decide if we were in or out. The runner was better and back running because of the stuff, this Chinese herb-food stuff, and even if she was exaggerating for TV, I wanted it. But the woman had saved the best till last – she told us the price. We left. We were 'out'. There was no way we could afford it.

I think the lamingtons were Colette's idea.

So relatives, neighbours, family, friends, everyone we had ever spoken to and many we never had, ate lamingtons for weeks so that we could buy two months' supply of another experimental remedy.

God, how it made me ill! I couldn't eat, couldn't get out of bed to pee, couldn't move. My glands sat like ping-pong balls behind my ears and at times, all I could muster to describe my situation was a groan. Mum rang the supplier in a panic: "What are you trying to do to my daughter? This stuff is killing her!"

"Oh good! It's the healing process. There's got to be a grand cleansing first! Tell her she can halve the number of meals she's having if it gets too much. It'll just stretch the process out a little longer, that's all."

I'd wanted to die often enough in the last 12 months, so if it was going to kill me, at least it would be final and relatively swift. I slept and moaned, for how long, I don't know. Then I was able to get up sometimes. And sometimes I was able to stay up for a little while after eating. Then I could read without forgetting how every sentence started. I had some days when I could smile and laugh, and every time I did, I would get so excited that I'd over-do it and end up in bed again for the next three days. But five weeks on, I started to paddle at the Manly Leagues Club pool and the water fed my parched soul. Seven weeks on and I started to train, tentatively. I was dodging mines, but actually dared to believe that the doctor may have been wrong.

A black and white photograph emerged from the fog – it was me, smiling, surrounded by ripples in the water.

* * *

People say that overcoming a serious illness gives them a reverence for life and a connection with their spirit that they never had before. Some say that trusting in a force greater than themselves is a comfort, and others say that faith comes naturally after a momentous fall. I don't really know why or how it happened for me, but I started to see connecting threads, chains of events and 'coincidences' that had conspired to lift me out of my impenetrable darkness.

Spirituality had never cropped up for me. I knew that Mum had been confirmed in the Lutheran church because she wanted a party and presents like her school friends, but Mum's parents had stayed away from churches because the priests did nothing but slander each other from their pulpits. I knew that Dad was Jewish, but his family hadn't practised ever since his grandmother had taken a goose to the rabbi to have it blessed – the rabbi said it wasn't kosher because of a malformed foot, but when she came back with a new goose, she found the original one smelling delicious on the rabbi's dinner table. But Collie and I had never been hooked up to any spiritual gang. So when I started to feel a sense of gratitude for having my life back, I began wondering who, exactly, I was thankful to.

Ask the question, and the answers will come. Through Jo's herb-food and one of my dad's academic colleagues, we met a man who introduced us to a woman who introduced us to a man with the answers.

The first man was Professor Ron Laura. We were introduced to him by my dad's work colleague who had undergone a miraculous physical transformation from fat to fit because of Professor Laura's weight training regime. I needed to relieve myself of the excess blubber I was still carrying, but I needed cross-training that was gentle, and this was it.

Ron Laura was a freak in every way possible. He was appointed to a Professorial Chair at 35; he was a visiting professor to Oxford, Cambridge and Harvard Universities; he was a champion body builder and on the judging panel for national body building competitions; he was a Martial Arts expert and a recording classical guitarist; he spoke seven languages fluently and had an extensive knowledge of Chinese herbs, most of which he cultivated in his garden; he had published many books and was a regular contributor to various health magazines. The picture of himself as a centaur that adorned the wall directly opposite the entrance to his private gymnasium was all that was needed to describe him.

But his training system made me physically stronger than I had ever been; leaner, too. Again I was grateful, but to whom?

Ron introduced us to Carmel, one of his students he knew was interested in health foods. We had become distributors of the 'miracle food' just to help reduce the ongoing cost of me eating it and were always on the look-out for prospective customers. She looked like an elegant blend of hippie witch and regal queen of ancient times. Her pale blue eyes looked past all surface appearances and the loose, grey top knot she wore gave her an air of Buddhist wisdom and she wanted two boxes of our herbs. No one wanted two boxes of our herbs without a trial.

"Why do you want two boxes?" Mum asked one evening as we sat in Carmel's lounge room. "You really should try one at a time."

"No, I need two. It sounds like exactly what I've been looking for," she said with a sweet, firm tone.

"Why two?" my mum persisted. "We can send you the second when you're ready." She sensed there was something Carmel wasn't saying and, unlike any reasonable person who knows when to mind their own business, she started to pry.

"I'm going away."
"Where to?"
"To India."
"To India? Oh… is there a particular reason why India?" Mum had always been interested in Eastern philosophies and India had some of the best holy men around. It made me squirm when she stuck her nose in like that. She did it all the time, and for some reason people found it endearing.
"Yes, I'm going to see someone."
"Oh, someone special?"
"God! Leave the poor woman alone!" I thought as I started to scan Carmel's bookshelves loaded with esoteric-sounding books – *A Course in Miracles, The Prophet, God Lives in India, The Tibetan Book of Living and Dying, Conversations with God, Autobiography of a Yogi.*
"A holy man," Carmel said matter-of-factly. And that was it. Mum leaned forward in her chair and after an hour of question and answer, she handed over the two boxes of herb-food and asked Carmel if she had anything she could read for more information.

A few days later the book arrived, *Divine Memories* by Diana Baskin, an American journalist. The blue cover showed a man with an afro hair-do in an oval frame. I didn't take much notice at first, but the Universe has a way of gently slapping you across the face until you recognise the answers to your questions.

* * *

I was not about to believe blindly. You take a new car for a test drive before you buy it; in fact, that's really what you do with most things, so why not with Faith?

What Mum read aloud from that blue book made sense but I found it hard to reconcile my past pain, still so raw in my bones, with the idea of a God who was looking out for us. Even though I had been living one life for a while – being 'me' whether I was in the water or out – and I was learning to like it; even though black and white had blended into shades of grey and John Konrads had came back out of the fog; even though I had learned which angel was good and which was bad and I was managing my moments of up and periods of down; despite all the moving forward I had done, I still found it hard to reconcile my past with the idea that I might be deeply grateful to 'God'.

No one had looked out for me. If there was a God, why didn't He help me when I was suffering rather than after the fact? If everything was just 'meant to be' and part of my 'life lessons', I wanted to know what I was supposed to have learned from the past 18 months. No one should have to feel the way I had, to be so desperate that they can see no way out of the pain. God needed to go on probation before I was going to accept Him as the answer to my universal questions.

So when Piccolo, our larger-than-life budgie, disappeared into the trees, I cut Him a deal. I think we all did, silently, out there on the back lawn, calling his name to the tangle of distant trees: "If You're so powerful, if You even exist, then You can fix this."

No flash of cheeky blue miraculously landed on my shoulder, therefore there was no God.

We were devastated at our little friend's disappearance. One of mum's work colleagues was staying at our place for the three days we would be in Canberra for my big come-back meet and she had been looking forward to taking care of our dumb dog and the budgie who made a game of calling out 'Where's Buffy?' while dive-bombing the dog as soon as she came to the sound of her name. She was saddened to know that Piccolo, with his precocious sense of adventure, would most likely be tormenting some local feline in no time.

On our third day in Canberra, between 1pm and 3pm, while I rested between heats and finals, my family was gently cheek-slapped by the universal consciousness. Reminder after reminder of our missing bird – his name all over packets of Christmas biscuits that Mutti normally sent from Germany; tables full of a rare plate that we used as his bath; a woman who shared the unusual name of Carmel's Indian holy man, Baba – they began to add up. Between 1pm and 3pm on that day, our friend in Sydney received a phone call, picked up a very tame, emaciated budgie some four suburbs away who, after a long sleep, declared, "Piccolo's a naughty boy!"

The thing I've learned about miracles is that they are relative and that you never dictate the terms. What is a miracle to me may just seem 'lucky' to you, unless we're talking about the big ones like materialisations, healings and packets of Tim Tams that never run out. But the everyday kind of miracle is one that makes you shiver on the inside, a feeling just like the tremor of anticipation before a race, a shudder that says, 'Yes, that means something to me'. It's the kind of feeling we're trained from a young age to rationalise away, but we all get it from time to time, even if we don't believe in it. Piccolo's return meant something to me.

Although it did take a while for me to be entirely convinced that God was alive and well and looking out for us in some strange kind of way, in the end I just got a kind of knowing; like a peace that I was never alone, even in the blackest times; a sense that something greater than myself had kept me here when I so desperately wanted out.

I did keep testing the universe to see if answers always came and it wasn't long before I inadvertently threw a real curve-ball. It was a good quality fuck-up that I desperately needed God's help to get out of.

Some lucky people get a second chance at life, but it's rare to get a third.

12.

"Sometimes you're the windshield; sometimes you're the bug"

– *"The Bug"*, Dire Straits

YEAR 11. Start of the New South Wales Higher School Certificate stress zone. 1992. Two weeks to the Barcelona Olympic Games. I wasn't going to be there. And all because I was an idiot; a damned stupid boy-mad idiot! Instead, I'd be at home in my lounge room, or maybe watching the fountain in our backyard ripple the surface of the fishpond, or maybe studying like senior students do. But I wasn't going to be watching The Games on TV. That would just bring back a shuddering memory of why I couldn't be there.

Life had been going so well. I was swimming fast again, I was happy again. Lynne, my new coach, was positive, my new squad was relaxed and I felt like I was in control. I could see myself in black and white, smiling that smile. But I was in love, and that's where it all went wrong.

Kevin was fully aware of his rippling attributes. He'd prance around the small Manly Leagues Club pool like it was his own private catwalk and the way I saw it, every king needed a queen. So, one Friday night after club races, I let my inner Cleopatra emerge. He suggested a game: who can dive out the furthest with their hands behind their backs? At 16, I should have been over such silly games, but flirtation knows no bounds, so I volunteered to go first.

"God, please let him be impressed," I prayed as I climbed onto the block, gut wobbling as though it was the race of my life. I leapt higher than ever before. I piked sharper than ever before. I hit the water vertically, followed immediately by the bottom of the 1.2m deep pool. Bloody hydrotherapy and their shallow pools.

They said I stayed under a long time. I don't know, but I remember my brain exploding with a thousand thoughts: "Fuck that hurt how embarrassing Kevin'll think I'm a loser I need air which way's up God I'm dizzy why can I taste blood I need air which way's up I feel weak I want to puke which way's up ooooooooh..."

I was holding the top of my head when I finally found oxygen. I'd ripped through the inside of my mouth with my teeth and broken a molar, I could tell. But overwhelmingly, I'd made a complete idiot of myself. As the first streams of blood trickled down the sides of my face to turn the grey tiles a deep burgundy, the majority of the crowd whispered from left to right and shot pathetic looks in my direction. That is, everyone except my mother, who had seen the whole thing transpire from the other side of the pool and was making quite the exasperated scene (and further humiliating me in the process).

Kevin had vanished.

Someone helped me out of the pool and gave me a towel to stop the bleeding. I was fine, apart from my bloody, throbbing, slightly spinning head and slowly swelling mouth. I was indignant all the way to the local medical centre where a doctor gave me an injection, pulled a splinter of pool tile out of my head and stitched me up.

"You'll be pretty sore tomorrow. You've probably just got whiplash, but Panadol will fix it. See you back on Wednesday to take your stitches out."

No one spoke on the way home. The silence squeezed me to inaudible tears. It was like a classical symphony – a sole violin plays that high E-minor for an age and the sound pierces through your throat as you hold your breath for the orchestra to thunder with a dramatic 'Da Da Da Dummmmmm'.

My disgrace was complete and I quietly stretched and massaged the whiplash. Panadol did squat. Mum wouldn't speak to me – I'd given her a heart attack and Dad's face was grey and distant. Collie sent silent glances of solidarity across the back seat and I loved her as she surreptitiously squeezed my hand. She was about to turn 13, and yet always managed to seem so poised in my chaotic moments. I wondered what she did when I was actually together and happy. I felt as though I didn't really know my sister, that I never paid her any real attention, and yet she was always there, like the little white witch I'd imagined her to be when we were young, spreading her magic when I needed it most.

By the end of the weekend, nothing had changed. My neck was stuck, seizing the whole top half of my body with the whiplash. We were five weeks out from the Barcelona trials. One day out of the water was a potential catastrophe! Mum convinced Dad to take me to our doctor on Monday morning to see if he knew a really good chiropractor in the area. She'd kind of forgiven my moment of lunacy, as mothers do, and she knew that Barcelona rested on getting rid of the whiplash.

The doctor came through. He booked me in with a chiro just down the road and we rose to leave, thanking him for getting us the appointment. I think the doctor was conscious of the fact that we were signing a Medicare slip for a two minute consultation, so he tried to stretch it out with, "So, any other aches and pains?"

"Um, it hurts the back of my neck when I swallow. Will that go away with the whiplash?" I was making him feel better. Of course it would go away with the whiplash. Everybody knew that.

He went the same shade of grey my dad had been since Friday night. "Sit down Nadine... I think you should have some X-rays before you go to the chiropractor. Just to be sure there's nothing we're missing."

Thirty minutes later I was in a green backless gown in a dark room, trying to hide my Bridget Jones underwear. Forty minutes later the three whispering doctors who were looking at ghoulish pictures of parts of my body I'd never seen, put me in a neck collar, handed me a big envelope and told us to go to the Royal North Shore Hospital for CAT scans.

Dad didn't say a word until we stepped outside. It had been a while since I'd seen his eyes red and moist like that. The thought of it still kills me.

"Do you know what this means?"
"I think so..."
I didn't.

The drive was another silent, slow one and somewhere in my head a voice was swearing. My stomach clenched slightly and my eyes got a little wider... the confused look that cows get when they know that where they're going isn't a happy place.

"He'll be right with you," said the nurse. Why she was so cheerful, surrounded by the moaning, sneezing, bloodied humanity in the emergency room, I'll never know. I was wretched. There's a reason they call you a 'patient'. 'Right with' means three and a half hours and I wondered how long it was for a non-emergency patient.

Dad rang work to cancel his classes for the day. I didn't try to imagine what he told them. I wasn't really thinking at all. I was too afraid of what my overactive imagination would conjure and how close it would be to the truth. I just kept repeating, "We'll be fine. Five weeks to trials. One day out is no biggie. We'll be fine..." Whoever I was trying to convince did not reply.

I was visited by an old doctor who looked remarkably like a garden gnome. With him he had a little plastic hammer that he knocked on the reflex points of my elbows and knees.

"Just checking your reflexes," he said, "making sure there's no nerve damage."

I watched, bewildered as my lower leg jumped to life involuntarily with every tap.

He tickled the palms of my hands.

"How's that? Feel it?" he asked. I wondered whether that constituted harassment. He pricked the soles of my feet with something cold and pointed and again asked if I could feel it, and with each nerve test, my nerves frayed. Fear crept in.

Finally, he nodded, grunted and kindly warned me, "Okay, well your nerves all seem fine, but just be careful not to move, you know, one slip and you could die."

That did little to comfort either my father or me. What was

the man talking about?!

It was like carrying an over-full cup of tea on a fine china saucer – the moment you think about it, it spills all over the place. Try sitting up in a bed in a room full of gurgling, groaning, moaning and tears, and then don't move your head. Not at all. Not a muscle. Don't move it when you need to go to the toilet. Don't move it when your dad, sitting next to you, asks if you want a drink. Don't move it when you sneeze from the formaldehyde in the air. Don't move it because some doctor told you that if you make one wrong move, you could die. I was spinning.

Our entire day was spent there. From that point all I really recall is my furious bargaining with God (if He existed) and the whirring of the CAT scanner. I was on the brink of meltdown when the spinal specialist finally arrived with coloured pictures of the inside of my neck.

He started to speak. "Miss Neumann, I understand you're a swimmer?"

I stared. 'Just get to it,' I thought.

"Yes, well that would explain how you got away with this. Well, that and a whole lot of help from above, I think."

I still stared.

"Right, well you're a very lucky young lady. You've broken your neck…"

He paused for a reaction and all I could think was, 'God, does he know I was flirting with Kevin?'

"If you look at these images here," he indicated three small lines in a coloured picture of a hollow disc, "this is your C1 vertebra, your Atlas, the one right at the top. See these lines?"

I could see them. I was numb.

"They're breaks. Big, clean breaks." He shook his head slightly in wonder and I heard my dad let out a short, sharp breath – the sound of his heart breaking. It killed me. He held my hand and I felt more guilty than I ever had.

"I'll explain why this is so remarkable," the doctor continued. I already knew what it meant, but didn't want to believe it.

"Okay, what normally happens is that the first vertebra shatters in an accident like yours; it normally explodes into tiny pieces that dislodge and either sever the spinal cord completely leaving the patient, well, dead or quadriplegic to put it bluntly. In that case, surgery is needed to clean up the mess and to fuse the spine to the skull, in simple terms…"

My mind wandered. Did he know I hated making my parents cry? Did he know I was going to the Olympics? Did he know that this couldn't happen to me? Not now.

"You know Superman?" he said in response to my blank expression. I was clearly not getting the full impact of his news. "Christopher Reeve? He had a similar accident to yours."

My mind gradually came around. 'It's broken. The first vertebra in three places… three neat slices of a cake. A broken neck. Fuck. All that effort. All those hours, those days swimming up and down a black line. All those years… I've wasted my life…'

"You know, Nadine, all those hours, all those years of swimming, it saved your life." The doctor was right.

I'd spent three days of stretching, massaging, playing around with a time bomb: don't move – might die.

"You know, there was a surfer came off the top of a wave and crashed into a sandbank and months later he drove over a speed bump and died. You're one very lucky young lady, Nadine! Somebody's looking out for you." Again, he was right.

Dad was so silent.

Denial helped me find my voice. "Will I be able to swim at the Olympic Trials? They're in five weeks, I should be fine by then…"

"You'll be in a cast for six weeks. You should be grateful to be alive. That your vertebra has held together is extraordinary. The impact was absolutely perpendicular, perfectly on top. If you'd hit on the slightest angle it could have been quite different." I could see he was bewildered. I was a greedy teenager without the slightest gratitude for the miracle my life had suddenly become.

But I didn't feel lucky right then. I couldn't comprehend

what the inside of my neck looked like, what my life could have been (especially given the number of speed bumps on the way into emergency), but I did understand that I wasn't even going to have the chance of getting to the Olympic Games and I was furious. I'd gone through enough to deserve it, so why would 'God' deny me that?!

I was strung up by the chin in the middle of a big metal frame that resembled a kid's swing set, my jaw clamped shut and the feeling of being strangled slowly becoming intolerable. The faultless ballerina posture made my lower back ache. For almost an hour the nurse heated, placed and sculpted strips of fibreglass mesh around my upper body, slowly, slowly transforming me into a Teenage Mutant Ninja Turtle... minus the ninja. Dad, tired and with hair now matching the pallor of his skin, looked on with the slightest glimmer of amusement. As the cast grew heavy, squeezed the air out of me and framed my face with white mesh, leaving a Frankenstein tuft of hair out the top, I finally grasped the enormity of what had just happened and did battle in my mind: Disappointment – my dream is gone; Relief – I am alive; Anger – this isn't fair; Shame – how dare I complain; Scorn – how could I be such an idiot; Wonder – how could I be so lucky?

There's something about being mummified that puts things into perspective. I had broken my first vertebra in a miraculous way – three breaks held together for three days by muscles developed through time spent in the very environment that broke me. Those three clean cuts would heal and on the last day of the Olympic Trials I would walk out of the hospital as though nothing had happened at all... but really, I should be dead. Everything here was too perfect and I had to concede that someone or something was looking out for me. I was not clever enough to orchestrate this on my own. I wanted to cry, but that would be ungrateful; I wanted to mourn the loss of Barcelona again, but I had life to celebrate. So I froze and did neither – control the sadness, show only relief.

I survived the suffocation of that first night in my casket but the weight, the heat and my gradually swelling body made it terrifying. I was constricted, couldn't breathe again, and again I felt like I was in an oven, only this time there really was no way out. Hot with panic. Jittery with claustrophobia. I had to use every scrap of my imagination to think myself into a vast green plain on a sunny day, daisies dancing in the soft, fresh, cool breeze brought to me by a pedestal fan. Exhaustion eventually reigned.

I survived being banished from my waterbed because my top heavy body sent the blood rushing to my swollen head when I lay down. The banana lounge was not nearly as comfy, but it was home for those six weeks. I learned not to sleep on my side perchance I amputate an arm with the pressure of my shell against it and I learned that if I lay face down on the coffee table, the back of my casing popped up just far enough for Mum to wipe a cool flannel against my prickling, stinking skin.

I survived the humiliation of my first day back at school being photo day – one of my friends confessed that her mother pointed, shocked at the sight of a big white beast in the centre and exclaimed, "What's that?!" I survived the many stumbles down stairs – it is hard to go down crowded stairwells without the luxury of looking at your feet. I survived the tormenting itch between my shoulder blades as my skin slowly rotted, thanks to Mr Trout's chalky metre-ruler – he placed it on my desk before every Biology lesson so it was there, waiting like a smiling friend as I walked in the door, and I'd spend the 40 minutes scratching.

I survived massive weight loss caused by my sudden inactivity, and because the cast became loose enough for me to crawl out of it, I relished the refitting that gave me the chance to shower, to wash away that old-sneaker stench that wafted around my face! I received flowers from people in my distant past who heard that I was in a wheelchair, paralysed for the rest of my life, and I was heartened to know the Ryde rumour-mill still worked so well.

Kevin loved me for the six weeks of my incarceration and then for one more week after that. But the sweetness of a younger woman and the removal of my one solid, white talking-point made me less alluring than he had originally thought. There's nothing quite like being dumped when you think you're finally normal.

The greatest pleasures in my six-week confinement came from being with my family and realising how unconditional their patience was. It came from feeling like I'd had a real life handed to me, one that included leisurely afternoons of awful children's game shows on TV – the terrestrial world exists between 3.30 and 6.30pm! I never knew! So, I decided to stay there a while.

I wouldn't train. School was more important since I'd missed The Games anyway, but I knew I'd never be able to leave the water completely. I could think there, and despite all the pain the water had given me as I plodded up and down the length of the pool in those endless hours of training, the music of the water still touched my core. To me, the sound of the water is the sound of heaven – the tinkle of bubbles as the surface breaks and swirls around your ears, the rhythmic, rumbling bass-drum of your breath, the roaring cymbals of your feet agitating the waves your body carves, the melodious movement of an element that supports you, surrounds you, becomes part of you, completely.

And the symphony plays through a silence that makes you feel the song is yours alone.

My song, locked away in a place of silence where a black and white photo waited for next time.

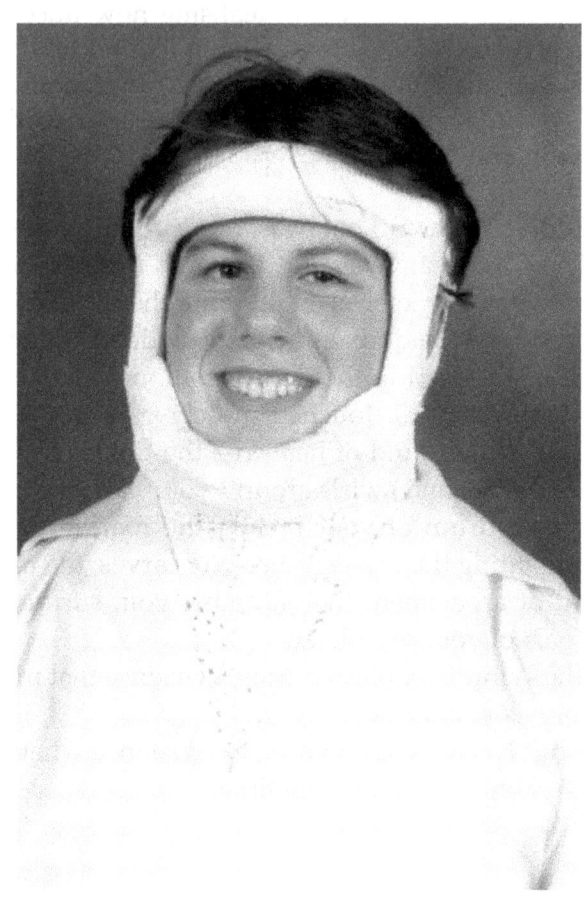

My first day back was school photos – the broken neck is eternalised.

13.

"Tonight we'll be starting all over again, and it feels like the first time"

    – *"Starting All Over Again"*, Bon Jovi

AT 18 I WAS TINGLING WITH THE HOPE of an eight-year-old again. It was the intermission that had renewed me; the two-year pause is where I gathered strength and strategy to go hunting for an Olympic flame again. It felt good to have reclaimed my focus and drive. It warmed me to think that, for the first time in two years, I would be on a mission where I'd dive into that cool expanse of blue and, looking back on those two years, feel such gratitude for the wisdom I had found. If I'd had it my way, I don't think I would have ever felt the kind of clarity and excitement I did then. Hindsight can teach us so very, very much.

Two years out is a long time in swimming. I still paddled from time to time for sanity and to cure the occasional bout of Higher School Certificate study-seizure, but most of the time I revelled in what it was to be kind of normal. I still never went to parties – I was still never invited because it was assumed I wouldn't go anyway, and they were probably right. A rigid lifestyle was so ingrained that TV and chocolate for afternoon tea was all the splurge I needed to feel utterly decadent and guilt-ridden.

    I was aiming for a result good enough to get into a Bachelor of Arts with a Diploma in Education at Macquarie University. I'd toyed with the idea of becoming a lawyer after a few successes with my school mock trial team, but I was too much of an idealist. There is a difference between justice and the law. Momentary thoughts of television journalism, acting and writing eventually gave way to the one career that would encompass it all – acting to entertain a class of 30 bored individuals, journalism to make my content relevant to their experience of the world, writing to report, to enthral, to inspire and to model, and all the time imbuing young minds with ideals of justice and morality. Put that way, I was aiming to be a saint, but it ultimately came down to the fact that the marks to get into teaching were lower than any of the other options I'd considered. And I was tired of aiming for lofty dreams. Really tired.

Then, suddenly, my school years were over and I was sad. School had become fun. I had found friendships with people who couldn't care less if I was a swimming goddess or not. I had found laughter and a sense of peace within myself and I relished the clarity with which my mind worked. Having been in the Chronic Fatigue fog for so long, learning and thinking was its own reward. I loved my teachers – they were my friends more than teachers. I loved a boy at school, Peter, a wiry, red-headed rebel with startling intelligence that contrasted his lax attitude to study. He was more interested in raves than in Shakespeare but I had managed to convince him to do 3-unit English with me. It took much cajoling, which I enjoyed enormously; making use of every one of my most charming faculties. Those late 3-unit afternoons with Mrs Hutchinson, 'Hutch', felt like being part of a privileged club. I loved debating the existence of God with my biology teacher, 'Troutie', during my many free periods – science clashing in a mental-gymnastic dance with philosophy. I even enjoyed the notoriety that came with being ex-communicated from the library for repeatedly creating a ruckus during my many free periods!

All aspects of my final two years at school left a gaping emptiness when that little bit of something secure ended. The rhythms of each day had become as comforting to me as the lapping of water in the pool gutters and I missed the absent-minded order of being governed by the bell.

I was meant to celebrate on the third of December. I was meant to look stunning with hair and makeup matching dress, shoes and handbag. I was meant to arrive at the flashy inner-city venue on Peter's arm and we'd dance with the others, reminisce and sing nostalgic songs as we squeezed tears from our eyes and swore we'd always stay in touch. It would have been a nice 18th birthday at my school formal, but instead it was spent in a small terrace house in Frankfurt, far from everything that was home. The end of my Higher School Certificate exams marked the beginning of the peak travel season, and to avoid paying almost double for airfares, November was when we had to leave. I had bled my parents of enough resources already with all my Chronic Fatigue treatments that I was in no position to argue. A birthday in Germany with my gorgeous grandmother, Mutti, was a privilege, even if I was a little nostalgic.

At first, the icy German winter had a dampening effect on everyone. Daylight leaked into the mornings at 9am and retreated at 3pm. People trudged through their days with internal shutters locked tightly against the chill and any sense of community, and the mood settled like a mouldy woollen blanket. We sat, chatted and ate; napped, chatted and ate; thought, played cards and ate… an endless, whispered cycle.

Mutti was on edge because we were going to 'God-forsaken, filthy, dangerous India to see a money-grabbing, brain-washing, cult-running, charlatan-guru' and since Colette, Dad and I had joined my mother in a vegetarian diet, the one talent Mutti was truly proud of became obsolete – her culinary skills were pedestrian when meat was stricken from the menu and her obsession with meal times made me bristle with memories of a world where the shape, size, tone and texture of your body was everything. Her angst was tangible.

It took three full weeks for the magic of a cold Christmas to eventually warm us: spangling lights of the evening Christmas Markets; steaming 'Glühwein' and roasted chestnuts; Christmas Eve at the Main River where the bells of the five Frankfurt churches tolled for an eternity, heralding Christ's birthday. The rain had not stopped since we arrived and Frankfurt was an inland sea – the idea of a white Christmas turned to sludge. The Main had burst its banks and swirled over the promenade that runs along its usual banks and only the very tops of the street lamps reached out of the water in an eerie SOS. The bells started as we arrived at the furious river and a hum of voices, crunching pebbles under heavy winter boots and the 'Aum' of the church bells transformed that rumble of water into an opus. Two swans fought against the surging current. I was mesmerised. The bells embraced me in the womb of the world...

I felt born to a new life that night. A life where I could be myself, where I would no longer reserve parts of me for different worlds and different circumstances. I would be Nadine regardless of land or water and love for my family overwhelmed me.

The rain stopped, and the snow fell on Christmas Day. Colette's big white smile matched the coating on our bedroom windowsill when I woke. She was pulling her hair up in a hurried ponytail as she breathlessly whispered, "Look, Nad!" Her twinkling almond eyes beamed as she layered jumpers and socks and rushed outside. She truly was beautiful, even if she annoyed me in the way only little sisters can.

On the fourth of January, we left Mutti's home, her cosy little haven, for India. Despite the quarrels, tears were plentiful. It aches to have a loved one so far away.

***

India.

Many an accomplished writer has managed to capture the spirit of India, the clamour of contrasts that is the most intriguing place on earth, to lay down the comical lilt of the Indian accent, the peculiarities of Indian-English grammar, the very distinct way of gesturing, moving, expressing through the body what words cannot convey. I am not one of those masters of words. I struggle to express the profound impact that place had on me, but it was in a village called Puttaparthi, four hours' drive from Bangalore, that my Olympic quest was truly resurrected. It was the turning point in my two-year absence from the pool, so I will try to explain how I, an 18-year-old at a crossroads, saw this most vibrant of countries.

It can only be experienced through the senses, all six of them – smells, sounds, tastes, sights, sensations of touch and instinct. Our senses had been pulverised by the time we got to Bangalore in the middle of the night after delays in Frankfurt; an hour on the tarmac in Delhi; a mysterious call for all passengers to 'go to the front of the plane immediately!' as we gathered speed down the Indira Ghandi Airport runway; eight hours without food, seating or ventilation in Bombay Airport; and a harrowing, bumpy ride in what sounded like a midair submarine, but smelled like a curry campout with a man starting up his mini stove to cook a meal in the aisle. The taxi ride from the Bombay International Airport to the domestic terminal still danced with me. India had jumped down my throat, tugged at my stomach, slapped me in the face, tickled me under the chin, caressed my heart, knocked my knees from under me and spun me until I was so dizzy that I wasn't sure if I liked the ride or if I wanted to be sick. Lady India was offensive in every way and I was enraptured.

She rolled out her poverty-stricken beauty before me with ferocious honesty, the kind that cuts sharpest when given with love. Immense concrete buildings loomed at inexplicable angles; balconies defied the gravitational pull that beckoned them to the road ten floors down; rain-stained shutters dangled precariously from single screws and framed filthy, jagged window panes; destitution mingled with purposeful strides and brilliant smiles that shared a joy I'd never seen before; intricate, vibrant fabrics fluttered from string that measured out doorways, walls and floors along sidewalks; crops of parcel-sized shacks made of ingenuity and scraps of anything handy glowed with colour and shade that could only exist at the rainbow's end. And while my brain blurred with the sights, my throat grappled with an overpowering yet undefinable sweet smell, like a slathering of day-old coconut milk combined with cheap aftershave and thick incense barely masking the rotting stench of excrement and humidity-saturated mankind. You could taste the thick perfumes, every curried, sugared, spiced, greased one of them. And the cacophony of ancient automobiles, cowbells, barks, shrieks, twangs and trumpeting, bustling bedlam pierced my temples and whisked my mind into an ecstatic celebration of life. Everything was oppressive.

And in that mayhem, The Lady holds up a mirror to your soul in which she reveals every part of your essence in a myriad of blacks and whites.

I reviled myself at times. Staying in an ashram offers no escape from other spiritual seekers, people trying to live their lives free from all things 'bad'. And on many occasions those do-gooders repulsed me. I was sickened by their superiority, their condescending virtue, their insincere platitudes that dribbled from pious fa ades. I hated them and their self-delusion. I hated them and their perfection. I hated them for their false serenity. And the more I judged the self-righteous as loathsome, the more despicable I felt. Who was I to condemn those I was ultimately jealous of? I'd rage and spend the next few hours treating everyone and everything around me with disdain. Until invariably, a smile, an act of generosity, a song would pierce the black cloud I carried with me and I'd cry, ashamed of the vile little teenager I was.

At other times I exalted in being me. I could laugh at the monkeys mating at full volume, perched high on the temple steeple, in front of an audience of thousands who turned their faces away from such irreverence. I could be compassionate toward the disgusting old woman with no teeth who stank of years without washing and who insisted on burping in our faces. I could work in a kitchen, peeling pineapple all day until my fingers burned in the acidic juice, and feel the joy of giving. I could adore my sister without restraint, I could kiss my mother with tender gratitude for all she had done and I could hug my father with warmth and pride. I was okay, and my Higher School Certificate results said I was smart, too (top five percent of the state smart, although I am fairly certain whoever marked my papers was drinking at the time). What more could a girl possibly need?

At times Lady India tests you in ways beyond imagination. On one particular morning, for no real reason, Colette, Mum and I decided to try the finest of local fashion. Struggling to wind the metres and metres of sparkling silk fabric around and around and around our waists, I felt certain that saris were invented by fathers as a kind of chastity belt to prevent hungry teenage hands from accessing the precious flesh of their daughters. After hours, we finally emerged from our unit into the village streets, gliding like royalty towards the ashram temple for the morning's ritual prayer and blessing. As we sat, patiently waiting to be allowed into the temple area, the heavens opened without warning and unleashed a biblical rain. The desperate crowd surged like a wave at the temple gates. We clutched each other's wrists as Colette's feet were lifted from the ground and she was swept away in the stampede. At that terrifying moment it was easy to imagine how hundreds may die in a crush.

"Just hang on!" I screamed to her.

"I can't! Don't let go!" Collette's panicked voice shrieked alarm.

"Lean back!" Mum shouted.

"Don't let go!"

"I won't. Just hang on... hang on..." I called.

The crowd bellowed, the heavens roared and trampling feet whipped the mud like a herd on the move. Finally the gates opened and the throng rushed at any form of shelter they could find, and no sooner had the mass of devotees cowered under archways and steeples, than the heavens cleared, revealing a brilliant Puttaparthi day. We were in no mood to stay, bedraggled and freezing, to pray; drenched in body and in spirit.

The three gliding princesses were a sight, schlepping home through an ankle deep river that coursed down the mud streets. Putrid with all manner of refuse, the flowing stream carried the odd floating cow pat and nappy directly into the foundations of the apartment block that was being hastily erected next door to ours. The brilliant blues and greens of Mum's sari ran in thick vertical stripes down her underskirt, and because her sari had shrunk to just below her knees she looked like a circus clown with a tutu bouncing over striped pantaloons. Colette's sari had gone in the opposite direction and wrapped itself around the soles of her feet so that each step made her teeter dangerously close to planting her face in the septic mud. My sari clung so tightly to every curve and crevice of my body that it left absolutely nothing to the imagination of bemused street vendors who still seemed to think it was appropriate to call out, "Sandals, madam, very fine, yes… incense very cheap for you, madam, only twenty rupees… jewels yes, madam, very lovely…"

Lady India laughed heartily that day. Alas, we did not.

Sometimes the mirror India held up to humanity's core would glint and she'd reveal scoundrels with no respect for others; adults mutilating small children's limbs to better fleece the tourists' consciences; innocent animals who, being left to starve, were mercilessly beaten by packs of bored youths; and in my impotence I was ashamed to call myself part of the human race… But only until She found a way to remind me of the goodness, the mystery and the variety of human existence: sometimes through a young child joking in French, German, Spanish, Italian, Telugu, Hindi, English, as he scanned and tallied the cost of bags of fruit with the precision of a computer system with no more than his big, cheeky eyes; or through an enormous group of sinister Kashmiri men dressed in jet-black robes with evil stares and a presence that sent people scurrying, asking for a photograph with our small, white-robed family because, "Black and white, little and big, is funny yes!" And at these times there was no greater gift than being alive.

The rhythm of the days in Prashanti Nilayam, Sai Baba's ashram, was slow and easy. We'd rise at four, a chorus of people hocking the phlegm from their sleepy throats acting as an alarm. A cold shower, followed by a mouthful of banana and we would head to the temple area. There we'd wait for almost three hours in disciplined lines, meditating, napping, listening to the muffled sounds of the world waking and men chanting the Vedas. When the little holy man emerged from his living quarters to greet the crowds, a cool breeze invariably caressed us, and after he had left, after the singing of devotional hymns was complete, we would slowly stretch our limbs, frozen from being crouched for hours on the bare earth, wander home, sleep and contemplate. The afternoon routine was the same as the morning, only hotter.

Sai Baba was a phenomenon. As he glided though the crowd, giving his blessing, talking to devotees, manifesting sacred ash, the wave of upliftment through the masses was tangible. People who had come seeking advice, healing, solace or simply out of curiosity were all touched in some way, and we were no different. This little man had one giant spirit, and just to watch the way he interacted with the crowds was enough to have me awestruck.

For me, the ashram life was about the inner transformation, the sense of peace and direction I eventually found after experiencing every high and low that we human beings can put upon ourselves. India gave me a perspective that made my dreams of being an Olympian seem embarrassing, pointless. How could I pursue a desire to swim for my country when millions of people were living in squalor without the chance of a satisfying meal? My social conscience plagued me with a need to find some more noble way of using my privilege than swimming up and down a pool really fast. But one day a rock, a tree and eight eagles made me change my mind.

I found a sense of certainty high up on that rocky hilltop, lying back on nature's baking tray under the overhanging branches of the Tamarind tree, the wish-fulfilling tree. Many miracles have been said to have happened there and pilgrims come to say their prayers, to send their wishes directly to the ears of their Gods. The Chithravathi riverbed, dry and sandy, snakes its way past the base of the mountain and into the green, leafy distance. On that day, the 'dhobis' (washer women) laid a spectrum out on the sand to be scorched dry as sounds of village bustle blended with Sanskrit hymns being chanted in the ashram below. It was the one place where a breeze brought relief from the heat and it carried the delicate sounds of life with it. As I lay wondering what the future back in Australia might hold, eight eagles began circling in the cobalt sky. I felt as though I knew them, like our spirits were in some way connected, familiar. I don't know how else to explain it.

I heard them without my ears. I felt their wisdom. They showed me how I had denied myself when I lived two lives.

They revealed the power in me if only I could stay true to my spirit, bringing the beauty of the land to the music of the water. I understood the secret to starting again in that instant. I just had to find a way to make it work, permanently.

And I did. I was tingling with the excitement of an eight-year-old again…

Glad to be back in the water, but training will have to wait until school is finished.

14.

"Make my make believe, believe in me"
- *"I've Been High"*, REM

My dad and I had a plan; a risky plan, but what did I have to lose?

We were going to trial Dad's training theory developed on a research trip to Paris. He was researching French literature, Claude Simon, Patrick Modiano, not swimming. But on the trip, he watched a florist with enormous paws arrange a bunch of flowers he had bought for Claude Simon's wife. That's when it hit my little professor. It was not the incongruity of the brute delicately arranging flowers, but the dexterity with which the man worked, despite holding an animated discussion about rugby, that was remarkable. He asked the florist, "How do you do that so quickly and so perfectly? No one's waiting, you can slow down."

The man's hands did not falter as he looked up. "I don't know. I've done it so often that it's automatic. And the funny thing is that when I think about it, when I try to slow down, I can't do it – they turn out shit."

It got him thinking. It was all about how the body was programmed. Traditional training methods have swimmers going a certain distance and then doing it over and over and over again, each time trying to get faster. But the overall effect, the professor reasoned, is that the body becomes accustomed to swimming at a below-par pace; the muscles become honed for swimming three kilometres of Breaststroke rather than 200m at goal speed. If we worked backwards, starting with getting the speed right and then building up endurance at that speed, the body would be programmed to go at race pace every time it hit the water... surely it would. It was a theory, but what coach would go along with it? Especially a coach with a full squad of aspirants? It would be one thing to experiment on myself, but no one would experiment with an entire squad.

But I found a coach who was willing to give me a go. Back at Ryde. With the devastating financial effects of the past few years, my parents' souls belonged to the bank, so they sold the house in Narraweena in an attempt to reclaim themselves. We moved back to the world of my childhood, renting. Ursula was still at the club, but a young coach, Greg, had taken over the senior squad, and it was with Greg that I made the deal.

"I train my way in the morning, on my own, no interference. I train with you, your way, in the afternoon, to my body's limits, as monitored by me. You get the credit for whatever I achieve. I take the responsibility for whatever I don't."

He was nice, he was innovative, and he was willing to let a demanding little miss play boss!

* * *

February 1994 and I laughed and I cried all at the same time. Was it possible to be excited and terrified, hopeful and crestfallen, sure and uncertain all at once?

John Konrads smiled at me from his perch in the entrance hall. I think he was pleased to see me. I'd forgotten he was there! I smiled back and sighed, "Hello again," remembering the oath I swore so vehemently when I was 14. "Guess I'm back." I'd forgotten how young they all looked. I felt so much older than their fresh Olympian faces already.

It had been months since the waters embraced me and I held my breath, wobbling to the core, and dived into that sparkling expanse of blue. Full of the moment of homecoming, I forgot that sucking in with face submerged leads to choking. I actually panicked and really had to think about it – breathe in, breathe out. The 50m leg had me gasping, holding my chest to contain a heart that threatened to beat right out and run away. How did I ever manage to swim that far? And how would I again? I had to learn everything from the start. I had so much to reclaim, so far to go that I couldn't even glimpse the horizon. It was too big, too long, too hard, too frightening... but I somehow couldn't wait for it to happen!

There began months of baby steps, swimming with the little tackers, watching as those I used to beat made it onto the Australian Team, as their times got faster and further from the plodding pace I could muster.

"Focus only on the size four feet in front of you... That's all you need to do for now... Catch those feet in front of you."

The strain of flogging my body again was softened by the fact I could train at civilised hours – 8am in the glorious outdoor pool was what swimming is all about. There was barely a soul around, the silence only broken by birds and the gentle splotch, swoosh, splotch, swoosh of the occasional lap swimmer cruising through their morning ritual. The sparkling shimmer of warm sunray days; the brooding, swirling embrace of grey cotton wool days; the heavy pummelling of stormy days; and the best vantage point in Sydney for rainbows.

I loved my morning swims. I loved the solitude. I loved that my dad came out of his way, every morning for a half hour or so, to time my race pace sets and keep track of our experiment. I think he liked the fact that they were civilised hours, too, and that I could finally drive myself to and from the pool. He was so good to have around: my grounding when I thought I was better than I was and my solace when I was flattened by lack of progress. He always knew what to say, and sometimes I secretly watched him standing on the side of the pool – one leg crossed behind the other; spotless white sneakers under dark blue jeans and immaculately ironed, pin-striped business shirt tucked in around a mini-barrel stomach that sat on twiggy legs; spectacles perched on his big crooked nose and scraggy bush of beard bunched under his chin as he studies my times and contemplates the statistics. At times like that I loved him so much I could have cried. It takes a special kind of person to get away with carrying a man-bag and rainbow umbrella; an even more special person to get away with socks in sandals.

Sometimes I thought I was so much like him that God gave my mother Colette, so she too could have a clone. I had his nose, so much larger and pointier than Colette's little German-style button. I had his crooked top tooth folding over the left-hand eye-tooth, so much smaller and yellower than Colette's big, white grin. I had his beady little chocolate Smartie eyes, so different to Colette's wide hazel gaze. I had his flat bottom, his stocky middle... I was my father's daughter and yet people said Collie and I were so alike. It made me wonder if I was missing something, if perhaps I just felt more like my father's daughter than I actually was. Or perhaps it was a bond that grew with every day he came to the pool, rain or shine, to stand by me, his swimming experiment. Maybe that's what it was.

Every day I returned to the pool with a taste for the challenge, like I did when I was small, regardless of the frustration along the way. It took nine full months of training with the tadpoles to get into Greg's squad, and my first day back in the 'top' league was made even sweeter by the renaissance of a childhood romance. Sean was back. Again.

Megan had quit swimming altogether, as far as I was aware; Jess had quit too; and Sean had been out of the water until he heard a rumour that I was back. So there I was, not two months after graduating to the top squad, and I was already reliving the tight chest and flushed cheeks, the turmoil I felt for the first time as an 11-year-old.

He was a strange duck, my Sean. He was barely taller than my father, with fine, straw-coloured hair that curled in unkempt waves. His hands looked old, but his face had the round, soft form of a cheeky three-year-old. There was a tenacity in him that continually surprised me.

Physically unremarkable as he was, I'm not sure what kind of power he had over me. I guess there's just something special about your first love and something deeply romantic about the prospect of that love re-blossoming. On the first day of his return, he smiled at me from the other end of the pool and he looked as though he had a secret. It intrigued me. He gave a short, dry, nervous cough as he left a conversation with another swimmer to approach me – his conversation had been nothing more than an attempt to cover how eagerly he was watching the entrance for my arrival. That much was clear. I knew I was in trouble. He hadn't changed.

"Hello there," he said, trying to mask a wicked sparkle in his eyes. "It's been a while."

"Yeah. Good to be back." I tried to be non-committal but couldn't help scanning his body – strong, but with a soft layer, his wiry legs lost in baggy shorts.

"Good to have you back," he said and chuckled at his own double meaning. Then went in for the kill. "Only reason I'm here."

He was ordinary in every way but I was stricken. It was absurd, but his brazen assumption that I'd be at all interested had me floored. It was wonderful to be so entranced, but at the same time to be so terrified. The on-again, off-again nature of our last relationship was fresh in my mind, but I convinced myself that we were both older now; we had been so young then. My parents still didn't like him in the least and I sensed trouble ahead.

Sean trained hard. He pushed me and challenged me in sessions with Greg's squad, but it was the mornings, on my own, Dad by my side, where I felt the improvements surge. I tried so hard to maintain the one life wherever I was – being the same person whether 'the driven, ambitious swimmer' at the pool; 'the spiritual, loving sister/daughter' at home; 'the bright English and education student' at uni – but it was hard and it got harder. It wasn't long before a double life began to emerge as I avoided mentioning Sean at home and I made every effort to prove he was no distraction. But the faster I swam, the more I was torn between the energy and attention he demanded and the passion I'd invested in my Olympic song. He wanted a normal girlfriend and I wanted him to understand my obsession. I was torn between two masters, two desires, and I didn't want to have to choose.

I needed Sean. I needed him more than I liked to acknowledge. His presence made me feel special in a way I'd always sought but never managed to find. Sometimes his childlike softness made me believe that he needed me more than anyone ever had, and I wanted to hold him, protect him from the world, love him more than I knew how. But at other times he was cold. Sometimes he was so flippant that I felt as though he was, in fact, just doing me a favour by hanging around, so I fought to please him in any way I could; to make him see it was worth staying with me. I'd never been so weak, so dependent, and that scared me.

I could understand why being my boyfriend might be a tall order, after all, who would want to put up with a moody swimmer driven beyond what is usually considered reasonable? He put up with it and my love was so much greater for it. Who would tolerate having a girlfriend who never went out because she had to be up and training in the morning? Who would adhere to strict visiting hours, curfews and regimented schedules to accommodate their girlfriend's sport? Who would stay with someone whose parents so obviously tolerated him just to keep the peace? Who else but someone as patient and generous as him? I was blessed that he stayed with me and I loved him all the more. But in the back of my mind, I remembered how it felt when we were young and I was afraid.

At training I was building up to my one test-run before the Atlanta Olympic Trials – the Australian Open Championships doubling as the Pan Pacific Trials. This meet would tell Dad if his experiment was working. If it was, it would let my competitors know they weren't alone in their quest for an Olympic berth, but if not, I would drown. I'd look like the girl who didn't know when to cut her losses. And I was afraid Sean would find someone faster, more gorgeous, more perfect than me again. So again, I tried too hard. I tried to maintain buoyancy at home to prove all was well in my world. I tried to maintain focus in the pool to prove all was well in my world. I tried to show Sean that he meant everything to me, to prove he was all that was well in my world. I gave him everything he wanted from me, whenever he demanded it, even if I didn't really want to. I did it just to keep him coming back. He needed to know that I loved him enough to give myself to him completely, body and heart. That was more important than anything else. Except my dream.

I prayed. I asked for guidance and strength and wisdom, but God was silent, or perhaps God only lived in India. So alone, I did the best I could to make it all work, I compromised to keep everyone happy.

But I would not, could not, compromise my dream.

15.

"Gonna climb that mountain, gonna do everything"
  – *"One Way Ticket"*, LeAnne Rimes

IN MY FANTASIES MY COME-BACK WAS GRAND AND DRAMATIC, but in the real world, I knew there was no way I'd make the Australian Team for the Pan Pacific Championships. It had been a long time. It was no surprise when I came fifth in the 200m Breaststroke. Dad's methods were working. It was a surprise, however, to receive a letter a few weeks later, congratulating me on making it onto the Australian World University Games Team.

I felt 14 again, on my way up! Sean strutted, chest all a-puff, but he gradually became more and more paranoid that I was drifting away, that my success would lead me to someone 'better' than him, an intellectual at uni or an Adonis in sport. I felt like saying, 'No Sean, you're the one who runs after "better" people, remember?' but I held my tongue. It became strenuous, my constant need to please him and my constant need to affirm how faithfully I adored him. It only enhanced my eagerness to step on that Fukuoka-bound plane in search of space to breathe. They say absence makes the heart grow fonder. What a joke!

Fukuoka, Japan: Vegas meets Bombay – without the dirt. I was nervous. I knew barely anyone. The athletes' village had been especially constructed for the occasion and our apartment, just like in India, still had builders' rubble on the floor, unhinged doors and raw support beams for separating walls that were not yet there. When you're confined to a small space with no privacy other than a dubious toilet door that locks automatically and unlocks unreliably, you get to know each other pretty fast.

I was dazzled by the Japanese flair for big events. The organisers had thought of everything – a social outdoor area surrounded by the flags of all nations was set aside for athletes to mingle beneath the fireball archway that burned day and night; a leisure pool and manmade beach for relaxation, a dance club for celebration; a dining hall to feed the famished masses (sadly short on vegetarian options, so I lived on rice and soy sauce, buttered Turkish toast and lime iceblocks), and bicycles to get from one end of the expansive village to the other.

It didn't take long for all the good bikes to go missing, stashed in secret hideaways, and I was silently pleased at the excuse not to ride. I could just see myself taking a dive a day before racing started and I was not going to have that happen again! The Japanese officials carried out reconnaissance raids on the bike bandits' hideouts from time to time, but it was never more than a few hours before those quality specimens were back in their secret stores, leaving bent forks, twisted handlebars and flat tyres for the bulk of commuters, and a relieved smile on my face – another day that I wouldn't have to explain a bike phobia that originated when a riding lesson on the Lane Cover River flats ended in a painful altercation with a tuft of grass.

It was in Fukuoka that I met Jade Adams, a breaststroker from Perth. She and I clicked in a way I had read about in novels and seen in movies: the lonely new kid finds a kindred spirit in her exact opposite. I'd never experienced an instant knowing like this before.

In the Fukuoka pool, it was us against a girl from South Africa, Penny Heyns. She had been training in the USA, had just burst onto the world scene and was using these games as a warm-up for the Pan Pacifics. She was fast, threatening-Sam-Riley's-crown kind of fast, and I felt like she was a level far beyond that of my own. We were in no way equals, and just as I had with Megan all those years ago, I found it impossible to speak to Penny. Jade did not. She seemed to regard everyone as equal and while her height, fine lips and delicate, silky hair make her appear aloof and serious, her genuine curiosity and thoughtfulness bridged every gap, however real or perceived. I admired that.

I came second to Penny in the 200m Breaststroke in my best time, although I was a long way behind her, and Jade's genuine excitement made me feel so accepted. I couldn't remember a time when a competitor was that thrilled for me. It would have been a riot to see someone with the poise and grace of a *prima ballerina* jumping and squealing with someone as stumpy and brash as me, acting as though they were sisters.

Before the 100m, Jade and I made a deal. She would come second behind Penny and I would snatch third – a tall order for someone whose body only ever seemed to wake up on lap three, but Jade's fire spurred me on to my best 100m Breaststroke ever. I broke the New South Wales record and kept my end of that bargain and I believed that together, Jade and I could accomplish anything. We were the happiest minor place getters in the history of the Uni Games and couldn't wait to hit the disco that, by all reports, was as tacky as Saturday Night Fever.

It seemed the officials were as surprised at my 100m as I was, because they were determined to delay my victory dance.

"Miss Neeoomunsun, you must come for drug test."

I was a little excited, until I realised what it entailed.

I'd spent far too long being coarse with the boys to be the bashful type, but this was something that required a whole new type of confidence. A quiet, unblinking little man watched everything I did from the moment I exited the competition pool at the end of my 100m race. He scrutinised every interaction with the coach and team manager, he opened fresh bottles of water for me, to ensure I was not drinking something uncouth, he observed every lap of my cool-down and followed me like a stalker when I went to get my clothes. I knew I would have to give a urine sample so I tried to get as much liquid into me as my stomach could hold but it's a vast space in there and I feared I'd be waiting for hours while the music played, "… Shake y'groove thaing! Shake y'groove thaing! Yeah-yeah! Show 'em how we do it nahw…"

In a back room of the competition pool, the little man watched as I sat, picking at my nail beds, foot tapping reassuringly, willing the officials at the table to call my name next. I was required to fill in and sign a number of forms declaring what medication I was and was not taking, I selected one vacuum sealed package containing a beaker and another one containing two bottles labelled A and B, and religiously recorded the random collection of numbers and letters that would become my sample code.

"Now, you fill up here," the lady said, indicating a mark on the beaker. It seemed like an awful lot, but by this stage I was blessedly bursting.

"Here some paper towel, if you spill…" I wondered why I couldn't use toilet paper. As I stood to 'go', the little man who had chaperoned me thus far smiled and nodded, but made no move to rise and I was quietly relieved I'd be able to do this bit in peace.

But no. The lady who had handed me the paper towel rose and gestured. "This way."

It was a large, tiled room, like any other toilet block, but it was lit like a movie set. In the centre of the tiled floor sat a bed-pan, directly under a bright spotlight. I edged around it, wondering what poor sod had to do their business under those interrogation conditions, and headed for the cubicles.

"No, no, no. Here!" She smiled and gestured elegantly towards the spot-lit pot as though she were showing me to my front row seat at the opera. The cubicle doors jeered, 'Wouldn't you like to hide behind one of us!'

I still had my swimsuit on because I had been conscious that my little watch dog would find it hard to deal with me going to the ladies to change, and I wanted this to be as smooth and fast as it could be. Racing suits are not designed to be worn for hours and by now it was beginning to cut into my skin. I gingerly placed my beaker on the ground and pulled the crotch of my cossie across to one side.

"No, no, no. Down!" She smiled again as she gestured for me to pull my entire costume off.

"Are you serious?!"

She smiled sweetly, nodded and reached for my straps.

"It's okay! I can do it myself." I stepped back and began to wriggle my way out of the skin tight fabric.

"This is not happening," I mumbled as I grazed the skin off my back and thighs with the costume that was made for a six-year-old frame.

I half squatted, held my beaker between my legs and tried to think of anything but the glaring fluorescent light on my naked body, or the scrutineer who stared me down with no sign of shame. It's one thing to bend over for mummy's help when you're two, a completely different thing to be bent over for a stranger at 19. I squeezed and prayed for rain, and as it proverbially does, it poured! I filled the beaker to the brim and couldn't stop. 'So that's what the paper towel's for...'

It continued, all over my hand, down the side of the beaker and still, the rain pelted in short, sharp spurts that echoed from the tiled walls like a machine gun, 'Rata tat tata tat … tatatatat… tat… tat… tatat…' I was grateful for the pot and the paper towel, but as she handed me a toilet roll, the paper towel drowned in the deluge and the machine gun kept firing. I couldn't look her in the eye.

By the time I finally rose out of my squatting position, my joints had set and the tiny swimming costume clung to my shins. Putting a wet costume on is hard at the best of times, but when it is three sizes too small and you're keeping a very watchful eye on your full sample beaker to ensure it is not spilled, tampered with or destroyed because you are damned if you're going to go through that again, it is a mammoth undertaking that simply cannot happen fast enough.

Puffing and crimson-faced, I carried my precious liquid back to the table. Now I had to pour the sample from my overfull beaker into the narrow-mouthed glass jars whilst athletes waiting for their turn at the table looked on. Had she not seen how much trouble I had had getting it into the beaker in the first place? Then it was checked. Strong enough? Acidic enough? I felt for the poor suckers whose samples failed this part of the test. And after an eternity I was free to scurry away, still flushed, still flustered and relieved I hadn't suffered the same fate as a Canadian boy I met while I was waiting for my turn at the table.

The previous year when he had had his first drug testing experience, he occupied himself by chatting up a very attractive lady-athlete as they waited, beakers full, for their chance to seal their jars and get out of there. As he smoothly crossed his legs in the direction of his prey to better lean in to her, he knocked his full sample beaker to the floor with an almighty splash that bounced upward and all over his prospective woman of the hour. He had to wait for another three hours before he was ready to go again and she told every other female at the meet to steer clear of his pick-up lines.

Jade and I finally did get to our disco, bright yellow kimonos, white freebie Coca-Cola hats, medals around necks and stuffed toy mascots under arms. We looked a sight and we danced like John Travolta until our limbs could fever no more. Bleary eyed the next morning we woke to the realisation that we would have to swim the 4x100m Medley Relay. None of us were in the mood. A few withdrawals had put us up from tenth to eighth place in the final. Leigh Habler was to swim the Backstroke, Jade was taking care of the Breaststroke, and Debbie Croucher, our sprint Freestyler, would anchor, which left yours truly to do the Butterfly. Behind the blocks I joked with the girls that I had better remember not to do a Breaststroke underwater pull-out. 'I'm doing Fly. I'm doing Fly...' I repeated to myself. But the jinx had been set.

Jade charged towards the wall. Poised on the blocks and ready to fly as soon as she touched, a surge of adrenalin rushed through me. The team cheered my name. I made way for automatic pilot just as Dad had trained me to do. I dived, hit the water and pulled my arms down in the start of a Breaststroke pull-out when I suddenly remembered:

'Oh, shit! I'm doing Butterfly!'

"What the hell is she doing?!" the crowd murmured. Tears welled in my goggles. What now? Stranded halfway between the surface and the bottom of the pool, I wriggled my body desperately like a mosquito larvae trying to get to the light. I managed, after an age, to heave myself to the surface without using my arms (we would have been disqualified if I had moved my arms) and I thrashed my way from one end of the pool to the other in a respectable time, but all hopes of a medal were dashed. The girls assured me that they hadn't even wanted to do the damned race so sixth was a bonus. I was mortified. Jade thought it was hysterical but attempted an earnest expression of concern as she wrapped a long arm around my shoulders: "Oh, Neumannsun!"

But the laughter was not far behind.

That was not the way I wanted my meet to end, so we played around to make up for it. A flag-stealing mission made our team motivator, Dawn Fraser, proud. We danced and talked to strangers; I explored the city of Fukuoka by day and scoured the universe for chocolate with the soccer boys by night. And I loved it.

Sean didn't like that I loved it.

"So you're having a good time?" His question was loaded, but I didn't bite. Instead, I gushed.

"Yeah, it's incredible. I've been having the best time of my life! It's just amazing and everyone's so nice and no one gives a shit if you swim fast or not, you're here doing the best you can and that's all that matters, and it's... it's just the best!"

"Better than with me?"

"What do you mean? No, it's just totally different."

"You never seem to have that much fun with me. Maybe you should just go off with one of your other boyfriends and forget about me..."

I was crestfallen. What had I done wrong? What had I said?

"Sean, what's with you? Why do you have to shit on my happiness? I'm just having a good time. Is that such a crime?"

"I'm not shitting on your happiness. I'm just saying..."

But I didn't want to hear what he was 'just' saying. I cut him off, "No, I don't want this tonight. We've fought every time I've called you, and I can't do this over the phone."

"What? You don't want us? You don't want our relationship? You can't break up with me over the phone? Is that it?" he said, hurt, defensive and looking for a way to turn me into the bad guy.

I wanted to scream, 'Fight, you moron. I don't want to fight, you paranoid halfwit!' but all I managed was a pleading, "Sean, please. Don't be stupid…"

"No, that's just fine, go off with your little buddies and have a good time if that's more important than our relationship," he blurted and hung up.

And after crying, again, I partied on.

I returned from Fukuoka with the title of Australian Universities' Athlete of the Year, and a firm determination to end it with Sean. It hurt to be with him and it hurt to be without him, but overwhelmingly, it was just too much hard work.

My parents were quietly, sombrely pleased. Sean was stung. But a day after I broke the news that we were over, he came over to my house to say a 'final and proper goodbye'.

We sat in my bedroom and he smiled with a sad and quiet serenity. "It's okay, I'm happy with my decision. I always knew I would die before I'd reach 30, so don't worry about me."

I couldn't believe what I was hearing. I folded. I cried. I couldn't be responsible for this. How could I hurt a person who loved me more than his own life like this? It was too hard to let him go, so we embraced and he smiled triumphantly again. When he left, I felt a lead weight choke me. My parents were silently, sombrely dismayed.

* * *

I sometimes doubted that the Olympics were worth striving for. For all I knew, it could have been nothing compared with the picture John Konrads painted in my mind every morning. How one moment of glory could possibly make up for years of effort, violent tears, paralysing exhaustion, the ever-present stench of chlorine oozing from your pores, often failed me. How could an instant wash away the demons that gnawed at me during eternal hours in the pool; during the continual beatings my fragile confidence suffered each time I performed below par? But Fukuoka showed me what a high is. It gave me a glimpse of what an Olympic Games might feel like, and if that was it, I wanted it more than ever! I wanted the Atlanta Olympics more than I had wanted Barcelona as I sat years before, being mummified in that cold hospital room. I wanted it more than I did during every one of those tortured hours of Chronic Fatigue. I wanted it more than I did when I gazed at Megan in all her glory and promise when I was small.

This time the Olympic Games were going to be mine and I would break the Ryde drought, my picture would hang on the wall beside John and Ilse Konrads, where I had imagined it all those little girl years ago. This time the music of the water and the fire in my belly would take me there. It was my turn to sing, to see my family beaming with triumph, to feel Sean's pride, to dance with Jade at the greatest competition on earth.

This time.

My two medals from the World University Games in Fukuoka, Japan, 1995.

16.

"I believe there comes a time, when everything just falls in line"

– *"All Fired Up"*, Pat Benetar

EVERY MORNING DAD PUT ME UP AGAINST THE CLOCK. Every Saturday morning was dedicated to skills as Mum and Greg ironed out flaws in my technique – dives, turns, push-offs, pull-outs, stroke, stroke, stroke. The lifeguards at the Ryde pool did their best to ensure I had a lane to myself whenever I needed it, and the regular 8am-ers had become like training partners to me. Rick, an intense man who was competitive enough with himself not to need any racing, would talk about anything contentious with the same fervour he put into every stroke. Then there was Peter, a wiry, graceful man who made a comeback to swimming every five years to break all the Butterfly world records in his Master's age group while he was at the young end of the spectrum, and then gracefully bowed out of competition until next time. He was a Professor at Macquarie University's Graduate School of Management and he never missed a morning, keeping close tabs on my progress. He was the aquatic version of my dad, even looked like him with a woolly white beard and the gentlest eyes.

One quiet, sunny morning when most of the regulars had slept in and a stupid child had frustrated my timed set by splashing across the lane in front of me, I found myself brooding in a foul mood despite the smiling sky. I was finishing off the last 1500m of my session, casually doing some kick with flippers, being lazy and seething about that idiot brat. I wondered if the kid could even comprehend what I was weeks away from doing – making a dash for the Olympic Team, trying to fulfil a lifelong dream, putting heart and soul on the line!

I pictured how it would be, every tiny detail of the marshalling area at the Sydney International Aquatic Centre in Homebush. I could see the crowds, what I was wearing, the colours, the faces, the cameras, the lights. I felt the nervous wobbles start in my gut and radiate outward until every nerve fired, every vein pulsed and every cell twitched with the tremor of readiness. My heart-rate increased, my face grew into a smile as I ambled, loose and limbered, onto pool deck, swinging my arms, hearing that song: "Give me one moment in time, when I'm more than I thought I could be..."

In my mind I waved as I was introduced to a prism of sound. I sensed the hush as we waited, poised, for the gun. I trembled. I puffed. I tensed and breathed in time as my mind swam the whole race in exact detail.

I won! I jumped and cheered, I hugged Greg on pool deck and was ushered over for the post-race interview where I answered every question with wisdom, humility and wit – the crowd loved me...

And I was still casually kicking with flippers in the warm sunlight. But my heart pounded and my body burned with that detached feeling of lactic acid numbing the synapses. It had been real. So real. So wonderfully real.

* * *

At the New South Wales Open Championships, my last race before the 1996 Atlanta Olympic Trials, I became the third Australian ever to break the 2.30 mark for the 200m Breaststroke. Rebecca Brown, the World Record Holder and Samantha Riley, the World Champion were the only other two who had ever done it. Not even Linley Frame, coming second at the World Championships in Perth in 1990, had managed to swim below 2.30. The media started to take notice.

* * *

The 100m Breaststroke at the Trials was on the program a couple of days before the 200m, which suited me perfectly. I always loved having a warm-up race to blow away any unconstructive big meet jitters and to get into the routine of up early, breakfast, warm up, race hard, cool down, lunch, sleep, up, eat, warm up, race harder, cool down, eat, sleep.

The 100m was Jade's main event. She had moved to South Australia to train with Glenn Beringen, a silver medallist in Seoul in the 200m Breaststroke, in preparation for this day. She'd given up life at home with her family for the chance at grasping what we all wanted. In the marshalling area I squeezed her shoulder and whispered, "Adamssun, wanna make a deal?"

She grinned and nodded.

"You win the one and I'll win the two."

She beamed. It was outlandish, but we'd made deals before. No more words were necessary. My heart sent her everything.

From my place in Lane 2, I cheered for Jade as the announcer introduced her. It was remarkable that I was even in the final of the 100m. I wasn't particularly focused. In fact, it would have been nice to sit in the stands and really get into screaming for her, to watch it all happen, and in my mind I did just that. I didn't even check for my time at the end of the race, but searched immediately for Lane 5.

She did it!

The media went berserk! 'Sam Riley Beaten', 'Sam's Form Slump', 'Pressure Mounts for Sam'… oh, yeah, and some chick called Jade Adams won. She was going to the Olympics and she laughed, "Now it's your turn!"

I couldn't wipe the smile off my face. Never had I felt so elated for another and I wanted to feel that way forever. If I was bursting, how must she have felt?!

That night I slept soundly, but the night after I couldn't rest. My stomach was alive, my mind paced. I watched the clock: 12.30am, 12.53am, 1.12am, 1.24am, 1.58am… I was excited, not afraid. I couldn't wait for my turn on the stage.

My heat swim was solid. It put me into Lane 3 for the final, next to Sam – exactly where I wanted to be. I had always been a pm-er, so lifting for my moment that night would come naturally. I had to touch first or second to make the team. I had to swim under 2.30 to make the qualifying time. John Konrads was in the stands. I wondered if he knew that he'd been talking to me for the last 12 years.

Media were everywhere, cameras beaming the event live to lounge rooms around the nation. Everyone I had ever known filled both sides of the grandstand. My whole extended family was there; even those whose bodies could not traverse the distance were holding their breaths on the other side of the globe for the telephone to give them a thumbs up or a thumbs down. Ursula had cancelled training for the afternoon so the entire club could be at Homebush. Many of the youngsters had volunteered as basket carriers and they cheered for their older club-mates from behind the starting blocks with baskets for competitors' clothes in their arms.

'I wonder what they'll say, if I'm the one to break the drought. Foul mouthed, boy-crazy Olympian...' The thought made me smile.

It seemed strange to imagine that some of those youngsters could be looking up to me the way I had adored Megan. A humbling thought. I had never considered that Megan might be a person like me. She was only ever a goddess in my eyes.

Tension built and I started seeing the evening in snapshots. The crowd. The pool. The cameras. The announcements. The warm air. The dazzling light. The pounding in my chest. The tremble in my gut. The smiles. The rituals.

There are moments when the world slows down for us, when time expands so that we can feel, see, smell acutely that instant, and we become aware that these few moments will change our life. I had a thousand thoughts that stopped rushing for a few minutes – just long enough for me to swim four laps of the pool that would play host to the Olympics of the millennium. All I felt was joy extending from my chest to the still, deep blue expanse winking before me. My feet were not connected to the earth. The passion of people in the grandstand radiated, and louder still was the itching of my muscles and the drumming of my heart in my throat. As I stepped from the marshalling area to parade along pool deck, surrounded by the very people

I had visualised would be there, wearing exactly what I had imagined in those weeks before, smelling the chlorine mingling with Dencorub, they were playing my song over the PA.

"Give me one moment in time
When I'm more than I thought I could be…"
I knew this was going to be a beautiful night.

Eight people on the blocks; a lifetime of dreams calling each one of us. Doubts, fears, hopes and courage clashing in the subconscious minds of every mother, father, sibling, friend and fan.

Suck in three last deep breaths.
Right arm stops shaking.
Toes curl tight.
Silence.
Go.

17.

"There in that one moment in time, I will feel, I will feel eternity"

– *"One Moment in Time"*, Whitney Houston

WORLD CHAMPIONS. Commonwealth champions. The world record holder. All eight of us capable of world-class times. All of us with world rankings. All of us fighting for two places.

The TV commentators call the race:

"Riley in front, Nadine Neumann in the yellow cap is there with her, and also Brooke Hanson. This is a good swim by Hanson and not far away too is Linley Frame, and beside her Rebecca Brown. Through the 100m they go in a time of 1.11.33 – less than a second between the first five."

"Nadine Neumann looks great in this race. She is keeping up with Sam Riley. Sam Riley is the second fastest swimmer in the history of this event, and Nadine Neumann is keeping up with her!"

"Neumann really is challenging. She is in a clear second position. They go through the last turn, the 150m mark. It's Riley in front of Neumann, back there in third place it's Hanson, then Brown, then Frame…"

And 40m to swim. It was deafening.

"It's the girl that suffered the broken neck, in the come-back now. Nadine Neumann, Brooke Hanson, Riley – three of them in the middle of the pool. Neumann in front of Riley, Hanson trying to challenge Riley… with 15m to swim and it is Nadine Neumann that's going to cause the boil-over here! Neumann! Neumann! In goes Neumann! 2.29.65! She's off to Atlanta!"

When your mind is still and your body is free to do what it knows best, you don't really hear with your ears. The thunder of the crowd coursed through me like a flash of inspiration and there it was: the indescribable song I had chased for so many years, through darkness into this moment of exhilarating light.

Euphoria.

I have no recollection of bounding out of the water, hugging Greg, beaming joy in his nerve-ravaged face. I don't recall doing a jig on the way to the poolside interview, but it was all over the papers the next morning! I don't remember being interviewed by Laurie Lawrence, but my consciousness returned when I found my dad. I hugged him and the world embraced me. This was real. His tears were real and for once he was crying for the right reason. We had actually done it!

Collie howled out of control, running her nail-chewed hands through her long brown hair in an attempt to regain her composure. At 16, you don't want to be seen on TV wailing and screeching like a madwoman, but what else could she do?! My mum trembled as though struck by lightning and she held her chest and her mouth alternately in wonder. She was speechless and tears filled her sparkling blue eyes. My uncle, cousins and two aunts couldn't stop laughing as though this were a moment too absurd, too bizarre to be true. Sean coughed his dry, nervous cough, not sure what to do with an overwhelming moment like this. He couldn't wait to get his hands on me!

After cool-down, dancing an absurd ring-a-rosie dance with Jade, accepting congratulations from everyone and anyone, I floated, bursting with joy, through the throng of young well-wishers, all wanting an autograph from the latest local hero. It took over 45 minutes to move through them, I signed my name so often that I forgot how to spell it. My face ached from grinning and the next day none of the fervour had died down. They all wanted the story of the broken neck come-back kid. It was the kind of thing that was perfect for the end of *Today Tonight* on a slow news day and every station wanted a version for their back-up shelves. I soaked it up, every flattering ooooh and aaaaah.

I floated in a dream and I never wanted to come down. We drank champagne. We laughed and relived the telecast over and over and over. I ate pizza and danced in the lounge room. I smiled, wide-eyed in bed, adrenalin keeping me wired. I stared at myself in the mirror and asked my reflection, 'Did we really do that? Was that really me?'

And on the last night of the Trials, as they announced the team, gave us our first item of Olympic clothing and walked us, one by one, along the pool deck, past an honour roll of swimming greats lined up to welcome us to the club for the best in the world, I shook his hand.

He said, "Congratulations, Nadine."

He patted me on the shoulder.

And I smiled, speechless.

John Konrads welcomed me to the Olympic Family, no longer in black and white.

In technicolour.

"We did it!"
With my dad on that glorious night in 1996.
A still from *Sports Sunday*, Channel 9, 28/4/96.
Reporter: Michael Magher.

18.

"It can cut you like a knife if the gift becomes the fire"
   – *"She's a Maniac"*, Michael Sembello

SPECULATION STARTED EARLY. Can Kieren Perkins find form by July? Can Susie O'Neill break Mary T Maher's world record? Can Scott Miller beat the Russian, Pankratov, in the men's 100m Butterfly? Can Sam Riley ever recover from her slump in form? How many medals? How many gold? My job was far from finished, but I had never considered what happens after you make it to the Olympics. I'd never thought beyond that triumphant moment at the Trials. What was supposed to come next?

It hit me hard. Back to training, back to the slog, back to the beginning to do it all over again. My expectations were childlike: 'Well, then you go to the Olympics and get a medal and then you'll be famous when you come home and everyone will love you and you'll get rich and you can retire on a high as a hero...'

The training cycle started with a shock, with the National Breaststroke Camp – an event I had only taken part in once, and that was a disaster. I'd hated every minute at the Australian Institute of Sport again and had spent more time with backstroker Christina Thorpe than I had with the other breaststrokers there. This time I felt like the frightened little girl in the middle of an expanse of trampoline, trying hard not to pee into her new leotard again. We are never too big to be frightened and when we are most frightened, all perspective leaves.

After a taper in my training volume lasting three weeks (the workload is reduced to allow the body to recover, rebuild and rest before competition), a week of competition with no real training and a week of real holiday, I found myself pounding up and down the pool like a maniac to prove to those I had displaced that I truly belonged on the Olympic team. I felt undeserving, afraid that I might again be shunned by those I had beaten and I wanted to justify my place there. I felt watched. I was the overnight success who didn't belong with these heroes of the sport. I was just little old me.

It is easy to forget that every swimmer is 'just little old me'. It's easy to forget they are as fragile as the next person, especially when you're in the lane beside them and they zoom past effortlessly, while you thrash with heart and soul but go nowhere. It was heartening to have Jade around. She was a slow trainer, made me look fast, but it didn't seem to bother her the way it did me. She hated training, but she had a kind of acceptance that she couldn't 'perform' the way some of the others did. I wished I could remain as dignified as her.

I don't know where the demons came from. Maybe I felt guilty for being the one to cause others such disappointment, for having made it back to form so quickly after my two-year absence. Maybe I wanted to look into their eyes without a sense of selfishness for denying them the Olympic dream and taking it for myself. I had never considered that it might be hard to be the one who got it right on the day.

The need to justify my place pushed me to a shoulder injury in camp week. A knife stabbed deep into the front of my right shoulder and burned its way through my chest and lungs. A tear and substantial inflammation in my right shoulder tendon stopped me from raising my arm at all. Putting on clothes was impossible. I couldn't find a comfortable position in bed at night. Anti-inflammatory drugs made me feel like a sea-sick blimp and the specialist's eagerness to put me under the knife had me worried.

The frozen peas I used as an ice pack at least four times a day made my shoulder pink and raw and Brent, my physio, was a masochistic bastard who'd make me writhe, sweat and swear on a whole new level. Luckily, he had the most beautiful face and ultimately, magic hands. I hated the exercises he made me do and I did take some small pleasure from seeing him beg, bribe, threaten and reason with me to do them. It took six weeks for my shoulder to heal sufficiently to cope with any substantial Breaststroke work and in the meantime my left shoulder flared because of the added strain it had to cope with. I had only six weeks to go.

* * *

For 12 weeks, I walked the same path with the same people I had since my return to the pool. Some days you think it's dull and you wonder if it's habit or hope that keeps you coming back. Some days, though, you notice the little things and your walk along that same path seems magic; you feel alive. Some days you share your happiness with the birds – song to song; and some days you fill the pool with your tears – water to water; but always you are driven by fire.

I knew where my path led. I knew its terrain well:

Phase 1 – Endurance: long, boring sessions that went on and on forever, lap after lap building basic fitness that formed the foundation for peaks to come.

Phase 2 – Race Specific: sessions that applied newly developed endurance to the demands of your specific program of events, distances, strokes.

Phase 3– Quality: where strength that was developed in Endurance and refined in Race Specific is honed into sparks of power that burn furiously and fast.

Phase 4 – Taper: where the body is rested, where fuel is stored and where the jitter of competition begins to tingle.

And all the while I relished those morning sessions in solitude, Dad taking notes and supporting with his presence. I knew that Greg would make it as interesting as training can be. I knew that I would rely on him for the rationale for every lap; I knew the levels of exhaustion that came with the varying terrain; I knew the mind games; I knew the sound of my white angel and the sound of the black. And I knew that Sean would be there, asking things of me that I could never give, and yet would try so valiantly to accommodate.

Drudgery was broken by the building excitement of letters in the mailbox emblazoned with the Olympic Rings (was the postman impressed?) – an invitation to model the Australian Team Uniform at its launch, forms to fill out – dietary requirements, profile details, what do you like to do on the weekend? I hadn't been asked such questions since I learned to lie about my hobbies in primary school.

And the night before departure it occurred to me, what do you take with you to the Olympic Games? I was completely unprepared for my trip down the rabbit hole. Was I still dreaming, still plodding up and down the Ryde pool with my flippers on, visualising my hopes for some distant future?

* * *

A personal entourage of 12 escorted me through the official media reception at Sydney International Airport. There were tables of t-shirts to be signed, cameras to be spoken to, orange juice to be sipped and sandwiches to be nibbled, then finally, away to the departure gate. Even Ursula came to see me off – I had broken the drought and all was forgiven, but my photo was not yet on the wall.

The farewell was harder than I expected. I couldn't believe I'd be there without them – my pesky sister, my vigilant mum and my quiet professor. It somehow seemed wrong to be doing it alone. They'd trodden the path with me and now, in the last moments, I wouldn't be able to see their faces. I didn't think I'd miss Sean, though I knew he'd call.

We hugged, one at a time, slowly.

Collie stopped breathing and she trembled as we did our silly little good luck routine – pretend hock and spit over each other's shoulder. I'd kiss her forehead, she'd kiss mine. "Om Sai Ram."

Mum cried and crushed my lungs with her vice-grip. She wanted to be there so very much.

Dad's eyes were moist and red, struggling to contain his emotion. He was churning, nervous.

Greg couldn't hide his nerves at all. He didn't know where to look, how to stand, how to say 'see ya'.

And Sean planted a kiss that made front page of the paper, among a barrage of dry, nervous coughs.

This was going to be one hell of a ride.

Three

Then a woman said, Speak to us of Joy and Sorrow.
And he answered:
'Your joy is your sorrow unmasked.
And the selfsame well from which your laughter rises was oftentimes filled with your tears.
And how else can it be?
The deeper that sorrow carves into your being, the more joy you can contain.
Is not the cup that holds your wine the very cup that was burned in the potter's oven?
And is not the lute that soothes your spirit the very wood that was hollowed with knives?
When you are joyous, look deep into your heart and you shall find it is only that which has given you sorrow
that is giving you joy.
When you are sorrowful, look again in your heart, and you shall see that in truth you are weeping for that which
has been your delight...'
   – Kahlil Gibran

19.

"And as I roll along I begin to find things aren't always just what they seem"

– *"Upside Down"*, Jack Johnson

YOU WATCH IT ON TV. You hear about the triumphs of our nation's heroes. You feel the magic of the Games, the fire that lifts every competitor to performances they barely dare to dream of. They return home legends. It's the 'Spirit of the Olympics', the flame that touches them and makes them stars.

I had heard of heroism in failure and how it was as much part of the Olympic magic – a runner who stops to help a competitor who has fallen, sacrificing a medal but helping another sportsman finish a race he's worked four years to run. I'd heard those stories of people battling insurmountable odds just to be there, but I listened more to stories about the bolt of 'Olympism' that turns an underdog into a champion – Jon Sieben toppling an unbeatable Michael Gross in the 200m Butterfly in 1984 and Duncan Armstrong repeating the moment in his 200m Freestyle in 1988. This was the folklore that floated through my veins... that was what I was going to become.

Sometimes it was like I'd followed the white rabbit to a tea party and a game of cards, but there was so much more of the mundane than the TV ever told me.

* * *

The Atlanta Olympic Games started with our flight being delayed at Sydney Airport. It was delayed again. And again. A complicated trek of missed connections and rerouting saw the nation's elite stretching in corridors, lying in lounges, on the floor, eating the air industry clean out of peanuts. Being vegetarian caused a stir. The team dietician kept asking if I wouldn't please consider eating meat, for health reasons, of course. I was unable to comprehend the fact that she existed solely for the benefit of the swimming team, let alone that she might be asking me to change my diet to make her job of catering easier. For 24 hours I didn't have a decent meal because ordering vegetarian on the plane had slipped someone's mind. I blessed Mum for the dried fruits she'd forced me to take in my hand-luggage.

Three days later, at midnight, I melted into bed opposite my roommate, Karen van Wirdum, in our tiny rectangle at the University of Georgia, aching for a swim. I hadn't been a day without my dose of chlorine for so long. It was as though the gravity on land was tearing at my muscles and I needed the weightlessness of my friend to realign. We would spend the next couple of weeks at the university – training, being outfitted, settling into the new time zone, climate and our new role as fair dinkum Olympians. It still didn't seem real.

Our entrance into the athletes' village was just as protracted as our arrival in Georgia – hand print scans, gender verification, accreditation badges, signatures, waiting for God only knows what, and when we finally made it to our rooms, they were no more than upmarket prison cells – grey, draughty holes in a noisy corridor that amplified every boom of the heavy fire doors and the tinkle of every droplet in the share-toilets. Many of us were still waiting on luggage that had gone astray on our trek over, but the buzz of finally being in the village made any discomfort nothing more than a mozzie bite.

What I didn't anticipate was the tension that comes with the three weeks on tour before an international competition starts. When I was preparing for the Trials and the World Uni Games, my three week taper was like any other phase in training. The only thing that changed was my energy level and a short peak of realisation on the first day of competition that this was it. But taper does strange things to people and when the stability of my dad's words was on the other end of a phone line once every couple of days, and when I was witnessing others go through their own turmoil with daily detail, when my peak realisation that 'this is it' arrived three weeks in advance, taper made me feel like I was in a sauna, slowly simmering to a boil.

Your body is sent into a tailspin when the workload is decreased and you go through a patch of literally forgetting how to swim. Everything feels wrong, aches and injuries resurface, you feel like you're dragging your lead arse along the bottom of the pool through thick sludge at a crawl. No matter how many times you go through it, you always get anxious. Its intensity impacts as much out of the pool as it does in. I'd never been through a taper where everyone around me was tense about the upcoming competition, and because different personalities react differently, I felt like I was in a nuthouse at times.

During taper I was a drastic mood-swinger (although some would say I was even at the best of times). I felt fantastic and I showed it on good days in the pool, but I seethed and brooded and bit when I swam like a lead weight. It was awful for those around me, but it also meant I could be unpredictable enough to feed off others and their energy. It was so good to have even-keel Jade around, but I hated the thought that I might be a drain on her.

Some people go completely crazy, hyperactive with unspent energy, and they can be exhausting to be around. Others get tired, mellow and down. When I was having a day like that, I looked around at my team mates and wondered what I was doing there. I felt completely out of place. I missed home. I was no longer thrilled by the cereal and salad bars, the fantastic, frightening bodies of athletes from every corner of the globe, the frequent visits to the day spa. I felt the pressure, and I knew everyone else did, too – the expectations were unreal, and while I floundered, the stars were doing what they knew best: they bunkered down.

Queensland's 'Super Squad' had separated themselves. Scott Volkers and his galaxy didn't come to the pool at the same time as everyone else, they rarely mingled with the rest of us, or maybe I was just imagining it. They didn't participate in team stretching before sessions, and though it was considered snubbing, it was somehow tolerated by management. We started referring to Scott and his Super Squad as 'the other Australian team' and the apparent presumption that they were somehow above the routines the rest of us lived by was only working, on my down days, to fuel the feeling that I was way out of my league. The Super Squad members seemed like the gods I saw everywhere on Olympus, warriors who would smite me if I offended them with my presence. I was 'utterly intimidated', as my mum had once observed.

The Atlanta experience was like India in some ways – all contrasts and contradictions. At times the excitement had me feeling as though competition had already started, while at others, the absence of distraction made me feel like I was waiting patiently for the sky to fall. It was hard to balance my desire for distraction with the need to wrap myself in cotton wool like the caution of a young car lover taking his dad's new MG for a spin – God forbid you blow a gasket at this early stage! And that was the test – to stay balanced in a world of wild extremes.

So, while exploring the athletes' village like a tourist, the free McDonald's on every street corner had to be added to a mental check-list for later, the pecan pie in the dining 'pavilion' had to be avoided in a similar fashion, the temptation to spend days in the laser games arcade had to be tempered with reminders of why we were here, walking had to be shared with tram rides, and attending concerts in the stadium across the road had to be exchanged for small group jam sessions with Laurie Lawrence's guitar.

Many an hour was spent with that guitar, especially in the last few days. If we weren't on the telephone to home in the long, open communications centre with 24 other athletes jabbering ('Oh, hello Mrs Dunn, it's Nadine here... I'm really well... Yes, just waiting for a call from home... Hold on a moment, I'm pretty sure Matt's here... Matty, it's your mum... No, he says he's waiting for an attractive blonde to call... just kidding! Here he is... yes, it was nice to chat to you too...'); or if we weren't sorting out the tens of thousands of letters and hero-faxes that came via the mail room to crates labelled 'Swim Team', 'Kieren P' or 'Susie O'Neill', and needed to be sorted into individual piles by anyone with a fetish for organising (Dear Nadine, Everyone else took the good people, so I'm writing to you to say Good Luck. I hope you win gold even though you are not as good as Sam. From Kellie); if not engaged in physical honing in the vast rooms of massage tables and physio benches, watching in awe as the gymnasts re-strapped ankles that screamed with open wounds from ripping old layers of tape meshed inextricably with skin; if not thus engaged, we chatted, laughed and sang.

Initially the sing-a-longs in our rooms started as a private thing for Jade and me, but soon gathered a crowd. Ryan Mitchell and Jade played most of the guitar and I sang without restraint. One night when only a few of the girls were left I sang that song, my Olympic song, 'One Moment in Time'. It wasn't easy to do, unaccompanied, but it felt right, and the girls loved it. Goose bumps all round, and that night I finally felt that I fitted in with people who shared similar passions and who liked my company as much as I enjoyed theirs. That was the night when Hayley Lewis became a real person to me and the night when Nicole Livingston was no longer daunting. Everything changed with that song.

Up to that night, Hayley had always struck me as dull and stuck up from her sudden rise to celebrity years before, but I'm not great with first impressions. She turned out to be a dark horse, sweetly taking the piss without batting an eyelid, always egging you on to give as good as she did, and she had me in stitches frequently with her deadpan comedy. Nicole was, by other reports, a harsh, crude, arrogant bitch, but I quickly discovered that Nicole was the only person of whom to ask questions because she was the only one with experience who would give a straight, no bullshit answer. Her curse was being too forthright with people whose sensitivities were scarred by her sledgehammer touch. I loved them both, even though they'd betray me a few nights later.

* * *

Laurie Lawrence, our Team Motivator, organised a full Australian Team sing-along to get us into the spirit a day before the Opening Ceremony. It was the first time we'd all been together in a casual setting, weightlifters, boxers, runners, gymnasts, cyclists, shot-putters, martial artists, swimmers – all gathered in the Australian courtyard under the stars. Physios and massage therapists, media liaison, management dropped in for a while and we even had a television crew trying to do an interview with a gymnasts while we carried on like Laurie Lawrence clones in the background. Paul Green, a 400m runner, wrote a song that the track and field team performed, Paul on guitar, Tim Forsyth on bass – it was a private concert where our best athletes revealed that they had many talents:

"And we're here to say: 'Give it all you've got,
Get on your marks, get ready, go!'"

I wished I could sit there, listening to their magic forever. We sang ocker-Aussie tunes like 'Home Among the Gum Trees' (complete with actions, of course) and 'Waltzing Matilda'; songs that at any other time are banned from the stereo, but at a time like that they managed to stir a patriotism I didn't know I had. Alas, Laurie's repertoire of songs dwindled far sooner than we would have liked, and after three versions of 'Land Down Under', the crowd was desperate for material. Hayley whispered to me, "You should sing that song!"

I killed her with my eyes. "Not a chance in hell!"

Nicole's ears piqued and with the devil's grin she put it out there as only Nicole could: "We want Nadine, we want Nadine…"

"Yeah, come on!" Hayley took up the chant and, bloody sheep, the rest of the swimmers joined the chorus, "Yeah, we want Nadine!"

Scott Miller tweaked the call with "We want Wobbles!" and I knew it was going to get ugly. A matter of moments and everyone there knew who Nadine was, and despite not knowing why they wanted me (or if indeed they did), they called.

"God! I'm no Paul Green. I'm a hack. I can't even sing karaoke," I protested for a moment and almost burst into tears, but hearing the name Wobbles reminded me that crying is the crappiest way to gain respect in a sporting arena. They had no idea what they were asking me to do. They'd laugh at me, feel sorry for me trying to warble through a song that was never meant to be performed without backup... never meant to be performed by me...

Nausea gnawed through me; no nervous wobbles, just a horrifying puke response. Terror burned my beetroot face and made my eyelids disappear into my sockets. My knee caps developed an independence that was mildly amusing and I watched them as they jumped and turned bluish green. The earth ignored my request for a chasm to swallow me whole and still they chanted. 'The only way out is through,' I told myself. 'Just get it over with as fast as musically possible...'

I rose. Silence descended. A tiny squeal of triumph from Hayley, and I slammed my eyes shut, trying to pretend I was in the shower; a cliché, I know, but who doesn't believe they are Maria Callas in the shower? I heard the music in my inner space, opened my mouth and a wavering squeak emanated.

'Press on!' my mind whispered.

I didn't move for fear of collapsing, and I didn't open my eyes for fear of remembering where I was. A dramatic pause consumed the courtyard as I finally belted the last note and slowly inhaled, and... an explosion of hands and whoops thundered through the night as I exhaled.

I opened my eyes, managed a weak grimace and bolted for my room.

Paul Kent, in his column "The Last Word" in *The Sun Herald* on July 21, reported:

"...swimmer Nadine Neumann inspired a few goose bumps with a solo of 'One Moment in Time', the theme from Barcelona."

Interesting how circles close – theme from Barcelona. If only Mr Kent had seen me as a dancing drag queen on rookie night, I could have had a real future in show biz.

The first group of rookies had to have dinner at the main dining hall at peak-hour in their swimming costumes and caps – not so onerous. We had to dress in drag and dance to 'I Love the Nightlife' by Alicia Bridges in the McDonald's restaurant across the road from our dorms – a somewhat more challenging prospect, not only in terms of discomfort, but our resourcefulness was given a thorough workout trying to come up with Priscilla costumes with very limited supplies. Tacky golden headbands for 50 cents from the village hairdresser, garish accessories made out of gold aluminium ashtrays nicked from McDonald's (ashtrays in an Olympic village baffle me), shiny swimming costumes and spangled party clothes pilfered from various female wardrobes, and a short routine to go with the chorus had us set.

Trent Steed was hot with his rolled up sock breasts perched a few inches too high and accented with two gold ashtrays pinned at the nipples. He had the moves for the table tops and quickly drew a crowd clamouring for a piece of that action as he flicked his skirt with a wink. Scott 'Cobber' Goodman surprised everyone with the most sociable, team-oriented display he had ever given – stiff, uncoordinated bopping, ashtray bling bouncing around his neck, socks in flip-flops, fumbling as he mocked everything we did – he had the team doubled over! He wasn't what I'd call an attractive trannie but there was something about him that just worked. Jade and I didn't need to do much other than try to look like men trying to look like women, and damn, we did that well!

With a rookie night stunt and singing debut under my belt, the prospect of swimming in front of thousands didn't register as any kind of a challenge. I was looking forward to finally doing something I knew how to do in front of an audience. I couldn't wait for that Olympic bolt of brilliance.

* * *

It was Colette's 17th birthday on the day of the Opening Ceremony. I had a mission – to get onto television with a 'Happy Birthday Ollie' sign. I still called her 'Collie', as I always had, but her school friends called her 'Ollie' and the publicity stunt was as much about making her a legend at Forest High as it was about me sending her a birthday greeting. She'd be chuffed, for sure, and she'd see it as a small perk for putting up with being 'Nadine's little sister' all her life. There had to be some benefit for her!

It was steamy and we sat in the holding pen (the Athletics warm-up arena) for what seemed an eternity, watching the ceremonial spectacular on giant screens, waiting like nervous performers who hadn't had the chance to rehearse. It took forever and by the time we were given our cue, lined up in neat rows of eight, ready to march in, we were thoroughly dehydrated and cursing those who felt it necessary to use 100% Australian merino just to make a symbol of us. It wasn't as though anyone was saying 'Ooooo, what a fine merino suit you have there, you must be very proud to be Australian with all those… sheep…' Instead they were saying, 'That looks hot!' And it bloody was. Cotton would have been fine! Releasing the lining of my skirt from the sticky sweat dripping down the backs of my thighs became a subconscious act that no one noticed because they were busy doing the same.

We were instructed to march in our neat rows of eight, like army cadets, but it only lasted as long as it took for the volunteers to say it. Climbing the steep ramp into the stadium, hearts in our mouths, I squealed like a toddler. I'd watched athletes enter the arena at past Olympic opening ceremonies, I had heard the announcer call 'Australia' as the packed grandstand erupted, but the experience is entirely different. TV lacks soul.

"AUSTRALIA!"

"Raaaaaaaaaaaaa!!!"

I hit the crest of the ramp and there it was – the Olympic bolt. The grandstand rose like a galaxy, cameras flashed an explosion of stars, humanity poured from a small opening as an almighty roar reverberated and I was an exalted witness to the birth of the world – light from darkness and life from the abyss.

Admittedly, I don't think God created us in alphabetical order. He may have created us with those smiles, but he certainly didn't need us to hang around in the fray for the next few hours as feet became sore and exhaustion set in. The bolt died fairly quickly and my roommate, Karen, and I jostled our way from the centre of the Australian pack to the edge of the track where we sat down next to volunteers' legs to get a less taxing, more uninterrupted view of the passing parade. Each time there was a break in the march of athletes, panting volunteers would scurry across the track, hand out frosty bottles of water and take away the empties. I sipped and sat, held up my 'Happy Birthday Ollie' sign every now and then, felt like part of a tiny ripple in the ocean, and I didn't realise that the Channel 7 camera zoomed in on us, the commentator announcing Collie's birthday to the nation.

My energy was flagging when the torch finally took centre stage. I expected Muhammed Ali to be an imposing figure, but there he stood – a trembling man, his broken body in the centre of the ultimate celebration of physical prowess. But something in him still shone; an element that transcended its mortal frame and touched me, burning my eyes. I knew that all of us were specks, tiny grains that together make the soil from which life springs. I had a million friends whom I may never meet, bound by a flame.

Later, as I tried to make sense of my Games experience, revisiting the highlights made me believe it was that secret unity that held me together despite the low-lights. Ever since leaving Australia, I'd been training under Glenn Beringen with Jade and Ryan Mitchell, and the bridges between me and those I had never spoken to before were built of the same stuff I saw in Ali. I really liked my stand-in squad. In general, coaches are chosen for Australian teams according to their athletes' performances, so not all swimmers have their home coaches with them on tour. I was one of the orphans allocated to someone with a suitable squad makeup and Glenn was great. His outwardly gentle nature reminded me of my dad at times. I understood why Jade chose to move to South Australia to train with him.

My satisfaction with my group showed in my swimming, too. A few days before the opening ceremony, I did one of my 250m time trials and absolutely flew. At the 200m mark, I was two seconds under my training goal time. Glenn raised his eyebrows, and the papers reported 'Neumann on track to break world record'. They loved extremes. I tried to take it in my stride, but I couldn't get the ache to race NOW out of my system.

A few days on, in the 100m Breaststroke, I could do nothing but watch and scream for my Adamssun. No miraculous bolt of Olympic strength – slower than her best, no final, only dark disappointment. But she had to pick herself up for a heat swim in the 4x100m Medley Relay, another chance a few days later. It was hard for her, and hard to watch on. At training, dodging other swimmers, I did my best time ever, faster than my bronze medal swim at the World Uni Games, and again Glenn raised his eyebrows. This time he smiled, too. God, I wanted to race.

In daily team meetings the captains reviewed what happened the night before, what the heats in the morning yielded, who'd made it into finals that night. Sometimes one of the coaches said a few words and the meetings would finish with a team cheer. But despite all the 'bonding', something was missing. There wasn't the togetherness, warmth and fun of the World Uni Games and I wondered why Ali's spirit didn't manifest as some magic glue in this instance. It was as though the underlying unity of an Olympic family was buried under the pressure.

On a few occasions head coach, Don Talbot, spoke to us at team meetings, but he was one harsh, negative man, echoing the media's scathing reports. Numerous personal best times and the fact that Australians weren't the only ones in the world who had been striving for those Olympic Games seemed to elude him, and instead of congratulating the great swims and encouraging others, instead of being positive, Don reminded us time and time again that: "If you can't at least do your best time, you have failed." "If you fail to make a final, then you at least have to do your best time, otherwise you've failed." "If you swim slower in the final at night than you did in the morning heats, you have failed." "We are having too many people missing finals because they are lazy on their skills." "Too many people are taking it easy in the heats and are missing out on good lanes in the finals, or they're missing out altogether." "No one is going to give you a medal for trying, you have to do better than just try."

It felt heavy and daunting and hard. It was not the sparkling, exciting event I had expected. It was serious and scary, like going to the doctor to hear the results of a test – you have broken your neck. I needed light, I wanted fun and celebration, and I knew I'd have to create it for myself.

* * *

By the time I was due to race, Laurie Lawrence had whispered a thousand times: "Nadine, ANYONE can win the 200m Breaststroke!" He'd say it at the end of a conversation, as a farewell, a greeting, in the middle of a sentence, at lunch, on the tram, at any random moment on any given day. I had had at least three arguments with Sean, almost 40 smiling faxes from long-lost friends, neighbours, family and strangers, and I'd spent over $200 on phone calls home. I had heard the crowds. I had seen the crazy flag-waving, banner-flying, face-painting Aussie fans. I had painted my bed sheet with some of the other girls – a giant boxing kangaroo standing on a jar of Vegemite. I had witnessed delight and despair and I had prayed that the bolt strike me, if no one else, because that's what has to happen at the Olympic Games, that's what John Konrads promised me from his position high on the wall. I would become an Olympian, I would win a medal, I would retire from the sport on a high and look back forevermore on an experience that made me realise that nothing was out of reach. That was the plan.

It was going to be a great day. I was fit, slimmer than ever (the days of 79kg were 22kg gone), I had swum faster than ever in my training run six days previous and I was itching to get on with it. But I hadn't felt brilliant in the water since my blitzing 100m time-trial. I put it down to nerves. I trusted my body to do the right thing in the real thing.

I was in the second seeded heat next to American favourite, Amanda Beard. Amanda was young and she'd clocked some dazzling times in the six months leading into her Trials. She was reasonably fast in the first half of the race, but was positively lethal in the second 100m. I had always been a 'back end' swimmer, but Amanda had perfected the 'storm home over the top of everyone in the last 50m' race plan. She swam her races exactly the way I aimed to, so I knew that I might not see anyone in front of me for most of the race, but I wouldn't be complacent because the threat would be cutting me down from behind. I was going to have to do my best time just to make the final.

* * *

On pool deck, swinging my arms and jumping around to get my body ready for its two and a half minute marathon, the announcer declared it was me, Nadine Neumann of Australia, in Lane 5. I wondered, momentarily, why the crowd cheered so loudly for someone incognito to them. Such is the spirit of The Games.

I was nervous. My stomach wobbled more than I was used to. I felt slightly faint, but as I knelt beside the block and dipped my hands into the cool water, I knew my body would slip into its rhythm as soon as the gun catapulted me into the blue.

I raced. I tried to control the urge to spin arms and legs at top speed. I gripped the water consciously. I stretched. I lunged. I saw nothing. I heard nothing.

2.29.91.

Third in my heat and 0.5 seconds slower than my personal best time.

I was crestfallen. "I can't make the final with that swim," I fumed.

In a confused state of disappointment and anger, I was accosted by a cheery Neil Brooks for the poolside interview. Poor Brooksie. I answered his congratulations with a curt, downcast reply that made him struggle to come up with the next question. I had to keep my composure. I pretended to be philosophical about my race. He finally let me go and I sulked out to the cool-down pool where Glen waited with a businesslike expression.

"How does Lane 1 tonight sound?" he asked casually.

"What?" I was in no mood for jokes.

"Lane 1."

"Me?"

"The bloke behind you." He was smiling now.

"You serious?! How?!"

"Just get in and swim down, we'll talk about the race later. You did a good job this morning, kiddo, we'll just cut a few seconds off that tonight, hey?" Glenn slapped me on the shoulder and I wanted to kiss him!

My limbs wouldn't plod slowly up and down, they wanted to dance! Pats on the back, "Nice job, Nads." "Way to go, Wobbles." Even Don had a relieved smile for me.

Cool down, food, phone home, bed.

First step done.

20.

"If there's something you wanna do, you'll know when you've seen it through"

– *"Live as You Dream"*, Beth Orton

THE RACE-DAY ROUTINE WAS THE SAME EACH TIME – warm up amid the thrashing throng who scratched, elbowed and kicked for a patch of water, dashed past, over or through slower swimmers, turned and pushed off on top of anyone stupid enough to stand in the way. I hated warm-up.

The ceremonial shower and change into racing costumes was usually exciting, but at the Games it was potentially damaging to the confidence of the uninitiated. The European and American women appeared more comfortable naked than clothed and the tiled change rooms became a psychological battlefield. Tall, tanned, tough bodies staring each other down as they engaged in lively conversation, secretly waiting to see who would cover themselves first. I didn't even pretend to be worthy of such a battle. A brief chat with Glenn was all I needed and I was away, alone.

The marshalling room at the Olympics, like the change room, is a universe where all rules of social etiquette are cast aside. You need to be absolutely clear on your race preparation and you have to make the surrounding environment suit your style. If you're a talker, you engage in conversation and keep it going at all costs. If you are not a talker, you need to shut the talkers out without losing your inner space. Those who succumb to another's race prep lose. I knew so little about that world.

As my moment drew closer, I noticed the absence of my wobbles too late. I'd succumbed. I didn't know what I had succumbed to, but I was not in control of my preparation; I hardly even knew what my race prep was. I jumped around, I listened to music, I breathed, visualised, reminded myself of the lifetime of effort so many give for a moment like this. 'This is THE OLYMPIC FINAL, for God's sake! Make it in this race and you'll be remembered forever! Where is the bloody bolt?'

I was calm. I had felt more nervous before some of my training swims, and all I could do was chuckle at the absurdity of the image – The Olympic Final; the setting sun sending a shaft of golden light down my lane, my lane only, bathing me in its spotlight; and me, shaking my arms as though getting ready for club races. Not even my screaming team mates in the stands to the left, or the spattering of Aussie spectators to the right, not the television cameras and photographers from around the world or the electronic scoreboard proclaiming 'Atlanta Olympic Games 1996' could stir me.

There was no bolt. I ran third for the first three laps, but I couldn't get a glimpse of other competitors to spur me into the fight. From Lane 1, I saw nothing. I heard cheers, but the swim felt like hard work, not the flowing smoothness I had felt at the Trials. With 25m to go, I stopped completely – 'piano on the back' they call it. Penny Heyns first, Amanda Beard second, Agnes Kovacs from Hungary third, then Sam Riley, a Japanese swimmer and I touched, the three of us almost together with Agnes.

Sixth. I had done my best time by over a second, but I somehow felt cheated. My Olympics were really over. I had tired where I was normally strongest and I hadn't even felt nervous. I immediately began searching for what went wrong, but I was in the awkward position of being one of the 'successful' ones. No one could ask for more than a personal best in the final. I ought to have been thrilled.

It's funny how when you're young you have this glorious image of how your life will go. It's even stranger that you feel cheated, surprised or baffled when your childhood visions don't turn out the way you expected. One part of your mind chides the other for believing in those silly fairytales: 'Everyone knows that the world doesn't work like that!' But still, we want to believe.

I wanted to be Duncan Armstrong. I wanted to be Jon Sieben. But I couldn't show that to a rational world of team mates who would have been happy to achieve what I had. I was stuck somewhere between ungrateful brat and pleased participant, so I drowned myself in supporting the others to distract me from a detailed analysis of what went astray. I thought exclusively about green and gold zinc, Australian flags and new cheers with which to scream myself hoarse. And I had a ball making a complete ass of myself! I ate pecan pie until my gut ached, I drank Coke and Fanta until my eyes watered and I played as though the village was my own private kingdom.

I finally did see the Olympic bolt strike – Kieren Perkins had been written off in the 1500m Freestyle. His stroke looked laboured while Daniel Kowalski glided comfortably in his lane, and Dan got the bulk of our noise for most of the race. But King KP, who'd locked himself in his room for the past two days, brought the world to its feet. I cried then. And I cried later when Jade received her silver medal for her efforts in the relay heats. Later, I cried again for no particular reason. And then I laughed at myself for crying.

When the swimming was over, I went to San Francisco to see my Aunt Marianne. I missed home terribly and eventually decided to leave America before the closing ceremony. The bomb on the last night of the swimming was enough of an excuse to avoid having to explain that I was just not excited anymore. I needed to find a future direction, a next step. I had always planned to retire on a high after the Olympics, but now it felt uneasy, unfinished somehow. My relationship with Sean was going under as well and I knew the past five weeks had changed me in a way I couldn't even begin to explain to him. I needed to make new choices, but I couldn't move forward in America. I needed to be home.

21.

"I'm gonna try something just a little bit different this time"
– *"Permission to Shine"*, Bachelor Girl

I FLEW INTO SYDNEY IN THE COCKPIT as the lights from Wollongong to Newcastle sparkled on a pitch black canvas, just like the camera flashes had sparkled around the arena in those opening moments of The Games. I held my breath as we drew closer to the largest cluster of stars and they slowly unfurled, separating to reveal streets and buildings, houses, freeways and towers. I stepped off the plane, sure that I had seen a metaphor for the coming weeks – it was all going to become clear, I just knew it.

Only a family can bring such welcoming warmth: a laughing, squealing band of people who adored me, standing with balloons, flowers and faces brighter than the lights I'd seen from God's window.

Sean was empty-handed, but his first words were all the homecoming gift I needed. "Were you with anyone?"

I smiled and whispered back, "No, and it's nice to see you, too."

I knew my heart and I was quite detached as I watched him rummage through my bags like a three-year-old, sniffing out what presents I had brought for him. A switch in my soul was flicked – lights out.

It wasn't until the Welcome Home Parade that I really understood what the whole 'Olympic thing' was really about. Not in the whole of my preparation for the Games, not even while I was in Atlanta, did I quite realise what I was part of, and the parade gave me the quiver of 'Olympism' that I had anticipated all along.

The streets were crammed with cheering masses of all ages and from all walks of life. Businessmen and women threw shredded office waste, construction workers clapped from scaffolds, tourists waved Australian flags, mothers sat with babies on picnic blankets right there on George Street, school children clambered for autographs, the wealthy, the struggling, sport lovers and the plain curious smiled and waved and cheered. Streamers, confetti, toilet paper poured from windows, danced in the wind and caught in trees making the city look like a snowscape on a glorious day. Banners welcoming back Australia's 'heroes' decorated balconies, building facades and shop fronts. I was overwhelmed and I understood.

The Olympics is not a rush of glory like being kissed for the first time: it's a mosaic of light and dark moments, a pattern of the small events over a lifetime, fragments of conversations, snippets of time, all woven into an intricate tapestry called 'Olympia'. Each person I spoke to, each moment of activity and idleness, each tear and laugh, each lap, each meal, each fax and school student's letter constitutes part of my tapestry, and it is, like Lady India, about the everyday made extraordinary. It is about people who find they are good at sport coming together to share a month. It's a carnival like every other swimming carnival where you do your best in the hope of achieving a moment of perfection. It's about everyday people in an exceptional place wobbling, falling, getting up and laughing just like they did when they were learning to walk.

Although my achievements had earned me the 'Australian Swimming Rookie of the Year' title, I had the sense I was not finished. I hadn't seen the best I could be, but with my new understanding I felt sure it was there to be seen. I found a sense of strength in knowing the emotional drain with Sean had to end. I realised that, while striving to live one life, I never truly acknowledged the impact each compartment had on the other. My sections labelled 'relationship' and 'family' and 'mission in life' could not be extracted from one another entirely. Unhappiness in one was bound to send ripples into the others. Perhaps that was not the ideal way to be, for an athlete competing at the highest levels, but I had lived with a brick wall between my lives and could not do it again. Instead, I would look for happiness and unity in all areas of my life and this meant dealing first with my greatest unhappiness.

Sean knew I had changed. He hurt, that day at my house. We cried, but he didn't bother trying his old manipulations. When a handsome stranger appeared at the door at exactly the wrong moment, he also knew that the stranger would be his replacement. I'd met Ben at uni about 12 months before, and really the only thing we'd had in common (apart from a love of Mazda MX5s) was that we were both under the spell of people we could not fathom. We commiserated. That day, Ben had arrived to take me for a drive in his dad's red Mazda. It was an awkward moment. Despite me being adamant that Ben was not my type, Sean was sure. "You'll be with him because you can't be on your own."

It smarted, that he thought I was that weak. I guess I had been weak with him, and he knew it.

In the end, it was Mum who set me up.

Ben had just arrived at our house for a third attempt at that MX5 drive when Colette surfaced from an hour-long telephone conversation with a boy she secretly adored. He had extended an impromptu invitation to join him at a friend's 17th birthday party in a park near the beach at Clontarf and her thrill was palpable. She confronted my fairly conservative parents with, "So, can I go?"

Mum was far from impressed at the short notice; Dad withheld judgement; and I felt awkward with Ben there to witness a family 'moment'. I tried to defuse the situation by offering to drive.

"Then why doesn't Ben go along? Do you have other plans for tonight, Ben?" Again, mother's subtlety rivalled that of Nicole Livingston's.

"Nope, that's great with me!" he agreed with a twinkle.

"Nadine...?" Spotlight on me. This was the last thing I needed.

"Oh? Really? Are you sure?" Fan-bloody-tastic! Could the moment be any more painful?

When he grinned and nodded, all I could do was squint and direct a 'you owe me so big-time' glare at Colette.

"Okay, let's go!" she piped, pleased that she'd have her big chance to kiss her man and completely ignoring my discomfort.

I wondered how I had ended up with a date to my sister's wanna-be boyfriend's friend's underage beachfront bash, when all I really wanted was to go for a drive, for Ben to go home and for me to finish the day with a hot chocolate and an early night. Colette didn't care, as long as I didn't hang around like a chaperone.

But…

The rest is cliché. Colette's hopes of kissing her boy were dashed for some reason I never found out, while Ben and I did kiss on the beach as I tried to figure out if it really was the cold or if I was shivering for a whole different reason.

So it seemed that life began at 20. I'd started on a new mission, with a new focus, a new approach, and this time I was going to get it right. I was no stranger to starting again, that was for sure, and I actually felt kind of blessed to be given so many chances to learn from past mistakes. Part of me thought that maybe God did exist everywhere, in everything. Maybe all those times of stumbling and falling were the Universe making sure I got what I needed, rather than what I thought I wanted. It's easy to be philosophical when your head and your heart feel clear.

I'd met 'the one'. In Ben, I found the fun and tenderness that I'd ached for. And my parents liked him! He could see my layers of defence and self-criticism, he peered through them and showed me where the little Nadine was, riding the waves. He reminded me of the fun there was in just having a go. So that's what I would do: no great, earth-shattering adjustments in training or diet or anything else, just the joy of having a go. I would just swim for the thrill of swimming fast. I would study for the joy of learning. I'd love for the freedom of loving, be me without trying.

With Ben's help, I was able to accept that what happened in Atlanta, that strange nothing that left me flat, was not my fault. To a large extent, it was the result of a less than perfect taper – not an error that couldn't be remedied in the future. I still had so much to learn and I was ready to just have a go, thanks to Ben.

I wanted to retire on the biggest high there is – the Olympics in four years' time, at the turn of the century, at home. I wanted success with a true understanding of what it is to be an Olympian. And until then I would keep humming along to the soundtrack of the water around my ears, I'd balance the happiness in every part of my life and I would be the one, whole, rock-solid Wobbles when the whistle called me to the starting blocks.

John Konrads was still smiling in black and white. I was ready. Onto Sydney, 2000.

22.

"But if you try sometimes you just might find you get what you need"

— *"You Can't Always Get What You Want"*, Rolling Stones

WHEN I HAD STARTED MY '96 OLYMPIC CAMPAIGN, I had no real expectations, no real assurance that I was good enough to make it. This time I knew I was good enough and everyone else did, too, but something had me uneasy. I felt permanently nervous and I didn't know why. By the time the 1997 swimming season was in full swing, I had sponsors – real ones that you normally only get if you're a big star with big star medals. They were taking a risk by backing me on the basis of my post-Atlanta-Trials media profile and the promise that I would have whatever magic it took to become really big. God, I hoped they were right.

D&R Henderson were the first to come onboard with a sizeable cheque. The 'R' in 'D&R' was a family friend who had been so impressed with my dedication that he just wanted to help out in any way he could. A particle board manufacturer sponsoring a swimmer over three years – Rob couldn't have expected any great promotional opportunities, so I knew it was simply because they wanted to encourage me, nothing more, and I felt the weight of that generosity.

Next, the Gundagai Ex-Tigers took a punt. This committee of sport nuts would scour the horizon for athletes who showed promise of reaching glory, but who still lurked on the periphery of fortune and fame. They gave me financial support twice, including two visits to the annual Snake Gully Cup race day where I had a flutter and won a grand total of $3.45. I was made a life member of the Ex-Tigers after a stage interview with Norman May. He'd had a rather long and jovial evening and after a string of suggestive questions and comments he asked what I planned to do to ensure I get to the Sydney Games. I made the error of using a colloquialism: "I'm gonna bust my butt."

"And a cute little one it is, I've been watching it all night," he declared with a wink as he leaned in to me.

"I don't know how you could've, considering I've been sitting on it," I replied and exited, stage centre, amid applause.

The Tigers loved it; I dare say Norm didn't.

Then there was Macquarie University, a sponsorship I got because I was studying education there, and because I made a stirring speech to the local business community requesting their support for a pool to be built at the uni. It was a dream the university community had had for almost 25 years, and the lead-up to the Sydney games was the perfect time to be appealing to the community, businesses and the government for support. The Vice Chancellor was so touched by my words and the fact that I was a 'home grown hero' that she announced, in her speech of thanks, that the university was to give me $10,000 a year until the 2000 Olympic Games. The Deputy Vice Chancellor nearly fainted and the Executive Officer of the Sports Association had me nominated for the Board. I was elected and served for many years.

Finally on the sponsorship front, there was the real humdinger with proper legal contracts and incentive bonuses and all the trimmings of a professional agreement – Nad's Personal Care Products. I got the deal thanks to the passing of my days as 'Wobbles' and the dawn of my life as 'Nads'. Only a rare few still called me Wobbles, and although my new name had convincing connotations of courage and strength, at the time I still felt very much like a Wobbles; if not physically, my confidence was definitely walking the line. The hair-removal manufacturer's faith in me was like a Hollywood script and they were not at all concerned about how uncouth it may sound for people to scream "Go, Nads!" from the stands, in fact, I think it may have been the seed of a marketing idea aimed at those hairier individuals looking for a sleeker solution. Alas, lacking the required anatomical features, I was not to be a part of that campaign.

When I look back, I think it's with all this good will that a darkly-clad fiend snuck in and took up a position on my left shoulder. I think Fear was with me from that point on, because while I knew I was looked after, financially, I sensed the weight of my responsibility to perform for others and I was beginning to feel more and more socially isolated.

When I started back at training after Atlanta I was a vastly different creature to the one who had left on an Olympic adventure – a cocktail of celebrity and outcast, suddenly serious about what I was doing at the pool and impatient with the trivialities of teenage crushes that absorbed 90% of the squad's focus. After two and a half months away from Ryde, I had suddenly become 'older' than the kids in the squad, and I was getting the sense that it made me a stranger to be observed from afar. I relied more and more on Greg's expertise and adult conversation and I loved him in the way only a needy athlete can. Of course I had friends whom I also loved – Beshy, Terry, Zoe – but I had been to the 'other side' and I knew what professionalism looked like. I missed it.

Ben had taken on some of the morning timing sessions that my dad had always covered, and I thought it was terribly romantic – him coming straight to the pool after night shift at the servo to watch me plod, pound or power through tedious laps. He'd developed a keen eye for my technique, but it was always my professor who knew what to say. Between the three of them, Greg, Ben and Dad, I had the perfect coach.

But I missed out on selection for the World Short Course Championships and I was only graciously offered a place on the B-team for the World Cup in Europe because another member of the team had to pull out. Greg was put on the team, too, but I knew only one other swimmer there and he still called me Wobbles. God, how I wished I had Jade's company.

* * *

Three days in Gelsenkirchen, Germany. We were a small team and we spent the short stay racing and walking the local streets. I got to know Kate, a second kindred spirit, like Jade. I was unsure whether she was an angel or a devil, but if her electric blue eyes and innocent blonde bob were anything to go by, she was a devil for sure. I couldn't help but kick myself for thinking this butterflier was a powder-puff bore to begin with – I was always jumping to conclusions. We shopped. She tried on a white lace dress and looked every piece the angel she pretended to be (apart from the antitheft disc perched on her left nipple) while I tried on a bright blue sequined number that matched her eyes and barely covered my buttocks. It is the one impulse purchase I regret not making. I also had the chance to have dinner with Mutti at an Italian restaurant one night. We were both so astounded at the tyre-on-a-B-double-sized wheel of parmesan in the foyer, that we took photos. It was magnificent to see her again, accompanied by Stefan, my German coach of so long ago.

I told him, "*Stefan, ich habe 'was' gemacht.*" Stefan, I've achieved something.

And he nodded, "*Ja, echt.*" No kidding.

The tour continued on. Three days in Imperia, Italy. Our hotel lift, made in approximately Four AD, claimed to carry five people safely, but it really only carried one valiant daredevil with a suitcase at a time. It was so slow that, had we all used the lift, it would have taken four hours to check in. My most memorable moment: (an event that was repeated so often it was like *Groundhog Day*) being unashamedly groped by the Italian male swimmers in the warm-up pool. Apparently helping oneself to a handful of tit or arse is customary, provided it is done during a turn; while passing a swimmer going the other way; while passing a swimmer going the same way; while waiting to push off the wall; entering or exiting the pool; while bobbing up and down in the water for no particular purpose other than to check out what you're getting a handful of; or during any other activity that could be argued is a part of regular warm-up procedures. Elbows, nails and the backs of heels became powerful defence weapons.

In the pool, I won two silver medals and was beaten on both occasions by a baby-faced Belgian terrier called Brigitte Bécue.

The tour moved on. Two days in Paris, France. I played charades with my dad's aunt who was a mad swimming fan (but who spoke absolutely no English) and her daughter. I mastered the sentence, "*Non, non, non, je ne parle pas français!*" (No, no, no, I don't speak French!) with such fluency that the French judges thought I was lying. One toad in particular was not convinced that I couldn't speak the language and he repeatedly threatened to disqualify me for 'an illegal Breaststroke kick', should I ever swim in France again. 'The Don' Talbot stepped up to the plate and asked the little man with the Napoleon complex to show him the kick that was so offensive. He couldn't, but it didn't stop him threatening me. It turned out this judge was a member of a club that was fierce rivals with the club offering me a full scholarship to swim for them at the French National Championships. Being the daughter of a Frenchman, and so a citizen, this would not have been a problem. But the fact that a little weasel, too scared to disqualify me on the world stage, felt that he could intimidate me every time I raced was enough to turn me off. The nail in the coffin of my French swimming career was when the officials (men and women alike) used the ladies' change rooms to line up for their glorious march onto pool deck every session, without warning swimmers who found themselves in various stages of undress, being ogled by a white army. I was not prepared to stand for that at every meet!

After the last night of competition in Paris, most of us were sick and exhausted from nine days of travel and racing in a European winter. The Don congratulated us with a speech that went something like, "You're soft... blah blah... easily distracted... blah blah... not going to make it to 2000 if you don't shape up... blah blah..." He hadn't improved since Atlanta, despite sticking up for me. I just didn't understand why he had to be so negative every time he addressed a team.

It had been a whirlwind trip but we managed to squeeze in a half day tour of 'The Sights' of Paris before heading to the airport. Kate dropped a candle in the 'make a prayer and light a candle' section in Notre Dame, snuffing three other people's prayers. Amid poorly contained giggles, we relit each one with an apologetic, "Dear God, so sorry. Please give these people what they prayed for…" before we scuttled, desperate to get out of there before we wet our pants with the pressure of remaining reverent. I loved those moments with Kate. Our photo hugging under the Eiffel Tower in the misty winter chill is one I cherish.

The return trek took three days with cancelled flights, missed connections and detours via Perth and Melbourne, but I finally arrived home with happier memories of the time spent out of the water than in it.

I loved being on tour and, as much as the interminable days of training could be a drag, I simply HAD to make it onto each Australian team in the lead-up to my Sydney Games. There was a joy in sharing a tour with people like Jade and Kate that I hadn't found anywhere else, and because I knew the swimming life could not last forever, I felt an urgency to get as much of it in as I possibly could. I felt alive with the prospect of sharing such rare moments with them, of racing and cheering them on.

But light casts shadows, and that shadow was something so hard to define.

23.

"But when she got too close to her expectations, well, the dream burned up like paper in fire"

– *"Paper in Fire"*, John Mellencamp

THE DARKLING FEAR ON MY SHOULDER slowly began working her magic. By the time the 1997 Pan Pacific Trials arrived, she had sent her talons so deep and had cast a spell so quiet and cloudy that she controlled my body. My focus was clear, my race preparation was solid, but my body would not follow my instructions, and I was sure it was Fear. I tried to meditate, to look for my inner space of calm and quiet, but there was a black so deep in there that I preferred to turn away.

I always liked having a warm-up event – something to blow away the cobwebs. I liked to have a splash in a lane on my own, get a sense for the atmosphere, the routines of the meet. I liked to listen to the unique sounds of the competition pool – how the water bounced off the walls, how it echoed in the gutters, how the crowd reverberated in a muffled, faraway boom or in a clear, metallic ssssshhhhhh, depending on how deep the water below me was.

The 400m Individual Medley was one of my warm-up events. It's an event for the all-rounder and I liked the special brand of sickness that the 400m Medley gave me as I turned from Backstroke to Breaststroke. Something in that particular muscle transition flipped me inside out. I won the 400m Individual Medley at the '97 Pan Pacific Trials. I made the team completely unexpectedly and I felt on top of a wave, riding it to an inevitably golden shore.

My main event, the 200m Breaststroke, started as normal – squirming stomach during morning warm-up, tight and slightly sluggish heat swim, nervous diarrhoea all afternoon, yawning in the marshalling area… But then, things changed.

Everything became slow and exaggerated, like I'd been sucked down a microscope. What used to be small signals of my body counting down to launch turned into overwhelming surges. I didn't quiver, I shook. I wasn't light and springy; I was light-headed and couldn't get enough air. As I approached the pool deck I was overcome with nausea, and weakness dumped me onto the chair behind the blocks. My head spun, my eyes wouldn't focus and I was drowning. It took every ounce of will to step up on the block and as I waited for the gun, vertigo wobbled me so violently I almost fell in. I was struck down by something intangible, it paralysed and confused me. Something was brewing, but I couldn't be sure what. I just knew I was afraid.

Every other event was fine, even fun, but the 200m Breaststroke had me stumped. I didn't make the team in the 200m and my only hope to swim it at the Pan Pacifics was that the rules were slightly more flexible and it would be up to the Head Coach's discretion. Given The Don's history, I didn't hold out much hope of swimming anything other than the 400m Individual Medley at the Pan Pacs in Fukuoka, but at least I was on tour; nothing else mattered. I was suddenly a Medley swimmer. No more Breaststroke.

It was actually quite nice to have something fresh to focus on; a new challenge would hopefully eradicate that sliver of darkness threatening my light, and by God it was going to be a challenge to get my Backstroke to the point where it wasn't slower than my Breaststroke. On a number of occasions, at formal dinners and swimming workshops, I had had the chance to get to know Murray Rose, and he always said I should try the 400m Individual Medley. He seemed to believe I could make a real go of cracking the Medley world with my stamina and my ability in Butterfly, Breaststroke and Freestyle, but to really crack it I was going to need help with my Backstroke! That's where Nicole came in.

I hadn't seen Nicole Livingston since a post-Atlanta cocktail party where, at the peak of the speeches, she dipped a corn chip into the fluorescent guacamole.

"...and it is an honour..." The chip cracked under the weight; she cursed.

"...on this most proud occasion..." She re-dunked, balanced an athlete-sized mouthful on a tender corner of corn just long enough to move it away from the bowl.

"...once an Olympian, always an Olympian..." It splattered across the pristinely starched, luminous tablecloth.

"...shall call upon you, our newest Olympians..." I held my breath and my laughter in one.

"...will treasure this moment..." She shoved the mess in her mouth with her fingers and surreptitiously manoeuvred a napkin over the bright green splat. All class and good humour.

So when Nicole offered to teach me Backstroke, I accepted before she finished her sentence. I couldn't imagine a better coach! She was a gem, but it turned out there weren't any major technical problems with my stroke. More than anything, I lacked strength in crucial areas. I needed to go to the gym and I needed a strength trainer to guide me there.

Three weeks after my first Nicole session, while I was again being lazy in the beautiful Ryde pool morning sun, a puffing and flushed ball of muscle muttered, "It's just not fair," as I glided into the wall. I wasn't sure if he was speaking to me.

He continued. "At least you've got one of those," he said as he pointed to the tattoo on my hip. "Doesn't make me feel quite as bad."

I smiled politely and nodded.

"D'you get that because you went or because you want to go?" he asked.

"Oh, my tattoo? Yeah, I got it because I went. To Atlanta." The Olympic Rings emblazoned on my hip were bound to get attention at some point.

"Wow. That's awesome. Sorry, I'm Wayne," he said, with an outstretched hand and I immediately knew where I'd seen him before. He was Wayne Pearce, rugby star and now coach of the Balmain Tigers. I remembered screaming for him from my lounge room on Saturday nights, copying the commentary streaming from my father and dancing in front of the TV with Collie, like cheerleaders, when he scored. I was suddenly embarrassed.

"I know. Nice to meet you, Wayne. I'm Nadine."

He was friendly and the conversation only ended when he was purple and shivering, some 30 minutes later. He suggested I visit him at the Balmain Leagues Club – he would introduce me to his team's strength trainer, Tim, and psychologist, Paul, "...see if we can't get rid of some of those demons, hey? Free of charge."

I was flattered he'd taken such an interest.

Psychology didn't go so well – apparently I was already very self-aware and my inner critic tended to speak up too often during self hypnosis – but Tim was exactly the strength trainer I needed. He was a bulldog, as wide as he was high with a bottom jaw bigger than his head and intelligent without a hint of brute in him; a tough trainer but all puppy-like fun outside the gym.

We worked hard, Tim and I. He turned me from a dolphin to a shark – honed, strong, fitter than I knew I could be, ready for anything. His sessions made me sweat in a way I'd never experienced; a kind of lather that coated my skin so it itched with tickling trickles. My brow would furrow, focusing under his stare as he willed me to do "just one more... that's good, now one more... come on, I'll do it with you... one more..." My limbs shook and ached so that stairs became my enemy and squatting for the toilet became a gym session in itself. But I loved training with him. He inspired me. I felt special to have my own private trainer, and he enjoyed working with someone who didn't laugh at the fact that he enjoyed reading history books. Sometimes I'd get him to tell me stories I'd already heard before, just so I could have a few more moments' rest, but he never fell for it. He'd talk while we crunched, lifted, jumped and stretched me into shape.

As the Australian Team gathered in Brisbane for our final 1997 Pan Pacific Championships preparations, I was certain I'd turned that mysterious darkling into a pumpkin. I felt ready for anything.

Photo by Reece Scannell

24.

"You've got to lose yourself in the music the moment you own it"

– *"Lose Yourself"*, Eminem

HE HAD ENTERED ME IN ALMOST EVERYTHING AT THE PAN PACS. Don Talbot had turned me into an all-rounder with one of the biggest programs on the books. The darkling Fear crept in under the cover of excitement. The Don was testing me.

Our first stop was Singapore for acclimatisation. Every day was thick pea soup and the pool (exactly the same temperature and consistency as the air) made it feel like aquatic and terrestrial environments had merged. Outside of training times we occupied ourselves by finding novel ways of staying cool. Naps in air-conditioned hotel rooms lost their lustre, so we sought out shopping centres. We contributed significantly to the Singapore economy that year, thanks to 'Rucky Praza' – clothes, cameras, Discmans and DVDs, what was compact and portable and preferably electronic. I must have missed the memo about portability. I bought a bloody indoor fountain in a mammoth box!

Our Pan Pacific Championship Team, 36 strong, included 16 rookies who used the post-Olympic lull to step up. Ian Thorpe, Grant Hackett, Geoff 'Skippy' Huegill – a cast that ensured rookie night was superb. Hacky and Skippy stole the show dressed up, very convincingly, as stunning gameshow hostesses, while the baby of the team, Thorpy, pretended to be the *Sale of the Century* host – they had all the moves! It was nice to be on the audience end of the rookie night ritual and I felt like part of the old guard already.

We were a pretty tight team because the media had started on us early. With the absence of the likes of Kieren Perkins and recent star of women's middle and distance Freestyle, Natasha Bowron, we were in for an ordinary meet, so they said. One reporter even had the hide to ask Craig Stevens (who had replaced Kieren on the team), "How does it feel to be the most hated man in Australia?" The papers didn't intimidate me the way they had in Atlanta. I'd changed enough to know that what they said was irrelevant until we'd raced and they had results to talk about. The press need to sell papers, so whatever headline works...

I was alert, ready to do something new and spectacular. But I kept overheating and dehydrating, and had the most extreme days of speed and slug that I had ever experienced in taper. My coach for the meet, Mark 'Reggie' Regan, watched from afar when appropriate and cracked bad jokes when perfectly inappropriate to keep our spirits up, and he did a golden job. I loved him for it, but I'm not sure he loved me!

Fukuoka hadn't changed: the dazzling glamour of Vegas lights and giant crystal chandeliers and golden pillars of marble hotel foyers; gambling 'halls' with long, whirring rows of poker machines lined up along one side of the narrow, fluorescent corridors no wider than a shopping aisle and with nothing more than a toilet at the far end for convenience; satellite dishes and shining new BMWs pitted against ancient, mossy, age-weathered statues that stood on shrines so old and overgrown that nobody remembered why they were sacred; gloomy alleyways where children played, tipping over-full garbage bins in their wake; and gleaming shop fronts that declared the latest and greatest to the wealth that passed by. The contrasts were wonderful.

Our hotel was glamorous – a smorgasbord of delights where the banquet hall decked out lobster and caviar at every meal. A chef stood by to sauté our every desire. Had they forgotten we were athletes? We ate Weet-Bix and noodles and steamed greens. We drank skim milk and fruit juice... and they had definitely forgotten me. Vegetarian options were limited and lean. Plain rice. Garden salad. Rice and salad. Salad and rice.

Yet, amid the luxury, our team was falling apart. A mystery bug spread like bad news – a gastro virus that was knocking us flat: Diana Calub, Geoff Huegill, Grant Hackett… Our team doctor, 'Doc Sando', was a well-experienced man on tour. He knew how to be prepared for people getting sick but he ran out of isolation rooms faster than anyone had anticipated.

Jade, despite her attempts at positive thinking, got sicker and sicker as competition approached. She was down and I wanted so much to help pick her up the way she had so often helped me. Before I had left on this trip, Ben had given me three precious little boxes – one marked Happiness, one Energy and one Magic. He had spent months with those boxes open beside his bed, willing the energy into them, pouring all his love and hope into them for me. I firmly believed in the power of those boxes: if the Universe is made of energy, then thoughts and intentions and will are energy too, and they surely have the power to change the world, just like a happy child can light up a room. Those little boxes had remained tightly closed since my departure, holding onto Ben's love, energy and magic for the times when I would need them. But I was flying high, and my friend was down. I was sure Ben wouldn't mind if I shared. Jade needed some Magic.

By day one of racing Jade was healthy, Kate had everyone enraptured with her electric blue eyes, Hacky had stroked and praised his pert backside at least eight times, my coach for the meet had repeated the same painful jokes for the 15th time and Don Talbot had given three of his not-so-stirring pep talks. I couldn't stop smiling. After a best time of 2.13 in the 200m Butterfly B-final I glowed with even more confidence. (I made the A-final, but each country was only allowed two representatives in the one race, so Susie O'Neill and Petria Thomas were the ones.) This was going to be a fine meet.

Day two, 400m Individual Medley. They say drowning is a peaceful way to die. I disagree. My first breath on the first stroke of the first lap in my 400m Medley brought a lungful of cold chlorine so unanticipated that I didn't actually get oxygen until 35m down the pool. Relief from choking came with the O$_2$, but it also began the coughing and spluttering that lasted for the next 65 meters. With that stress in the first 100m, I was dying, so by the time I had turned over for the Backstroke, I was so relieved to have my face in the air that the breathing pattern and leg rhythm Nicole had taught me never even started. I kicked too hard, completely lost any grip I had on a race plan, and thrashed frantically to make up for lost ground for the rest of the race. I had no legs left in the Freestyle and it felt like Satan himself sat on my chest with his big arse blocking my airway. He prodded around my throat with his pitch-fork and sent hellfire to every corner of my body while his demons did a fine job of messing with my head.

But I still made the final in a good time! I was hopeful for a much better performance in the evening final. My best time again? Perhaps a shot at my first international medal? Maybe a thrilling tussle for the wall? Or the feeling of flying effortlessly through the water, like I did in my first international Individual Medley when I was 14? Whatever the outcome, it would be much more pleasant than the heat swim!

"That was a good swim this morning, Nardine," Don Talbot said. "You set for tonight?"

Miss Mason used to call me 'Nardine'. For some reason, it felt like the first time Don had actually addressed me directly, by name.

"Thanks. Yeah. Should be good," I stammered.

"Good, good." He came straight to the point, "How would you like to swim in the relay?"

"Tonight?"

"Yes. I know it's after the IM. Do you think you'll be up for it? It'll be tough to back up but we'll put you at anchor; give you a few more minutes' recovery. What do you think?"

What do I think?! I'd never dreamed of being in a relay at this level. I just wasn't fast enough; not a sprinter. But here was Don Talbot offering me the chance to anchor the 4x200m Freestyle relay! What do I think?! 'Oh shit!' is what I thought. 'He must be desperate… It must've been that 200m time trial I did in Singapore… broke my best time by about seven seconds – not hard since I hadn't done a 200m Freestyle for about ten years... went 2.04... was stoked but didn't realise he'd noticed...'

"That would be awesome! Really?" is what I said.

"Great. Better get resting then!" he replied with a smile, satisfied.

I'd always thought of him as 'The Don', like the fearsome godfather of swimming, but I'd taken to facetiously calling him 'Uncle Don' whenever I talked about him with the others, mocking his lack of warmth. I suddenly felt sheepish. He had been very pleasant. I was a bitch. Still too quick to judge.

The 400m Medley hurt. Personal best again and I came sixth, but I barely registered any of it. My whole heart was focused on the relay. Susie O'Neill led off and got us to a good head start; Sarah Ryan went second and held Susie's lead. I wobbled more and more as the seconds passed. I was all out of sorts. When do I take off my top? When do I splash myself with the pool water? How soon is too soon to start jumping around? And how late is too late to get up on the blocks? I'd never done this on an international scale. I was nervous and so alive! Kate leapt from the blocks third and my heart rattled my throat.

"Just don't break," I told my twitching legs as I climbed deliberately up the step and onto the block, toes curling tight over the edge. Kate was charging for me, a Japanese swimmer in the lane next to her nipping at her toes. We were in third and when I hit the water, all I knew was that no one was going to take that medal from me. I flew the first 100m – did my best time in the split – and by halfway down the last lap the Japanese girl had all but reeled me in. I screamed into the water. I held my breath. I felt nothing but an almighty fire somewhere below my pounding head and the roar of the home crowd willing their champion on to snatch that bronze away from me.

But they didn't count on a Breaststroker, a Medley swimmer, a distance Freestyler who was learning on the job how to sprint. I lunged for the wall at full stretch to hold onto the most satisfying third place I'd ever experienced. I felt like a freight train had used me for tracks, but the girls were thrilled and Sarah reached over the blocks to pat me on the head.

"Great job, Nads! Awesome!"

Don was relieved. He'd made the right choice... just.

"That was very good! Very tough. Well done. What have you got tomorrow? Just make sure you keep your head now, hey? Good work." He patted me on the back.

The four of us on the medal dais grinned like naughty kids who got away with nicking the teacher's jellybeans!

The Optus network covered the race. They had Natasha Bowron in as guest commentator since she was too unwell to compete. She seemed to forget who was watching when, sitting pretty, she oozed something along the lines of, "Well, they can't be too disappointed with that performance because they really only had one 200m Freestyler in that team, Susie, and she did an okay time. The other girls, well, I guess they just did the job, you know. They got in there and did what they could and luckily came out with a bronze, so they can't be too disappointed with themselves..."

The implication that without her we never really had much hope made many a parent boil. Kate and Sarah were offended that in Natasha's eyes, they weren't really 200m Freestylers. Susie was annoyed by comments Natasha had made about her personality and training habits, to which she had muttered, "I'm not nice. How dare she say I'm nice? She doesn't even know me..."

Tongues wagged and attitudes fired and I wanted nothing more than to beat Natasha's 800m time; knock her off the pedestal she'd placed herself on.

* * *

Our 4x200m Relay team stayed the same for the 4x100m Freestyle relay. If sprinting 200m had me shaken, the 100m taught me that I was really glad I wasn't a sprinter! That last leg of the 4x100m Freestyle relay was more nervous tension than I could take! I was pitted against the same Japanese girl as in the 4x200m and she was out for revenge. The race was identical. She flew up behind me and she was there, eyeball-to-eyeball so quickly. I panicked. My arms spun. I had no grip and I couldn't see the wall. I took an extra stroke right when I should have stretched to touch and I almost hit the wall with my forehead. She must have done the same thing because I got there by .09 seconds. Another bronze. I could almost hear them gasp as I took that stroke. I'm sure Don had a heart attack. I was flying high!

I had eight races under my belt and my shoulders were beyond relaxing. There is only so much cooling down and massaging you can do before the lactic acid catches up with you. Eventually you get sore. But I had only one race to go. It was a long one. I didn't have a race plan. I was just going to go out hard and see if I could get into a trance-like rhythm at speed. It was all I could do and I figured if Hacky could do it for 1500m as sick as he was, a little extra warmth in my shoulders would be nothing to complain about. If I was going to beat Natasha's 8.41 in the 800m Freestyle, I was going to have to do my best time by eight seconds. Only one second per 100m. Only half a second per lap. Just good technique and great turns. I could do that.

I walked out onto pool deck watching the head in front of me. It belonged to another Australian, my roommate, Brooke Townsend. Her neck was grey with blotches of crimson that screamed, 'I'm nervous!' The familiar shimmer in my stomach was there and my cheeks were flushed. I could feel the shadow of the Amazon behind me looming over my shoulder. Her arms were so long I feared they'd connect with my head as she swung them. Her name was Claudia Poll, from Costa Rica... somehow. She sounded German when she spoke. She looked German. She was Goliath and I knew she would start like the wind. She'd be trying to stick with Brooke Bennett from America in Lane 4, so I planned to stick to Claudia's hip as long as I could – I'd never reach her shoulders because they were so far above my head already.

"Take your marks!"

The Blu-Tack in my ears amplified my breathing and dulled every other sound. I felt like I was in an aquarium. I consciously relaxed and set my muscles to spring.

We were off.

'Count in 100s and there's only eight… when you've done four, you're halfway…" I held on to Claudia just as I planned, my arms ticked like a metronome, but no trance came.

'Focus on the breath…' Each lap I made a little ground on the endless woman beside me, but on each lap she took three fewer strokes to get to the wall and she killed me on every turn.

By 400m I was spent, my legs were no longer mine and I had a stitch that threatened to double me over and tie me in a reef-knot. I was wheezing and light headed. I could feel the vomit rising. I couldn't bear the thought of another hundred so I began to count in 50m lots, convincing myself that each lap was the start of a fresh, new race, but my body shouted, 'LIAR!'

I counted in 25m lots and I could see Jade and Kate marching along the pool deck, spinning tracksuit jackets and towels above their heads, screaming and whistling, leading the rest of the team in a roar. I lifted.

I saw them again on the next lap and I held on.

I looked for them on the next lap and they were there, so I held on.

Again.

And again.

I could only see Claudia's wash beside me. There was no one else around, but Jade and Kate were there, screaming, willing me forward, and I turned for the last lap. I couldn't push off the wall. My body wouldn't straighten, but I held on…

8.40.

Fourth.

I was elated. I used to say fourth was the first loser, but that night I won.

Don nodded and smiled and patted me on the back. I floated. I couldn't find the words to thank my friends. Energy can come from many sources, but they are always precious.

After that race I was ranked number one in the Commonwealth in the 800m Freestyle.

On TV, Duncan Armstrong remarked, "…if there was a wood-chop event, Nadine would probably be in that, too. She's just everywhere!" and in *The Sunday Telegraph* on 17th August, magic words were written:

"Yet the woman whose praises were most loudly being sung by Talbot was Miss Versatility NSW, Nadine Neumann. She was thrown all sorts of curve balls by the coach – 'She basically learned to Freestyle here in the relays because we had no one else to call on,' as Talbot explained – and hit them all out of the park."

* * *

Everything changed for me on that trip – my events, my professionalism, my role in the team was no longer 'rookie' but 'mum' to many of the younger ones. I felt as though I'd grown and learned again. I was no longer a little girl trying to be like John Konrads, I was a sports-woman who belonged in her own right. I had transcended that awkward space between amateur and professional and I knew Don Talbot could see that taking shape. Perhaps he was just a man under enormous pressure in a thankless position, not a heartless tyrant as I had assumed. Perhaps I would have the chance to find out for sure at the World Championships… if I could stay this high and make it there.

25.

"And what could make you whole was simply out of reach"
- *"Have You Ever"*, Offspring

"What goes through your head? It must be so boring: just looking at that black line."

"Well, the line generally isn't black," is usually my first reaction to that kind of question, but that's being facetious. The simple answer I give to someone I don't really want to talk to is, "Nothing and everything" - which is sometimes the truth. The pious answer I give to TV cameras and live audiences is, "Well, you're really focusing on your technique, breathing, you know, all the little things that make a difference in a race," - and sometimes that's the truth. But the whole truth is that, when you're training, you're either thinking of the next witty remark you'll make in a conversation conducted in snatches between sets, or you're battling demons of one kind or another: demons of distraction that make you daydream while going through the motions; demons that make you focus on the pain and question why and how much longer you'll keep it up; demons of anger that make you seethe about inconsequential things simply because you have the time to think about them; and the worst kind of demons - the ones of fear, doubt and perfectionism.

In the four months before the 1998 World Championships in Perth, I battled. I felt like I was living a big fat lie all over again. I was perpetually unhappy, searching for that one magic ingredient that would bring me a constant stream of the euphoria I had felt at the Pan Pacific Championships and at the Atlanta Trials. I wanted that feeling to last; I didn't want the rollercoaster of training through good days and bad. At the same time I was acutely aware of how I affected those I loved with my restless and unpredictable disenchantment. My parents did everything they could to make my life as easy as possible – Mum cooked and washed and cleaned up after me, Dad traipsed to and from the pool every day, Colette, now studying at uni sporadically, working casual jobs and going out like normal young people do, made no attempt to rub in the fact that she had a life and I did not – I just couldn't get rid of the darkness.

So I dusted off and, despite all the promises I had made, reapplied my happy face. One face for the world outside and another for the world within.

In truth I had nothing to be unhappy about and I knew it. I was an Olympian and had been successful at the Pan Pacifics – but it was not good enough for me. I had media attention – but not the right kind, not often enough and not about the things I wanted. I had sponsors – but I could do better for them, make them treasure me more, get them more coverage and they could pay me more, if only I could swim faster, really make it big. I had a father who was the perfect supportive sporting parent, who was proud of me and spent every waking hour thinking about me – but I never quite managed to get that glittering prize I wanted so much to give him. I had a sister who tolerated my crap and still wept tears of joy when I did well and loved me when I didn't – but I never managed to make it worth her while. I had a boyfriend who adored me – but I always felt like a failure as a girlfriend because I couldn't do the things the average girlfriend does. And I had a mother who, never missing a step, cared for me, nurtured me, laughed for me and watched each change in me with the vigilance only a mother has – but I somehow always managed to hurt her.

I wanted so much more for all of them, I wanted to reward them and I hated myself for being so thankless in the misery that brewed beneath my smiling veneer.

I searched for the reasons, whipped myself until there was nothing but emptiness, but I couldn't figure out where the sadness sprung from. I could see old patterns emerging but was helpless to stop them – falling asleep on the way to training and only waking when an irritated motorist alerted me to the fact I'd just run a red light again; snapping at anyone at any time and brooding the rest of the time. I was plagued by the feeling that I was always falling short – I wasn't strong enough, my technique not good enough, my body not lean enough, my mind not tough enough, my training not hard enough, my times not fast enough. I wanted perfection so badly. I was terrified – of losing and the tirade my inner critic would unleash; of the pain of every session; of the guilt that came with rest when I needed it and yet petrified of the Chronic Fatigue relapse I could see just ahead of me; afraid of making mistakes, afraid of failing, afraid of being imperfect.

Fear. How do you defeat it?

I tried creatine, a compound that your body makes naturally, but a lot of athletes were taking the supplement to help reduce the effects of lactic acid build-up, reducing recovery time and helping in protein synthesis. Perhaps it would help me develop more lean muscle and I'd have more power, swim faster and then I'd be happy.

It worked instantly. I bulked up like one of Tim's rugby league front rowers, but it did nothing to promote agility or speed. I jumped from 58kg to the 67kg mark in less than two months and the crap made me feel like a waterlogged corpse. Try as we might, Tim and I couldn't get my bulk down and I swam the World Championship trials feeling like an ancient oak barrel bobbing in the ocean. Still, I made the team and, although I was momentarily happy, the feeling was fleeting.

I began to pick fault with everything and everyone. Ben was too different from me. I couldn't relate to his bond with his mates and his fascination with cars and, as much as he appeared to try, he had no desire to discuss anything of 'consequence'. Every conversation felt like small talk and I was bored of it. Ben and I belonged in different worlds and, although I loved him, I felt as though he was not in the least interested in what lay beneath my happy face. He should instinctively have known that something was not right. He should have wanted to find out. He should have asked and probed to find my hiding soul. I ached at the thought that I would never truly connect with him and the sinkhole gradually swallowed up our ability to talk at all.

I was coming undone but there were no answers.

I looked to Tim, my bulldog of a strength trainer. He always knew how to make me laugh. He understood me. He made me feel important, if only for a little while. What I had to say meant something, if only to him. Being a self-obsessed swimmer was beautiful, if only to him. I was okay, if only for swift moments at the gym. I lost sight of what was really going on, my big, fat happy-faced lie got bigger and fatter and I compromised myself the same way I had with Sean. I just went with the flow to gain the approval I couldn't give myself. The pressure of the impending World Championships and being sick in the week before the meet finally made me snap. I had to cut Ben loose; Tim would look after me.

Finally on tour, I was rooming with my two favourite people – Jade and Kate – in a glorious apartment on Scarborough Beach in Perth. The World Championships were days away and I had long telephone calls with Tim and my mum; short ones with Ben. The darkling, Fear, who had taken up permanent residence on my shoulder, constantly rocked my foundations.

Ben arrived in Perth the day before competition started. I took one look at him and he knew. God, how we cried. It was even harder to break up because I couldn't really explain why I was running. I didn't know what it was that made me want out, made everything that had been true suddenly black with shadow. I didn't know what had stolen the flutter in my chest when I saw him, heard his voice, thought of him. Why was I left with a vacant space in my mind when he was on the other end of a conversation? He was alone in a strange city, supporting me the way he always had, and I threw his heart in his face. Tim arrived in Perth and consoled me. And I let him. I was determined that this turmoil was not going to ruin my World Championships. I would separate the aquatic and terrestrial worlds again. I would resurrect that brick wall. I had to.

But it was too late. I did a freakish personal best in the heats of the 400m Individual Medley to qualify fifth for the final and I drew confidence from that. But in the final I drowned... and cried. Later, I drowned in the 200m Breaststroke... and cried. And again, I drowned in the 800m Freestyle... and cried.

Each time I pieced myself together, partly to spare my roommates and partly to prepare for the next race; but each time I tried too hard and failed. Each time, Ben was in the stands – watching, cheering, hurting, questioning what he'd done that was so wrong. I just wished he'd go home. He was the problem. I was sure of it.

Somehow, through it all, my happy face held up well and I actually did feel a genuine smile when Jade won a silver medal in the 100m Breaststroke in her home pool. But it was a hollow happiness, gnawed out by what Fear had turned me into.

* * *

I was curled in a corner, red-eyed and snivelling like a pathetic baby after my 200m Breaststroke final. The pool was quiet. The last bus had left and I was still hiding there, too embarrassed and drained to be bothered moving. I didn't know how I'd get back to the apartment and I didn't much care. I deserved to be the little girl forgotten and locked in the pool overnight. God! What a drama queen.

Don stood over me and held out a hand. I cringed. Now I was really ashamed. Why did it have to be him? He hated me because I'd told him his relay selections were crap. I'd told him I thought they were based on a bias towards swimmers whose coaches were running the teams, always convinced of a conspiracy. Why did I challenge him directly like that? Was I mad? I'd never seen anything so scary. He had spat, "How dare you..." and turned a deathly grey spotted with blood. He'd been furious. I couldn't take that again. Not when I was at such a low point, although I probably deserved it.

He insisted I get a lift with him. "A quick dose of acid rain is all I need," I muttered to myself, but I didn't have the fortitude to stand up to him again.

He started with an arm around my shoulder and a gentle, "How are you?"

He gave me a hug.

He told me he believed in me, that I had a lot of growing up to do, mentally, if I was going to achieve the heights he believed I was capable of. He understood that my heart was broken and my mind was working overtime to find answers. He asked about my beliefs, about my hopes and my plans. He was warmer than I thought possible and I realised that I needed a friend. I needed kindness to remove that happy mask and look into my sad eyes. I needed someone who didn't want anything from me. Someone who cared.

Unlike so many who back away, speechless, when you disgrace yourself, Don Talbot found words. And those words found me hiding in a corner of my mind, cowering from what I'd become.

26.

"Sometimes I feel the fear of uncertainty stinging clear"
- *"Drive"*, Incubus

WHEN THOSE WRETCHED WORLD CHAMPIONSHIPS WERE OVER, I returned home with a week before I was due to compete at the World Cup in Sydney. I just wanted to run, scream, hit someone, anything but deal with Tim's arm around my shoulder and Ben's tears on my cheeks. An escape in the form of a second family visit to Lady India was fast approaching, but it couldn't save me from committing to something outlandish.

Jamie Barklay, the Manager of the Sydney International Aquatic Centre (the 2000 Olympic Games pool), asked me, "How would you feel about singing the National Anthem to open the World Cup?"

Part of my mind shrieked, 'What is so hard about saying 'no'?' But my lips said, "Are you serious? Oh, my God! Um, okay, I guess so." My mind was unimpressed. 'Air head. Well done. Now what? In over your head again. It's one thing to sing to the steering wheel, but the national anthem at the World bloody Cup?! Just great.'

One brief rehearsal and I wasn't impressed with the sound that flooded the centre, so I cajoled myself into believing I actually sounded like Julie Anthony. It was a strange preparation for an international singing debut, but I was glad for the distraction of warming up for the 100m Breaststroke. I was meant to be focusing on swimming, but singing and memories of Atlanta had my stomach jittery. I finished my warm-up swim early so I could change into something completely inappropriate for a swimming competition and in an instant Ken Sutcliffe introduced me, the music started, I strode along the catwalk in my bright red ball gown to a stage set up in the middle of the pool, and launched, "Australians all, let us rejoice…"

It had been a big secret. No one knew I was doing it, so it caused quite a stir and the sheer adrenalin of getting through the anthem made me swim a personal best in the 100m Breaststroke. It was a nice way to be reminded that when I just let go, when I stopped trying so damned hard, I actually flowed like the water and the successes followed naturally. I just needed to sing more, or think less, or both.

* * *

In India again with my family, I found space to gather my thoughts, to take stock of what had happened over the past few months. It was a deeply moving trip in so many ways, and again Sai Baba's ashram in Puttaparthi gave me a sense of clarity and peace. It was a reflective trip. I spent a lot of time alone, in my own mind, and I felt as though I was beginning to find my own way of connecting with 'the source'. My mother loved the devotional aspects of daily life in the ashram – seeing her guru gave her all the lift she needed. My dad loved feeling the energy of the place – watching the joy others found in the ashram gave him joy. Collie loved the vibrancy of the ashram – the colour, the variety, the opportunity to explore the whole world in a microcosm. For me, being there became symbolic of a pilgrimage to my self – a way of removing all of my daily distractions and concerns in order to find what my heart was truly trying to say. I knew that eventually I would have to find a way of connecting to that inner space without travelling to another continent, but for the time being, India was the vehicle for my connection to Spirit.

Again, Lady India showed me the way forward. In my world, everything had been governed by strength – a strong, lean body, with a strong, focused mind and a strong, ruthless desire all combined to make a strong trainer, competitor, winner. At least that's what my experience had taught me. I had always strived to be like a rock – unbreakable, not a crack of weakness, resilient in constitution, unbending in belief, and eternal in dedication. But all rocks eventually crumble and I didn't want to be worn away.

Water was different. If I could be the water, I'd be truly indestructible, beautiful and wild; swirling around obstacles, transforming when the sun was hot or when the air was cold; patient, life sustaining and powerful. If I could be that kind of strong, when the time came, I could overcome anything.

The challenge was going to be maintaining that sense of vitality and power, not getting lost in the mundane and not allowing my focus to narrow like it had been. That was all – simple!

* * *

Alas, human beings become accustomed to their surroundings quickly and the renewed vigour I had found in India was absorbed, on our return to Sydney, by my reunion with Ben, the resumption of studies and training. Routine snuck up on me and jaded my vision. My insight about rocks and water was relegated to backdrop in a heartbeat.

It was the smell of the pool that eventually pushed me over the edge. Our training venue had changed – moved from the glorious outdoors at Ryde to the homogenous indoors at Homebush where the sweet stench of stale chlorine mixed with countless pairs of uncovered feet that were never really allowed to dry so they gradually rotted layer after layer of calloused skin inside old sneakers. Sometimes the stench of a troubled bowel or a lolly-induced vomit wafted past, and there was always the acrid odour of yesterday's swimsuit and towel stuffed, still damp, in my bag. The stench smacked me in the face as soon as the glass doors slid open to welcome me to training every day. I missed my outdoor pool and I could ill afford to hate Homebush, venue for my Olympic Games in just two years' time, but this was where our squad trained, and that was final.

Ryde Council had demolished 'my' pool with the hallway of black and white photos. They pinched my university's proposal for a second water polo venue for the Olympic Games; at least that's what I had reason to believe. The former mayor was part of Macquarie's pool committee and had free access to the information on the university's tender, so it seemed odd that the Council should submit (late) something that sounded awfully similar to Macquarie's bid. Council's proposal was based on the claim that the existing outdoor pool was so riddled with concrete cancer that it really needed to be put down. Ironically, the Council excused their complete lack of community consultation by citing the confidentiality rules imposed on Olympic bids – I wondered what happened to that rule when the former mayor borrowed Macquarie University's plans. When the small Ryde resistance began to dig up some strong ammunition against Council, I was happy to be part of the front line. My whole family was.

The Council was going to sell land that was not legally theirs to sell; they would absolve themselves of all responsibility for the pool, allowing private owners to fleece the community for a swim; they would include squash courts that would put the squash centre across the road out of business; they were even considering pokies and a bar! They would replace the home of my black and white inspiration with razzle-dazzle. All on the basis of an assessment that the concrete cancer was incurable – an assessment made by the same engineer who was going to help build the new multimillion-dollar centre; an assessment that was negated by our own engineer.

It was a big deal in the Ryde area. So big, in fact, the local paper interviewed me as the resident Olympian and I didn't hold back. But before the story even went to press, I was met at training by a mystery man in a navy blue suit that he obviously thought was black when he bought it. His sunglasses were too big for his face and he wore too much product in his hair, making it shine slick rather than textured. His shoes were polished and square at the toe, like a trendy stockbroker's, but the laces were frayed at the ends giving the overall impression of a school boy playing tough.

"I understand you spoke with a reporter yesterday." His voice had a veneer of ice.

"Yes, I did, he is doing a story on the pool drama, and wanted my opinion." Mine was defiant.

"I see, well the General Manager understands how this issue must be very troubling for you and she would like to meet with you to discuss your concerns."

I raised my eyebrows.

"Tomorrow afternoon at three, shall we say? At the Council Chambers?"

"Sure," I said with a lot more confidence than I now felt. He did not intimidate me, but the stories of 'The Bulldog GM' did.

"Good. Well, it was nice to meet you," he said and stalked away. He had never even introduced himself.

I didn't know what weapons to take into this battle, one I hadn't anticipated having to engage in head-on. I knew I couldn't play politics at this level, I couldn't threaten anybody with anything or rage or fire at will, but I also knew I couldn't just sheepishly sit and allow the Council to believe I was happy about their plans. I wouldn't shut up the way so many of the Ryde Club members had, just because they'd been bullied or because they didn't care enough. I did care and I had to stand up for my swimming heritage. So I took the best weapons I had – a smile and my dad.

We arrived to what turned out to be a meeting between a swimmer and the Ryde Council bigwigs, including the woman who'd started it all, a General Manager and a few councillors I didn't recognise. She had hoped to convince me of the merits of her swimming pool project and for me to be a poster girl for her grand development. But their 'Pride of Ryde' wasn't interested. I voiced my concerns and my opinions and, although they fell on deaf ears, I at least had the opportunity to use the line, "With all due respect, I think your handling of this situation has been absolutely disgraceful." It felt good to say 'with all due respect' when I felt none was due.

Hundreds of people swarmed on the next Council meeting. Eight people gave speeches damning the new development from all angles – they were tearing down a piece of Australian swimming history; they were making a huge economic mistake; they were breaching their own protocols – and eventually the meeting was cancelled because of the vocal crowd. We were warriors, strong and persistent as the tide.

But in the end, we lost to the power of politics. The demolition of our pool went ahead. An edited version of my interview appeared in the paper. A new, sterile, indoor leisure centre was built where the rainbows once shone. My black and white photo never made it onto the wall with John Konrads'. And I found myself training at Homebush with foot and vomit smells.

Greg did his best to maintain my enthusiasm; Tim did his best, although he'd been quiet ever since Ben and I had reconciled; even the teenies that made up the bulk of my squad – Beshy, Terry, Zoe – they did their best, but I was a crotchety old woman, regularly so overwhelmed by the terror of pain in training that I cried and couldn't put my cap on. I think we must be programmed to see each day as a fresh chance, because I kept going back. I was the ocean carving a cliff face one tiny grain at a time. But God, I needed a change of scenery, I needed to find that inner space where my Spirit used to speak a language I could understand.

I needed to get away. Again.

Training in the glorious outdoors as a teenager.
The old Ryde Aquatic Centre

27.

"You want it all but you can't have it"
 – *"Epic"*, Faith No More

WITH MY GROWING RESTLESSNESS, I found a way to force a fake kind of sunny 'positivity' – the Pollyanna perspective, I called it. Sometimes, if you force it long enough, you may even start to believe it. I gained selection on the Commonwealth Games Team in the three events I botched at the World Championships and the Kuala Lumpur Games were the best chance I had ever had of a fabulous meet. My best times ranked me number one in the Commonwealth for the 800m Freestyle, number two for the 400m Individual Medley and number three for the 200m Breaststroke. I needed to believe in my Pollyanna perspective, so I sought out ways to make it stick.

I gave motivational speeches at schools, corporate functions, board meetings, dinners, forums, conventions. I'd tell my story, share a short moment, 20 minutes, an hour of my day and feel hearts talking to one another in a language I couldn't articulate. They'd laugh and gasp in all the right places. I'd feel no different to any one of my audience, and yet somehow they made me feel precious, like I had something powerful to offer. I reminded them that no matter how ugly it gets along the way, what you learn about yourself and about life is enough to make every hard moment worth it; win or lose. And I gradually came to believe my own words because the audience believed me. I'd laugh at my own foibles, at the times I wobbled and fell. I'd laugh because I was still here, going forward. And I felt like I could make a difference. These were the invisible rewards for simply being part of the international swimming world. I had overlooked these precious gifts because I so very much wanted the shiny, physical, stand-on-the-dais-and-sing-the-national-anthem rewards, but the more I shared my journey, the more I felt blessed to be on it.

The Commonwealth Games in Kuala Lumpur were special in the same way that giving those motivational speeches was special. I learned to value the special moments beyond what happened in the pool, maintaining a positive outlook despite the fact that I swam like shit. The swimming was only part of my Games. I was elected as the Girls Swimming Team Captain and I wanted to focus on what going away with a team really meant to me and in the end I deemed my Commonwealth Games to be a smashing success!

* * *

My taper was mixed up. I crashed in the 400m Individual Medley and Jennifer Reilley won the medal I thought was mine. I came fourth in the 200m Breaststroke and again proclaimed myself 'first loser'. Greg's pep talk for the 800m Freestyle was, "Well, I guess we just haven't done enough work, so you'll have to go out there, try to hang on and see what happens. Good luck," but he knew damn well I'd done the work. No one had ever denied that I worked hard and I wanted to hit him. I came last and found myself consoling the Canadian girl who came seventh – she was crying because she'd gone four seconds slower than her best time, but she finally cracked a smile when I told her I had swum 15 seconds slower than my best, a time that may have won the race if I could just get my shit together on the day. I had a very public fight with Greg about his 'encouraging' words and then cried violently into the phone where my family hurt for me. I had had a CFS relapse and that Fear demon on my shoulder loved it. But Jade had become a Commonwealth Games gold medallist and I had a lot to forget, so we felt it was only right to party!

On the last night, after the wretched 800m Freestyle, I finally emerged from the change rooms with eyes burning with tears. The cricket team were at the pool again and I wondered why they were so excited at the idea of being around the swimmers.

They were the sporting superstars, the ones that made the mind go blank in awe, not the likes of Kieren Perkins – he'd whine that breaststrokers are 'just so slow', but when I told him to bite my bum, he dutifully dunked under the water; hardly a superstar! Or Ian Thorpe who was just a goofy kid in a body three sizes too big for him. Or Susie O'Neill who did a dance on skit night with a bunch of the other girls that involved bananas stashed down their bike shorts. Or Matt Dunn who danced around with a big Matilda Kangaroo head on. Even Michael Klim took part in our rip-off fashion parade of the Games uniform – he stared down the camera with bedroom eyes as Jade zoomed in to reveal baby-poo-olive trouser legs tucked into green and yellow sports socks that sat halfway up his shins, clashing with his over-sized, brown boat shoes, his swinging hips emphasised the price tag attached to his back pocket, while Ryan Mitchell, sideburns grown for the occasion and tie resting somewhere just below his sternum, commentated, "… and you will notice the taaaag still fashionably attached so you can brag to your friends about how much this fine, fine ensemble cost…" They were just the 'guys' and they'd all seen me cry before, but the Australian Cricket Team were something else all together, so I made an effort to put on my happy face. The race was over. Nothing more I could do. Let it go and deal with it later. I donned my giant green and gold jester's hat and jingled to our team seating area.

A conversation began behind me:

"D'you know her?" Steve Waugh asked.

"Nup, but I will soon," said Gavin Robertson.

"Face doesn't suit the hat," observed the captain.

"Nah. Must've swum bad."

I was crestfallen that Steve Waugh should notice me because I looked like a sour-faced loser. Gavin slid down onto the bench next to me.

"Rough night?"

"Yeah, but that's over. Party now," I said, tipping my hat.

The conversation flowed easily. Steve talked about his charity work and his family. It was good to focus my mind on something else. I spent a lot of time with Gavin after that night. He was a sportsman, well aware of the ups and the too frequent downs, and he never once trotted out the 'but you have achieved so much, you should be so proud of yourself' clichés that drive disappointed athletes to hair-tearing distraction. He knew there was nothing anyone could say to make the sting disappear, so he didn't even try. And it was wonderful.

Gav was funny. We had a drink at the beer garden in Kuala Lumpur's purpose-built athletes' village. Chris Fydler tried to introduce us for the third time with, "Gav, have you met Nads? Hasn't she got the best lips?" and I choked on my vodka.

Gavin talked about his life, his wife and three beautiful children. His face was like a beacon when he talked about them and, although he loved cricket, he missed them when he was gone for such long stretches. He was the perfect antidote to the jaded, pessimistic creature I was in danger of becoming. He spoke with such enthusiasm that it was hard to keep a straight face. He never completed a sentence. It was like listening to three conversations at once – too much to be passionate about, too much to say, no structure in which to say it. It was infectious, and I found myself lifted by this man who had fallen as often and as far as I had. He retained his exuberance without a trace of the resentment that sometimes engulfed me.

We got well drunk together. He challenged me to a swimming race and I accepted without hesitation – always the competitor. We decided the challenge absolutely had to be settled immediately, so we searched for a way into the competition pool. Alas, it was 2.30am and I wanted to scale the fence but a security guard suspected we were up to no good. Our story that I was the swimmer, he was my coach and we had to train didn't sit right with the guard for some reason, so I tried the truth – we were there for a swimming race, I was to give Gavin a 25m head start and beat him over 100m. It was a very important race. But the guard remained unimpressed. Our race was postponed, so we wandered around the village for the next two hours contemplating the penalties for break-and-enter and trespassing in Malaysia.

Gav eventually won the race that was staged in the 10m leisure pool near our block. Jade said he cheated. He said he'd brag anyway. I was happy with a silver medal and a new friend I could watch on the pitch.

Long nights at the village beer garden, clubbing in town, drinking more and sleeping less than any human being ought to – these were privileges of only a small band of ten swimmers, the rebels who refused to return home to prepare for the World Short Course Trials scheduled nine days after the end of the swimming program and just two days after the end of the Games. Our team manager, Alan Thompson, the poor guy who got to stay behind, had one rule: be at the pool at 7.30 every morning for a swim. The state in which we made it was irrelevant, as long as we were alive and able to float.

Thommo reminded me of my biology teacher. He was a mountainous man and his voice was epic. When he was disappointed he'd lower it, very teacher-like, and rumble his disapproval. When he laughed it vibrated through the ground, up your legs and into your belly, but God help the man who raised Thommo's ire. I've only seen it happen once, when Sam Riley and I were in the marshalling area for the 200m Breaststroke final.

A little Malaysian marshal began his check of swimmers' costumes, caps, towels and clothing to make sure there were no sponsor logos that breached the size regulations imposed by the International Federation, FINA – yes, sport is all about advertising on TV. Our logos seemed to have miraculously grown since the previous night, because he insisted Sam and I take our swimsuits off!

"You want us to swim naked? Do you think the TV cameras would like that?" I was cocky.

He was a little embarrassed, but insisted we get changed.

"We'll get our manager," I said as I turned to leave.

"No, no, you must not leave the marshalling room!"

"Okay... so how do you want us to get changed?" A good point from Sam.

"No, no, you cannot leave. You cannot swim in that suit!" he went on.

The assistant manager noticed the commotion and called Thommo to deal with this poor man who had got himself into such a corner that he became like a yapping Chihuahua, unsure if he was barking because he was scared or brave: 'Do I bark and run or bark and attack? Run? Attack? Run? Attack?'

The Chihuahua was still yapping as our Saint Bernard bowled down the door.

"If you have a problem, you talk to me. Do you understand? You do not distract my swimmers. You do not talk to my swimmers. You do not address my swimmers! Especially when they are about to race! You take these issues up with me and I will tell you that the suits are fine! They will wear their suits and there will be no more discussion about them. Do you hear me?"

Everyone within 12 blocks of the aquatic centre heard him. I didn't see the official again.

With Thommo's blessing, we played. We cheered the hockey girls to a gold medal. We danced to the Malaysian version of Backstreet Boys at the closing ceremony. Gav saved me at the after-closing-party from a footballer who was trying to seduce me with a coffee mug of port while Steve Waugh, emboldened by a little bit of Jess magic, stood on a table and tried to get the throng of celebrating Aussie athletes to sing 'Ke San' with him. It took three or four attempts of going solo for the captain to gather his troops, but when Gav and I took pity, began urging some of the others nearby to join us in the chorus, what a mighty moment it was... the room erupted, "Well the last plane out of Sydney's almost gone..." An Australian hero wearing his team cap, 'Hi Rosie' smeared across the front in zinc, stirring the spirit with a little bit of Jimmy Barnes; a room full of world-class athletes, arms around any shoulder that was nearby, saluting Australianness with drinks and voices raised high. A perfect ending.

The ten rebels and our manager left Kuala Lumpur the next morning, not sorry to be saying goodbye to the crappy cardboard-cut-out food. I finally felt free of the black cloud that had shadowed me, if a little weary. And every one of the rebels made the team for the Short Course World Championships in Hong Kong, despite the fact we'd been cavorting while the others prepared.

Kuala Lumpur was the rush of being part of something so much bigger than I was, the joy of sharing it with people of like mind; the synergy of a unified group striving to achieve the same thing; the unreserved thrill of experiencing each exclusive instant. I learned there that my success lay in the memories that made me laugh, in the moments, faces, camaraderie that I always missed when I was back home in my silent lane, surrounded by chlorine and foot odour.

Every trip was an Olympic experience.

28.

"Do you know what the time is? Is it messing with your monkeys"

– *"Pacifier"*, Shihad

MONUMENTAL EVENTS AFFECT CHANGE – I break my neck, I don't swim for two years for example – but it's the deeper, more evolutionary changes that you only recognise when comparing the little things of the present with the nuances of the past. It's the nuances that reveal paradigm shifts.

November 1998, after the Commonwealth Games, Ben and I went on a holiday – a little thing, but to me profoundly significant. It was a normal person thing to do with your boyfriend. Byron Bay, day trips to all the trashy Gold Coast tourist spots, a holiday with no consideration for where the nearest pool was, how much ice cream I ate or how late I went to bed. We laughed. We enjoyed being in each other's company and it was easy. He called me his partner – solid, permanent, no longer the vocabulary of teenage crushes.

Christmas Eve 1998, my mum called Mutti in Germany. She was sick and alone and the night before she had nearly suffocated on her own phlegm. There was no one around to help her. Mum was distraught. It took some convincing, but by 3am Colette and I had both parents packed, I had bought two tickets for the next flight to Frankfurt with my sponsorship money, and we were about to spend the first Christmas and New Year apart. The kids took charge – acknowledgement of our adulthood.

Christmas Day 1998, Colette joined Ben and me with his family. With no more than an hour's notice, they not only accommodated the extra body, they had gifts for her under the tree. Their willingness to share a family day with my sister, whom they had met a handful of times, was more touching than I'd expected. Their kindness embraced me and mine as part of theirs.

New Year 1999, Colette called me from Byron Bay, drunk and singing. We laughed as she told me all about the party she had crashed and the backpacker she'd pashed, and I told her about my ulcers and disappointing lack of high from smoking a joint. It was a conversation between friends rather than a 'responsible' elder and a 'reckless' younger sister.

January 1999, my mum's birthday, the four Neumanns stood in front of a brand new, four-bedroom, split-level house in a battle-axe block in West Pennant Hills and our collective heart-rates jumped. My parents loved it. They wanted it. They didn't have enough for the deposit, still, after our financially disastrous move to the Northern Beaches. I gave them the shortfall and we bought the house. A new sense of responsibility and freedom for me and the joy of being able to give back.

It's the little things – being surrounded by people who want the same things as you, who understand the way you think, who can support you; adult conversation; a new environment. I was in the right frame of mind for a real change.

So I went to Adelaide to visit Jade and spend a refreshing week training with Glenn Beringen. Although she had also lost motivation at times, Glenn and his elite squad kept Jade going and since we both tended to think too much (wanting to know the why and how of everything), I figured that if Glenn could handle one of us, he wouldn't mind the occasional visit from a second. I had floated the idea of a regular trip to Adelaide with Greg and he thought it was just what I needed to get through my stale patches, so the intention was that I'd have a holiday every six weeks or so.

I was nervous for my first session at the Adelaide Aquatic Centre. There was something about visiting a squad of only elite-level performers that made me feel like the little kid in her shiny new leotard approaching the almighty trampoline yet again. The session was an ugly threshold set – pounding at about 70% pace for a long, long, long time with only itsy bits of rest. I was swimming last in Ryan's lane. He was a nice person, but I was intimidated by him for some reason and to be busting my gut with him speeding up behind me was more stress than I needed on my first day. I didn't want to get in his way on his turf – the ghost of Simon Upton at the Carlile Club haunted me still.

But halfway through the set, a girl called Tammy hollered, "Okay guys, great job, hold it up!" and one of the others replied, "Let's go, Tam! Go Megan..." I wasn't sure if they were for real. It was the kind of rev-up display you see footballers put on during a match, but in a swimming squad? 'Should I laugh? Is it an in joke that I don't get?' I wondered.

But in the next break Ryan said, "Keep it up, Nads! Hold it up!"

"Did he say I am holding him up?" I was mortified.

Then another responded, "Keep it going!" and it finally clicked that they were genuine.

They were actually encouraging each other. They were all as stuffed as I was, they all couldn't breathe, they all hurt and yet they were willing each other on! I had never, ever been encouraged by my peers except in a race. I had never had a squad member give a shit about how I was feeling. This was like having Jade and Kate running up and down the side of the pool all session; like being in a movie. Perfect!

Their discipline was incredible. Every person counted their strokes, took heart-rates, touched and turned every lap like it was the real thing, like they couldn't comprehend training any other way. They had a sports scientist, Bernard, recording times, stroke counts, heart-rates, doing lactate tests. He was at almost every session. And he got into the encouragements, too, as though they had all taken positive pills... and I wanted some!

They stretched together; they did strength training and recovery sessions in the spa and sauna together; they had a weekly meeting for God's sake! And all of this had been going on without me knowing. I had stumbled upon $E=mc^2$ and I hadn't felt so motivated since before Atlanta.

That first night I went to bed actually happy with my training – I had enjoyed the pain, the challenge, the process and I couldn't remember when that had happened last. Despite a 4.30 start the next morning (only three hours earlier than normal!), I looked forward to it. By Tuesday afternoon the miniature details of how these people trained had built up to a dilemma. I didn't want to go home.

Jade and I sat in the spa after another hard session. The acid fumes stung my eyes and the jets kept propelling me off the narrow tile step you're expected to be able to balance on. There was a man with bad skin and thinning hair trying not to look at us. I knew how he felt – I was trying not to look at Jade because she knew what was going on in my head. Not that a battle between the forces of 'Oh my God, you have to do this…' and 'Oh my God, you are too scared to do this…' can be easily hidden from a friend, but I knew I'd cry if I looked at her.

"Neumann, it's so good to have you here!" She was always going to speak eventually.

"It's amazing, I didn't know it could be like this," I said, and instantly wanted to retract the last part of the sentence because it brought the tears straight from my throat. I blinked and pretended it was the spa fumes.

I thought I heard a faint, excited laugh as she clenched her fists and blurted, "Oh, Neumannsun, you would love it here. I would love you to be here… for purely selfish reasons, of course!" and she stopped.

I was quiet as I raised my eyes. I hesitated.

"I have to do it!" came from I don't know where, but it stood like a pillar in the middle of the bubbling pool.

"I know it's an awful, awful decision. I cried for days when I did it, but it's been the best thing! And I know it's terrible for you. Your family is so close, and Ben, and… oh, Neumann, I know it's so hard but…" and there was another long pause before her face cracked and she laughed out loud, "…but I'm here and you want to live near me so we can play guitar and go to sushi train and party!"

Our excitement bubbled over and made the balding man openly stare.

Wednesday morning, as I sat on Jade's kitchen bench, I started my ritual round of phone calls.

"Hey, Ben."

"Nad! Hey! How are you?"

"I'm good... really good."

"Training good? How's Jade?" He sounded so upbeat.

"Yeah she's good. She's gorgeous. Training's been amazing. I'm shattered though."

"That's good. You got the morning off?"

"Yeah, but hey, listen, I'm um..." I was hesitant. How do you tell someone you love that you're going to move interstate?

"What's up?" He sensed trouble. I stumbled. "Gorgeous, what's up? You okay?"

I sucked in a lungful and said, "Okay, as crude and as fast as I can..." I got off the kitchen bench and started pacing the lounge room.

"What's going on?"

"I have to move to Adelaide."

And without hesitation he said, "Okay. When are we going?"

I did that weird crying, laughing, hyperventilating thing. He was so certain, so confident. He never asked me why, he just accepted that it must be what I needed and he would be part of that completely. I was going to move from Sydney to Adelaide to train in a way that I was not sure I could cope with, to support myself doing the cooking and cleaning and washing that my mother had always done for me, to swim with a squad I was not sure I belonged in, all in pursuit of a goal I had been doubting I could achieve. And that 'I' had suddenly become a 'we'.

Telling my parents was easy. They were always in full support of anything I needed to do, but they only managed to thinly veil their concerns – Would I train too hard? Would I cope with training and doing all the chores my mother had done for years? Would they be kept in the dark about my progress the way they had with the Carlile Club when I got so desperately sick? How would we afford rent? What would we do without our regular hugs? How would I continue studying? What would Ben do? Would us living together even work? Parents always worry.

Telling Collie was like letting her in on a secret she already knew. Her intuition had seen it coming a mile off.

When I got back to Sydney I had to tell Greg what was brewing. That was hard. I had a fabulous speech well rehearsed, but when the pathetic puppy look overtook my face, "I'm moving to Adelaide," was all I could come up with.

"I thought you might," he said with equal aplomb.

We stared at each other for a few moments, both of us blank, and then started to speak at the same time,

"It's not that I don't like training with you…"

"I know you've been really unhappy lately…"

God, it was awful. Although he was hurt, he didn't hate me. It's just hard to split from someone you've spent so much time with, shared so much with, someone who's worked so hard for you. How can you express your appreciation, your love for what they have helped you become, but at the same time tell them it's not enough? You can't, really, so it either goes okay or really badly, and I was glad that Greg made sure it was okay.

The move was almost instant. I stayed with Glenn in Adelaide for the three weeks before we headed to Brisbane for the 1999 Pan Pacific Championship Trials followed by the World Short Course Championships in Hong Kong. Jade helped me house hunt and Ben moved all our belongings while I was overseas swimming the way I always seemed to at international events. Badly. The Pan Pacific Championships 1999 would be different though, I was sure.

29.

"My name is might have been, my name is never was, my name's forgotten"

– *"Celebrity Skin"*, Hole

I WAS NEW. I was no longer anything of what I was. I imagined that Wobbles was gone, that Nads the Rock had been reborn as water in a life far from the home she once knew; a life where her own feet and her own judgement were all that stood between success and devastation. And I liked to think that I was wise enough and strong enough and brave enough to make the right decisions.

I was finally living the life it really took to find perfection. I was sure of it. I had already tried separating my worlds completely and being a different person in each, but the duplicity had destroyed me. Living a compartmentalised life where one section was allowed little impact on the others had proved that cross-contamination was inevitable. I had even tried living an integrated life where all aspects flowed freely together, but they had jostled and clashed and torn each other down. Living in a world where my ambition was everything was the only path untried and I felt sure this was what being an athlete was all about. The water and the work were my only friends. Everything else existed to support that one purpose. Ben was there, but his role was support. My family was there, but their role was support. My studies, speeches, sponsors were all still there, but their roles were all just support. I ate for my goal. I slept for my goal. I structured my activities for my goal. I breathed it and the whole world revolved around it. A black and white image at the centre of the universe.

But not everything is as it first seems.

A life like that cannot last. A squad like that is unbalanced. What I scorned as amateurish at Ryde turned out to be exactly what I missed in Adelaide. We were a school of indomitable big fish squeezed into a tiny desktop tank. Too many serious contenders, all dealing with stress in our own, often incompatible ways just like during taper on tour, only this was every day. Shakespeare understood the need for frivolous comic relief (that's why his plays, in reflecting human nature, all involved a fool of some kind) and it was precisely what I needed. As the 2000 Games drew closer, governments threw more and more money at breeding programs for Sydney 2000 heroes and the number of scholarship holders in our South Australian Sports Institute (SASI) squad grew. Glenn was under immense pressure to service his increasing crop of king carps, but we all needed kingly attention, and that was impossible.

The way I saw it, the result was a reluctant hierarchy that could really only be grasped from the inside. Glenn, Bernard and Ryan were the ruling triumvirate. Ryan was a young Glenn. Trained as Glenn trained, his body responded the same way to the same things. He raced in a similar way. They approached things with the same attitude and Ryan was destined for the same kind of 200m Breaststroke successes his coach had had – a medal at the Olympic Games. Bernard, like the others, was warm and likeable, but his sheer physical stature gave him the intimidating aura of a ruler. All three of them were charismatic, making it impossible to resent their status in the same way it is hard to hate the popular kids in a school playground. They were popular for a reason.

I saw myself and the other 'seniors' as the second tier. The triumvirate kept a close eye on the girls because we were volatile and incomprehensible, far too emotional for our own good, and although they genuinely liked us, we didn't really fit the mould of tough, controlled, methodical machines. The 'juniors', or those who had not yet made a senior Australian team, existed in the third tier and were largely looked after by Louise, the assistant coach.

There weren't many articulated rules in our world, but I picked up on some unspoken principles quickly. Everybody worked hard, weakness was not tolerated in any form and offenders were first delicately encouraged to shape up, then jokingly told to do so, and finally pressured with an energy so subtle you couldn't really say where it came from or how it was created, it was just there and palpable: blank faces, silence, meaning-filled eye contact between the strong, turned backs as though it was too difficult to look upon the weak. It was always Glenn's, Bernard's and Ryan's opinions that meant the most to me and, like a dog desperate to please her master, I'd sit when told, roll over when instructed, shake and hop up, wagging my tail with pleading eyes, waiting for their praise. When they scowled, I was crushed, whether the scowl was directed at me or not.

While part of me panted like an eager pet, another part of me hated the circus animal I felt I had become, resentful of feeling judged but basing my self-worth on that judgment. I did enough criticising myself. But still, I worked to impress and in the lead-up to the 1999 Pan Pacific Championships I had held up well. Despite Jade not being on the team for the first time since our international debuts, I felt confident. I knew I would miss her terribly, especially since she had become such a part of my every day, but like everything else in my life, her presence or lack thereof would have to be secondary. My swimming took centre stage.

The Pan Pacifics were crucial as the launching pad towards Sydney 2000, as well as being the first international long course meet to be held in the 'all new' format. We now had eight days of competition instead of six and semi-finals for all events up to and including 200m. It spelled potential disaster for some swimmers because it almost doubled the amount of racing for the benefit of TV and ticket sales and it meant that many of the more versatile swimmers ended up with clashes, myself included. On one hand, we had to make some hard choices about the events we would and would not contest, but on the other hand, it opened many events up for newcomers. Racing strategies had to change, experimenting was crucial and I didn't like it, so close to the Games, but that was the way it was for everyone.

The 1999 Pan Pacific Championships were held in Sydney at the soon-to-be Olympic venue and I was a has-been – the name on the program that was always there, claiming to be capable of something she had never actually done. Again, I was in the middle of a big hole and swimming through sludge thanks to that damned phase in training where the workload is reduced to 'rest' the body, that damned phase called 'taper'. It was becoming boring – the cycle of train, get hopes up, be positive, fall flat, analyse errors, start again. It had gone on too long. The only comfort was that I wasn't alone in my hole. Every one of the SASI squad members on the Pan Pac team misfired and Glenn was keeping his devastation well below his own version of the happy face until I opened my big mouth.

I'd done enough stuff-up debriefing over the past few years to know when I'd done the kind of training I needed, but I was the new kid in the squad and I had left all my lessons behind for the glorious promise I saw in that first week in Adelaide. Glenn was completely confident in his training methods and his attention to detail. He took great pride in his work and I trusted him implicitly. I wanted to believe he knew better than I did. I didn't want the full responsibility of working differently anymore and in Glenn's home of the elite, why should I need to? And when I reflected on the toughest training cycle I had ever experienced, I realised that I needed to air my concerns with Glenn, new kid or not.

There had been days when I hurt so much that I went numb, then pushed harder in the hope the numbness would stay; weeks where I had forgotten what it felt like not to burn with acid chewing my muscles to pulp. I had only survived because I had slept for three/four hours every day. My parents had worried and every time we spoke, we argued about it. Why was I allowing myself to be pushed so hard? Why was I not telling Glenn that I needed to incorporate Dad's training in my sessions? Why did I repeatedly get sucked into the same old over-training trap? I was old and experienced enough to speak up for myself; why, why, why?

Had I ever considered quitting in that last training cycle? Did I ever think I might not really be as good as I hoped? That perhaps I had already seen my finest hour and I was doing nothing more than hanging onto a fantasy that could never be? Of course I did. No person can swim 100k in a week and not wonder if this is really the destiny the heavens had in store for them. You can't hear them call, 'Anyone who pukes gets a Mars Bar' and not wonder why, in God's name, you find that motivating. It's impossible to lie like a beached and dying whale on the side of the pool, reeling with the rush of relief that comes from simply stopping and not wonder whether this masochistic life is really what you want. But always, the thought of walking away brought a sense of loss too profound for me to carry it through. My mind would turn to black and white as tears choked me and I'd be filled with a knowing more certain than miles and hours in the pool, that my time had not yet come.

But after reflection in the post-'99 Pan Pacifics carnage, I knew it hadn't worked. The outcome of that training cycle had been the same as every other outcome since Atlanta and I needed to give the determined, desperate part of me a voice. Finally.

So Glenn saw me at my fiery best. A fierce, self-directed outburst came first. What had I done wrong? But Glenn shouldered the responsibility, said that he and Bernard must have miscalculated the amount of rest we'd all need to balance the increased workload. I appreciated his willingness, but it didn't help ease the urgency I felt rising in my throat, like a panic that it would all be sorted out too late. I needed a solution now. This was my last chance to get it right and I was damned if I was going to find myself at the 2000 Olympic Trials wondering what might have been. We needed to talk about getting my dad's methods into my program and I needed it to happen NOW!

On the last night of the Pan Pacifics, I sat between Glenn and Bernard, two bulky, shaven-headed men, and I was mildly amused at the intimidating situation.

Bernard quipped, "Huh! Rose between thorns," and that was all he had to say.

Glenn started with daggers – any discussion of my meddling father's methods was not on his agenda. "Let's get one thing straight from the start. This is between you and me, not your parents!"

"I only want you to talk to my dad because he can explain what we did better than I can." I was determined not to turn this into an argument. I didn't want him to feel under attack.

"I don't really care what you did," Glenn said. "I want you to lift to the next level."

"But what we did worked and this clearly hasn't."

"I've already told you why. Bernard and I have already accepted responsibility for that."

"But that's not what I'm talking about, Glenn. I have to manage Chronic Fatigue and I can't do what everyone else does. I'm not Ryan. I don't care if we swim the same events! What he needs is not what I need and that's what it feels like we've all been doing! Everybody's different and just because he can train like a freak every session, doesn't mean everyone can. Just because he doesn't need rest, doesn't mean that I don't and if that means I'm weak then maybe I am but I can't be Ryan and I can't be treated the same as him! I need to do what works for me." It came out as a release, but exactly how it shouldn't have – a jumble of words that cut.

His face turned red, his eyes clouded and his voice wavered. "I don't need to sit here and listen to you criticise me and I don't need to hear from Bernard that your boyfriend is throwing his opinions around, and I certainly don't need to meet with your parents to listen to them telling me how they would do my job so much better! They weren't there every day watching you swim so they don't have all the information and they don't have the right to judge my program!"

"No one's judging your program..." I started.

But Glenn cut me off. "I won't discuss this with you while you're emotional!"

"I'm not being emotional. I'm just saying..."

"We'll talk about this in a couple of weeks when we have all had time to calm down and when we can be rational about it." As far as Glenn was concerned, that was the end of the conversation, but I was not finished.

"I'm not being emotional and no one's criticising you. My dad just wants to share his knowledge and experience with you. I know that parents don't count for much as far as coaching goes, but he has watched me for a hell of a lot longer than you have, and he knows me better than anyone does. No one's saying that you're doing a bad job, I'm just trying to help come up with a solution to my problem."

But the meeting was over. Bernard kept his gaze firmly set in the distance. He hadn't said a word.

* * *

It wasn't until January 2000 that Glenn finally gave in. He was so frustrated with my lack of progress despite training as hard as anyone that, in an exasperated moment after another poor performance at the World Cup round in Sydney, he conceded he had no idea what made me tick.

I had come to the conclusion that there was no such thing as perfection because everyone is unique and what is 'bad' for one is 'perfect' to another. The difficulty in sport is that you're constantly aiming to achieve a standard that is measured by another person's attainment of 'perfection'. So everyone who wants to swim a 400m Freestyle starts copying Thorpey. Everyone who wants to swim a 1500m copies Hackey. It requires bravery from so many people, warriors who will risk wandering off the accepted path to find that unique way to an individual's own brand of perfection. Glenn met with my dad to hear about my possible path to perfection and he made arrangements for me to start incorporating the training I had done since 1994 – the back-to-front, 'get the pace right then increase the distance' sets I had done with my dad every morning for years. From the day I started I could feel my long-departed confidence begin to return, but I never got the sense that the others in the squad felt comfortable with it. I couldn't bear the thought that my Sydney campaign might end up the same way as all my big meets had over the last four years, so I had to put the squad out of my mind and simply do what was right for me. Maybe it wasn't just the training, but a combination of that and the work I had been doing with the demons in my head that slowly ushered in the shift. Either way, something changed.

30.

"I place it, replace it, and try to change"
  – *"Never an Easy Way"*, Morcheeba

I WAS POSSESSED BY AN URGE TO RIP EVERYTHING out of my mind's cupboard and chuck out all the crap. I wanted to organise and reorganise everything. It always sounds like a good idea at the time, the whole purging thing, until you're sitting in the middle of the room with shit everywhere and no way to get to the door. That's when you consider just shoving it all under the bed, but you know it's never going to fit. The only option is to take a big breath and hope it turns out to be easier than it looks.

It never does.

Our last training campaign started with a break from swimming after the Pan Pacific Championships. I had two weeks completely out of the water and another two where our squad was meant to just exercise up to five times a week and maintain a little fitness and flexibility. Above all, we had to maintain our skin-fold levels. Every couple of weeks our body fat was measured and we were given a total in millimetres derived from the readings on seven parts of our bodies. I still had night terrors about skin-folds after my teenage Chronic Fatigue traumas in the 100-club, but I had managed to get a reading below 60 – just once, and only just!

Our final skin-fold reading after the two weeks of 'staying fit' would determine who would go to America for the World Cup and who would stay behind. For someone like me who constantly battled fluctuating weight, it would be a greater challenge than for many others, especially the boys. To add drama, when I returned from Sydney after my two blissful weeks out of the water, and just before I was about to start on my five fitness-maintaining sessions each week, I had a shower after Ben had left for work and, as I lathered the shampoo in my hair, I hit the ceramic, cemented-into-the-wall soap holder with my elbow.

Splinters crashed to the shower floor. I broke it clean in half! As I bent, swearing, to pick up the shards my head spun and blood dripped onto the tiles. I squatted. I wheezed. I passed out. When I came to, my instinct told me to call Ben. He'd saved me once before when I had stepped out of the car and suddenly fell in the gutter writhing with what turned out to be a tear in my right quad. He'd save me again, but how to get to the phone? I couldn't stand. I was so weak I could barely turn the water off and when I finally managed to crawl, soapy and bleeding, to the bedroom, I just hoped he hadn't started his Monday morning sales meeting yet. His office was not far away, but if he had an early morning run, if he had customers to see or if the team was already strategising for the week, I'd be stuck on the bed for a long time.

I was still on the bed, still soapy when Ben arrived 15 minutes later. The doctor was impressed that I had managed to cut myself so neatly and deeply on the back side of my elbow, and when she heard the fate of the ceramic soap dish, she almost applauded. I'd actually managed to cut the tendon, but not sever it – a delicate balance, I am told. One internal and three external stitches, no contact with the water for three weeks, no use of that elbow for a further three and only very light, limited use for another three after that. My preparation for the Sydney Olympic Trials was off to a flying start! Staying fit was a challenge, and as a result, on skin-fold test day, five millimetres was the difference between me showing evidence of dedication and not. Instead, I stayed home (while the others went to the US) and I started to work on my psyche.

Mediation, as much as I tried, just didn't cut it when it came to throwing out the mental junk and rearranging. I needed something stronger, so while the squad was away, I started making headway.

* * *

I'd never had much luck with psychologists. I received some spontaneous help from Bec – the cutest, toughest, smartest and most 'in-tune' massage therapist known to planet Earth – but I needed more. Bec was great as a mouthpiece for the Universe, saying exactly the right thing at exactly the right moment, like a flash of light-filled inspiration, but relying on Bec to give me the shot in the arm I needed whenever I needed it was not going to work. I had to get the 'messages' directly and permanently.

Jade had introduced me to Maryanne, who had taught her about creative goal setting, and this was a good start. When I first met Maryanne at Mamma Carmella's Café in Norwood, I have to confess, I thought it was all going to be a bit too cheesy for me. I'd sat through plenty of lectures about goal setting with the presenters raving about how you need to write your goals on Post-It notes and cover your house with them, surrounding yourself with pictures of your dream car, and in an instant you will have it all! It was a standard part of the multilevel marketing distributor's spiel. My family had been there with the Chinese herb food that had saved me from the Chronic Fatigue fog, but I didn't want my toilet door proclaiming to the world, 'Nadine wants to win an Olympic Gold Medal!'

But Jade had been keen, and I trusted her, so I went along to the meeting. It couldn't hurt.

Maryanne was like a brown field mouse with exhausting enthusiasm and a voice that twittered so fast it initially took all my brain power to keep up with her. I could feel a dopey smile with 'what's going on?' written in my eyes from the moment she started. There we were: a box of folders on the floor, magazines and cut-up bits of paper strewn all over the table, coloured textas, glue and scissors from one end of the alcove to the next. I was a little kid at kindy being asked to 'make a picture of yourself', and somehow it felt right.

Between sips of skim milk iced coffee (no cream or ice cream, thank you), I learned about the processes of the mind: the conscious, the sub-conscious and the super-conscious. She elaborated on the reasons why writing goals down is important as a translation of thought to deliberate action. She explained the rules by which they need to be written so that our super-conscious can provide exactly what we want with no communication glitches – only positive, present tense with no negative 'root words'. She clarified every throwaway suggestion I had heard about goal setting thus far, and showed me why being positive, why living our dreams as though they were already a reality was so important, why the use of colour was encouraged, and why images and symbols are vastly underestimated tools. Every word she said made sense... every one that I caught, anyway.

And it was bloody hard to put into practice! My thoughts 'I don't want to be fat, I want to lose weight' made my super-conscious mind say, 'Okay, fat and wanting' so I was always going to be wanting and always going to struggle with my ideal racing weight. As soon as I wrote down: I am 58kg and have 50mm skin-folds, my super-conscious said 'Okay' and my ultra-vigilant discipline with food actually started having an effect! I managed to drop the excess bulk I'd been trying to shift ever since I took that bloody creatine supplement before the Commonwealth Games Trials. It was incredible!

Every time I spoke with Maryanne, I learned. She invariably called when I was depressed, when I had a problem that seemed insurmountable and she helped me see through the language I was using, the messages I was sending myself, and showed me how to turn them around. Jade and I worked on helping each other get it right, but I still needed more.

* * *

I looked to Brian, the man who helped Jade get her mind ready for the Perth World Championships. He called himself a 'mental coach' and I didn't know what I expected, but his grandfatherly figure was certainly not it.

I sat in his bear-hug leather armchair in an unremarkable but comfortable home office. Brian's voice was gentle and rumbling but I was out of my comfort zone. I didn't like the idea of hypnosis, not being in control, allowing a stranger to put me 'under', but again I trusted Jade and she trusted Brian. He took my mind back to a time...

"...where you first felt an emotion that is now holding your swimming back."

My hand instantly clenched, my jaw set and I was filled with RAGE and a burning sense of inadequacy that forced the tears from my eyes. It was completely and physically overwhelming, but part of my mind was strangely detached, like a person watching a movie. I was suspended between clear, controlled consciousness and the drifting confusion of an afternoon nap, part of my mind commenting on what the other part appeared to be cooking up on the spot.

"What do you see?" Brian's voice came through the fog.

"There's a girl, she's like me. I think six. She's pretty and has big blue eyes with long eyelashes and bouncy blonde curly hair. She is so pretty and she's dancing like a ballerina, twirling in my backyard, and all the adults are watching her with smiling faces. They're clapping for her and they love her more than me. Katie's my friend but they love her more than me. I want to be like her but I'm ugly and clumsy and no one clapped when I danced. They just giggled."

"Bizarre," the impassionate observer in me said.

He took me away from that scene and to another time I felt the same way.

Jess was gossiping about me, excluding me from her fun. I was sure it was just because I swam faster than her. She pretended to be my friend, but she made everyone turn away from me. She made me feel alone, insignificant, an outcast.

I found the lair of many a demon in this way. Guilt at taking my parents' attention away from Collie, guilt at making my family sacrifice so much for my quest, the burden of responsibility to succeed for their sake, and the big one: FEAR. She was so large with so many faces that she had hideouts all over my consciousness. Fear of experiencing Chronic Fatigue again; fear of being a failure; fear of not fitting in; fear of being special; fear of being inconsequential; fear of pain; fear of losing; fear of succeeding and what that success might mean.

I cried a lot during our sessions. I looked directly at my demons, but accepting them and forgiving the source of those feelings was another matter entirely. There was so much there that we ran out of time and needed to prepare my mind for the race ahead with visualisations and affirmations that felt like I was telling myself bold-faced lies. But I said them anyway, just in case.

I surrounded myself with anything positive. I read uplifting stories, listened to positive music, avoided people who were down or sick or having a rough day. For the first time I was one of those people who runs from the person in despair because I needed to be selfish with my energy. I needed to get it right for me. Compassion could wait.

And as the trials approached, I felt something that had been hiding for a long, long time.

I was excited to race.

31.

"All that shall remain is a token of what we've said and done"
— *"Roses From My Friends"*, Ben Harper

BEN AND I WENT HOME FOR CHRISTMAS. I was still training, but home.

My family could see the difference in me. I had some of my pre-Atlanta sparkle back. Mutti, at 85 and the size of an oak wine barrel, had come to visit and she was thrilled that she would finally meet Ben. Mum hired a wheelchair so Mutti was comfortable and mobile, and she was like a little dictator on her throne, directing dutiful pushers this way and that. When she ordered "Halt," we stopped, when she wanted to walk, she got up and trundled along, pushing her own chair. Only one person could tell her what to do. Ben. He spoke less German than anyone I knew, but he managed to boss her around and she loved it.

Two memories stayed with me when we returned to Adelaide for the last stretch of Trials preparation. They were the thoughts that could bring back a smile after the guilt of ripping Ben's head off for the slightest misdemeanour – an event that occurred more and more frequently as the tension increased. One was of Mutti demanding that she be left sitting at the top of the hill, under the roof at my parents' local West Pymble pool. She wanted to watch me swim from there, because it was 'too complicated and too far and too steep' for her to get down to pool deck. Ben took no notice and, in response to her protests, "*Laβ mich!*" (Leave me!), Ben would retort, "*Ach Quatsch!*" It was the only thing he had learned to say and it meant 'Oh rubbish!' They were to-ing and fro-ing all down the hill, like something out of *The Two Ronnies*. Her indignant face and his placid stubbornness made me smile. The other was the image of Ben sitting in Mutti's wheelchair while she pushed him everywhere he didn't want to go – the image of a bond I have never seen between two people who can't understand a word the other says. It reminded me of the unspoken language between a swimmer and the water. We know its signals and it knows our will. It carries us, accepting our force on its body, to where we want to go, and we love it completely.

Not long before the Trials, Speedo developed their 'Fastskin' suit. It was supposed to create or eliminate, depending on which way you looked at it, that minuscule difference which separates the good athlete from the great. We didn't have much time to get used to it. One afternoon of trying suits with arms covered or 'no arms', and we had to decide which we preferred, or if we liked them at all and it was hard to answer all the 'What ifs' – What if they do make a difference? What if everyone is wearing them? What if I'm so uncomfortable that I can't swim? What if I decide not to wear it and then miss out on the team? What if it wrecks my timing and slows me down? Eventually you just had to let go and decide.

I loved the way the suit made me feel like a javelin when I dived in or pushed off the wall. The glide was endless, tight, without a wobble. I loved the way it supported my body, but it was tiring to fight against the suit to get my legs up into the right breaststroke kick position and I didn't really trust the way my legs slipped through my already dubious Breaststroke kick. But eventually I decided I'd wear it if it had the potential to make that bit of difference.

And then, as if in a dream, the Sydney Olympic Trials arrived.

Warm-up races, rests, tension, relaxation, building… building… building momentum.

To now.

This moment.

Here, teetering towards the blue where I see it all played out before me like a film – every laughing, screaming, singing moment.

* * *

I crouch on the blocks, toes curled tight, poised. Final heartbeats before the gun. Breath is soft, almost imperceptible with anticipation.

Wait for it. It will be all over if I jump the gun.

Wait for it.

One final prayer on the block:

"God, I know you hear me. My warm-up race got me into the predicament I'm in. I got stuck in the draughty marshalling area for too long in my wet suit. I feel sick."

A slow breath in and I remember how:

Jade missed out on the Sydney Team in her 100m Breaststroke. I wanted success for her at these Trials as passionately as I want it for myself. We had talked about what might happen, of course we had, but it had been tough to put her disappointment out of my mind, hard to let go. She was so brave, and she'd said, "Neumannsun, it doesn't mean anything for you. You are so strong and you've done everything right and you're ready. Perth Worlds was my home meet. Sydney is yours," and I believed her. So she didn't mourn near me. She wouldn't until I was ready to celebrate, then we'd do what we did in Kuala Lumpur when things were the other way around.

But secretly, I had cried for her anyway.

A slow breath out and I pray:

"Then yesterday, God, I swam the heats of my 200m. My head has been getting stuffier and my throat has been on fire. I swam well in the heats, just as I knew I would and made it through to the semi comfortably. I pumped the zinc and C, garlic and echinacea into myself, but yesterday I had to ask Bernard for the Panadol and gargle. I've held it off until now, but the killer flu that everyone else has had has got me..."

A short breath in. Tighten the legs. The starter's trigger finger tenses. I can hear it.

I remember last night, in the semi-final, swimming about a second faster than the morning, but well off the pace I need tonight. I scraped into the final in Lane 1 and the demons coaxed, 'You are sick! You need to rest!' They spoke gently, like they were concerned. I was scared they were right. My body was aching and my head was in a vice. I didn't come to the pool this morning. I stayed to rest; to talk my mind around, to release. I had all of Ben's boxes open, but there was no 'Miracle' box.

Hold the breath. The moment is here and I pray:

"So now, as I stand on the blocks, teetering towards the blue, in this final moment, I'm asking you, God.

"Can you hear me? I need you to make that miracle for me. You've done it before, when you healed my body after being so sick. You did it when you protected my spinal cord, my life.

"You know I deserve it. You know I need it.

"I've done everything I can. Now I need you."

Go

Let me not pray to be sheltered from
dangers but to be fearless in facing
them.
Let me not beg for the stilling of
my pain but for the heart to conquer it.
Let me not look for allies in life's
battlefield but to my own strength.
Let me not crave in anxious fear to
be saved but hope for the patience to
win my freedom.
Grant me that I may not be a
coward, feeling your mercy in my
success alone; but let me find the grasp
of your hand in my failure.

– *Rabindranath Tagore*

32.

"I'll gather up my past and make some sense at last"
 – *"This is the Moment"*, Eric Santos

THE WORLD HOLDS ITS BREATH.
 Now.
 I'm flying, everything gently tense. The cold water shocks me. The underwater stillness shocks me. The movement of my muscles shocks me. I'm no longer in control. The music takes over. Rhythm. There is only the rhythm: an undulating symphony of silence and sound; a roaring world watching and underwater solitude of breath. The beat is kept by the metronomic squeak of my shoulders on my cap just behind my ears as I surge through every stroke. An ancient Sanskrit mantra gives my conscious mind its part and we sing down lap one, 'Aum Bhagawan Sri Sathya Sai Babaya Namaha...' The wall looms at first chorus.
 Even the pause as I glide off the wall, underwater, lungs aflame, is perfectly in time with the demands of my unseen conductor. My initial frantic burst settles into a fierce routine. This is the lap where the stroke is refined, where the technique is perfected, where the stage is set.
 Lap three. Always the number three. This is the lap I come to life. My body shimmers, limbs slightly ache. It's a comforting warmth. 'Lunge – keep the rhythm; Lunge – keep the rhythm; Lunge – keep the rhythm flowing smoothly...' My breath becomes strained and my head pulls back.
 'Forward, forward, drive it forward...' My lungs tighten and the warmth in my muscles becomes acid as I hit the wall on a half stroke. 'Shit...'
 My hands are lazy releasing from the wall. 'Snap it around. Tighten the streamline. Hold it... Hold it... You can breathe later... HOLD IT!'

My head strains as I break the surface from my underwater stroke, desperately sucking in air. My limbs are screaming now. My stomach knots. I'm melting. I reach with every stroke, but my arms won't fully extend. I can't feel my legs. I will not let go.

25m to the wall. I lose control of my hands. My fingers cross and flail in the water's resistance as I force my arms forward to semi-extension. My shoulders are a concrete block, and my wrists are rubber.

'Hold it. Precision. Technique. Stretch. Keep the rhythm…' a voice from far away orders. It is not my voice. Mine is still singing; refusing to acknowledge what is now scorching every cell. I will not let go.

10m to the wall. My breath is wheezing. My neck is tight. I can't feel anything but my gut being wrenched through my throat. I will not let go.

5m to the wall. I can't see the finish. My eyes roll back in my head. I will not let go.

I touch.

I gasp.

I can't find the step.

I force my arm up to hold the wall.

It slips.

My head hangs and bobs.

I turn to the scoreboard, to face fate…

33.

"Closing time; every new beginning comes from some other beginning's end"

– *"Closing Time"*, Semisonic

NOT FAST ENOUGH.

Gasping for air and clinging to the cool familiar tiles above my head, I search for... something. Sam Riley is in the lane next to me. My sorrow is on her face. She wasn't fast enough either.

"Looks like the old ducks aren't going," I pant and the celebratory exuberance creates a cruel backdrop. Our eyes embrace – tired, broken, alone. We climb out of the pool, automatic pilot still engaged, and limp into the media-filled tunnel to reclaim our belongings and collect our thoughts. Cameras rolling, reporters shouting, "This is a sensation: Sam Riley didn't make The Team!" I'm grateful I am no longer remembered.

Out of the corner of my eye, I see a mother lunge at the lens of a hungry cameraman, indignant at the shamelessness of the media's need to capture anguish for a newsflash. Why can't they focus on the come-back sensation who won the race, or don't they like that kind of story anymore? In his misery my father shows sportsmanlike steel and goes to encourage the young girl who has swum so far above herself at this meet. She just missed out in the 200m, and he knows all about disappointment, but she made the team in the 100m and he also knows the power of that kind of opportunity.

"You have a very bright future. That was a great swim."

Her mother chooses to ignore him. She turns up her nose and her contempt is mimicked by her daughter, a sour picture of scorn. I briefly remember what it feels like to hear 'You should be so proud of yourself' in moments of disappointment, how you want to scream 'But I want it now!' We all want it now and I still despise them for their lack of sportsmanship. She's on the Olympic Team anyway and she's still so young, so what the hell is she complaining about?

"You'll get your own," I sneer under my breath in defence of all of us who have somehow fallen below the lofty heights of the new generation. I am angry and cold.

As Sam does, I scurry for the relative privacy of the change room. We're like fugitives, desperate not to be judged for our crimes of failure. Brooke Hanson joins us. Despite having swum under the 2.30 barrier for the first time, she was not fast enough either.

As the three of us look around, suddenly awkward in each other's company, my heart finally gives in and a salty stream drowns the fire that once torched my soul. It is extinguished with a pathetic, indignant splutter; tears wash my black and white photograph to a blur of grey.

Nothing will ever be the same.

Beyond

All that is gold does not glitter,
Not all those who wander are lost;
The old that is strong does not wither,
Deep roots are not reached by the frost.
From the ashes a fire shall be woken,
A light from the shadows shall spring;
Renewed shall be blade that was broken,
The crownless again shall be king.

    – *J.R.R. Tolkien*

Photo by Reece Scannell

34.

"Hello darkness, my old friend, I've come to talk with you again"

– *"Sounds of Silence"*, Simon & Garfunkle

NUMBNESS. Relief. Terror.
    Anger, sadness, excitement, fear.
    Confusion-turmoil-strength-weakness-emptiness.
    What-do-I-do-now-and-where-do-I-turn-I-can't-do-this-but-I-can't-do-that-anymore.
    Black.

We were sad. We were stunned. We were strong for each other, but we each held our bellies in silent recognition of the churning sorrow. Sometimes our wounds surfaced and we shed tears of loss and bitterness, but mostly, we tried to march forward, grim-faced and resolute. This was not the end of the world, merely the passing of a phase in life... a long, arduous, all-consuming, identity-defining phase.

I was not alone. For the first time I felt people coming towards me in my darkness and I was able to smile in that sad way people do at funerals. Everyone knew I had done all I could. I knew I had done all I could. And yet it was no consolation when, on the last night of the trials, as they announced the Olympic Team for the 2000 Games, I stood where John Konrads had stood four years earlier, welcoming the newest Olympians into the club. It tore my heart out and I bled until there was nothing left in my soul.

I was empty.

The void grew in the following days, when everyone went home and Ben and I spent a weekend at a little B&B in the Southern Highlands of New South Wales. His mum had bought us the weekend for 'some space to celebrate... or commiserate.'

I sat in the spa and cried. I drank champagne and cried. I ate chocolate and cried. We looked forward and planned all the things we could do now that we would have time and energy and freedom to explore a 'normal' life. And through it all, he held me and hurt with me.

Back in our home in Adelaide there was silence, so much silence.

I ate more chocolate. I ate ice-cream and chips. I lived on the couch. I spent my days with *Sesame Street*, *Jerry Springer* and *The Young and the Restless*. I built a wall around me. I was afraid of going outside, for fear people might ask me that question we all ask once introductions are done: "So, what do you do?"

I used to know the answer, but I lost my identity when my black and white photo was torn and how can you explain to a stranger that all you do is mourn the loss of a dream? So, I built a fortress around my couch as Ben looked on. I didn't want to look forward anymore. It was too frightening to have to create a new future.

After many weeks of hiding, I gathered the courage to walk to the pool from time to time, just to smell the place, that familiar chlorine fog. I wanted to re-gather something of the old me. I'd always found clarity in the water, I needed to feel okay again, but I couldn't bring myself to get into the pool and I didn't know what to say to Glenn anymore. Many of the others had left or decided to take time off. Jade was gone – back to Perth, then to the US in search of the pure joy she used to feel when she swam, before it all became serious. I missed her. I missed it. I was lost and I wanted my family – my mum to hold me, my dad to assure me it would all be okay, my sister to make me smile again. I didn't know how to do those things by myself anymore and Ben didn't know how he could help me. He was helpless to heal the hurt that was devouring my soul, and he hated it. He just held me as I cried every night, afraid of the depression that was paralysing me.

It was black for a long, long time. Sometimes the light came back for a brief while – enjoying a coffee and cake without guilt; waking at 4.30 and smiling as I snuggled deeper into the covers to go back to sleep; planning a weekend away without thought of how it might impact my training schedule – but it never lasted long. The silence always returned.

I don't really know how long my darkness lasted. Days were much the same as nights and I didn't have training phases or log books to keep track of time, but I guess many weeks passed before I started to record one thing each day that made me happy, or at least made me feel as though I'd achieved something... anything: 'I ate a salad sandwich', 'I did the washing', 'I went for a walk'.

Then, one day, my rose blossomed. It was a golden-yellow rose that Mum had bought for me, called 'Olympic Gold' and bred in honour of the Sydney Games. It lived in a small pot against the Colourbond fence that bounded our rear courtyard. In the 40-degree summer sun it had frazzled to a charcoal stick of thorns, which I thought was a nice symbol of what my Olympics had become. But then, one day, it bloomed.

35.

"Have you ever told a lie that was true more than truth"
 – *"Misere"*, The Cat Empire

AT SOME POINT YOU HAVE TO ACCEPT THAT EVERYONE, some time or another, is a fraud. Sometimes it's a little, harmless lie created to get you out of a sticky spot, sometimes a lie born out of fear or desperation or dissatisfaction with life the way it is. Wherever it comes from, it's a lie. I told lots of lies after that flower bloomed and it was those lies that dragged me back into the world, still sad, still hollow, but back with a chance to find my sparkle again.

I told myself I was okay – lie. I told myself I had nothing to be ashamed of – lie. I told myself I was stronger than this and that I had a whole life to look forward to – lie.

Then I started to lie to others. I resumed giving motivational speeches at schools, forcing my mind to focus on the gifts I had received from my swimming career, making myself look at a future without swimming in a positive light, telling those young students that they could achieve anything because I had. I hoped that the more I said it, the more I would believe it. It was the only strategy I knew. But when I got home and Ben was there beside me, the lies tumbled like an angry child's building blocks. It was too hard to lie to him. And he kept holding me, wondering where that invincible, driven, passionate woman he had fallen in love with had gone.

I knew that if I was going to get out of this hole I would have to do two things: leave Adelaide, the city that held nothing but silence for me anymore; and I would have to stare my loss square in the face. I had to go to Sydney for the Games. Masochistic, perhaps, but I lied and said it would be therapeutic.

* * *

On the 14th of July 2000, Ben and I picked up my family from Adelaide Airport. The following morning Ben's family arrived, and at 8.25am on the 15th of July, I stood on my street corner, dressed in white shorts and a long-sleeved white top while the footpaths pulsed with excited crowds. The sun shone a glorious winter morning, making my nose tingle with warmth in the cool air. People had set up their barbeques on their front lawns, breakfast bacon and eggs crackled amid the chinking of champagne glasses. Children clambered to see the torch I was given by a round policeman astride his gleaming blue Harley Davidson.

The children's jostling and shoving and cries of, "I was there first! Mu-u-u-um, he pushed in!" made me expand. I was standing at the centre of something so much greater than myself and instinct told me the moment had to be shared with the little ones at the beginning of their journey. A boy of about five reached up tentatively to touch the shiny blue and white torch and I caught his eye.

"You want to hold it?" I asked and his mouth gaped as he held his breath. I placed the Olympic torch in his hands and he glowed, reverently passed it to the next child who also fell silent, then exploded with an inexplicable buzz as soon as the torch had passed to the next little pair of hands. The jostling intensified and parents called, "Amy, you be careful with that! Oh God, don't let her drop it!"

Ben stood back from the crowd with the hint of a tear glistening in the corner of his tired eyes. The morning of the 15th of July was the first time he had seen me smile in over two months. Really smile. No lies.

"Okay, everyone back behind the barriers, thanks. Grab your torch, Ma'am, 'cause here she comes!" As they scuttled back, necks craning as far as they would go, a convoy of bikes, cars and buses rumbled towards us.

I squeezed my escort runner's hand. She was nervous. I breathed in the anticipation and bowed my torch to meet the man who carried the flame. He lowered his torch, the flame burning unmistakably in his chest, and he exhaled, "She's all yours."

What is it about the flame? It was like being lifted by a force beyond this world. I felt that if I jumped at that moment I would fly. The road disappeared under my feet and the crowds were a long way away, cheering and waving in uninhibited joy. That flame had consumed me for so many years, my quest to capture it had destroyed me, but in that moment, it really was all worthwhile. No lie.

The fire sang as I jogged and smiled and waved, in a dream:

"I am the light that calls the brave. I am their initiation fire. I am warmth and their destruction. I am the Spirit of the warrior's path."

As the next runner held her torch high, as I bowed mine down to kiss hers, my part in the relay over in a flash, the flame winked goodbye and whispered, "Did you notice?"

"Notice what?" I wondered, aching to be able to hold on to that light just a little longer.

"I shine brightest when I'm shared."

* * *

Our time in Adelaide drew to a close quickly. Ben was granted a job transfer, after explaining to his boss that I couldn't stay in Adelaide. I don't think I'll ever really know how hard that was for him. He loved his work, he'd set up a life in South Australia because I had asked him to, and now I asked him to undo it all again, for me. He did, without complaining, if it meant that he would get his fiery Nadine back.

I found work tutoring primary school English and mathematics in an attempt to do something 'worthwhile'. I continued my studies, desperate to finally finish my degree and get into the real world to which my peers had disappeared years before. I felt like I'd missed the train to the Promised Land. They had all partied through uni together, travelled together, found jobs, lived with flatmates. I had swum. And now that I was finally back on campus, I was effectively a mature-age student. Again I didn't fit in. I trudged through my studies, lying to myself that once I got into working, I'd feel the buzz of inspiration I had once felt in a classroom.

Truth was I was uninspired, full stop. My happy face had become my permanent façade and Ben was not fooled by it. He could see the black in my eyes. I couldn't survive without my mask and he was still waiting for the old me to spring from the ashes. His patience was rapidly fading. Mine was rapidly fading also but as long as I had no idea how to find satisfaction in a world without water, the new Nadine, complete with happy face, was here to stay.

I had thought about going to counselling, but psychologists had never done me any good. I considered medication, but I didn't trust doctors. I occasionally talked to my friends – people who had also felt the inertia of competitive sport and who now found themselves floating in a world without gravity, people like Jade. They offered comfort and understanding, but all their words of wisdom and kindness seemed little more than stars obscured by storm clouds. I was sure their patience was wearing thin as well. It was just swimming, after all, and now I could really live, so what was I whinging about?

The funny thing with lies is that if you tell them often enough, you start to believe them. Gradually, my lies gave way to half-truths. When people asked how I was enjoying life free from the demanding regimen of training, I'd tell them, "I love not having to get up in the morning, not having to worry about everything that goes in my mouth… yeah, it's good!" but I'd leave out the parts about hating the soft, podgy blimp I was becoming, missing the sense of purpose and drive, missing the friendships, the adrenalin rush of competing, the indescribable high of winning, the ability to get up a flight of stairs without puffing, the reason to get out of bed at all. Nobody needed to know all that.

They'd ask, "So what are your plans?"

And I'd say, "I'm really looking forward to finishing my degree and getting into a classroom, enjoying actually earning a regular income, and you know, just relaxing a bit."

They'd nod in agreement – it seemed a solid plan – but I'd leave out the parts about not really knowing where I was going or why, not actually being certain that I was capable of holding down a regular job because I kept suffering from bouts of what I could only describe as Chronic Fatigue despair. I didn't mention that I was unsure whether I even wanted to teach and that the idea of an average life bored me, while the thought of trying to find a passion made me tired. Nobody needed to hear that kind of melodrama.

A couple of weeks before the Games were due to start, I got the shot up the backside I'd been waiting for. It sent adrenalin pumping and made my heart race again. A volunteer position, 'International Federation Liaison Officer' for aquatic sports during the Olympic Games, had become vacant. The job was to 'do whatever the International Federation (FINA) members need you to do to ensure an outstanding Olympic experience for all their delegates'. Did I want it?

I didn't allow myself time to think for fear the miserable voice in my head would convince me that I couldn't do it. Yes, this was the chance to stare my loss in the face I'd been looking for.

I'd be at the Games, at the pool, in the stands for every aquatic session. I'd be there, watching with the VIPs. I'd be on show, in the belly of the beast and I was thrillingly terrified.

36.

"Got a bowling ball in my stomach, got a desert in my mouth"

– *"Crucify"*, Tori Amos

Sydney Olympic Park is a beautiful place when it's empty. The quiet swirls in the same way as the water's musical embrace. Anticipation, like the heavy calm that descends before the first thunderclap of a summer storm, sighed in the colossal spectator stands. Each day revealed another layer of adornment as the precinct was dressed for its gala performance on the world stage. I cried – no, sobbed – one night as I walked along the empty boulevard to the car I'd been given for the duration of the Games. The night was warm, the fairy lights in the trees danced and swirling laser images of the Olympic rings spun on the pavement making the road look like a river of dreams. They weren't bitter tears. For the first time I almost felt appreciation for what I was part of. They were warm tears pouring into my smile. I liked those quiet days of preparation.

But then, a couple of days later, the swimming teams arrived on pool deck and I ran in the opposite direction. I choked and hid until Don Talbot spotted me. As I winced, he reached out for a hug, something I'd never seen him do, and I wondered where his Big Bad Wolf reputation had ever come from. He was kind and warm and he knew what being here meant to me. God how I wanted to swim! How I wanted to show him that his belief in me had not been misguided, that I could do all the great things he thought I could, we thought I could.

Some of the swimmers rushed to say 'hi'. Some turned, busy and focused on getting their cap on right, and I wasn't hurt. It was a strange, mixed up kind of sensation. I was overwhelmed by how much I missed some of them, and I felt like I was watching my life from the wrong side of a glass door to which no one had the key.

I snivelled into my champagne as we watched the Opening Ceremony from my parents' lounge room, glad that I'd returned the free ticket I had been offered. Sitting three rows from the front as the Australians marched by would have killed me. Collie was working that night, at the Stamford Hotel in North Ryde, and she had to excuse herself from the front desk as the big screen in the foyer announced 'Australia'. How could she explain to guests that she wanted her sister to be marching that track so badly? That we had all wanted it and now it was really gone?

When the women's 200m Breaststroke finally came up on the program, I thought I had prepared myself enough to be able to watch, but it was the longest four laps of Breaststroke I had ever seen. I gritted my teeth, my fists clenched, and I couldn't move from my position behind one of Chelsea Clinton's giant bodyguards. The Australians didn't fare well. Their times were slow overall and it felt like a punch in the guts. I hid in the ladies' toilet and silently wept for what might have, could have, should have been mine, and I realised that I was truly sick to death of crying like a petulant baby denied the right to play with the big kids.

When I finally managed to slap myself into consciousness, give myself a firm talking to and whip myself into shape, I emerged, shoulders back, head high, happy face on. But Cornel, the head of the Federation, whom I had been working with for the past two weeks, noticed my bloodshot eyes and with a paternal fury burst, "What's wrong! Who did this to you? Where can I find them? I will fix it!"

"No one did anything, Cornel," I sighed.

"Tell me, I will hit them! Who made you upset?"

Cornel was about five foot four inches but, like a bull-terrier, he had a fiery temper that made the thought of him beating anyone up a little less absurd than his appearance suggested.

"I'm just a bit sad. That was my event a little while ago."

"Oh..." he said, with genuine sympathy. "It is not easy... but you are so beautiful! I am glad you were not swimming because then I would not have you working with me!" He grinned and laughed, "That is good, yes?!"

"Yes, it is good," I smiled at his stilted English and his enthusiasm as he turned to an unsuspecting passer-by to declare, "You see this beautiful lady? She can do anything! She is wonderful!"

All I could do was shake my head and laugh. Perhaps it really was that simple.

From that night on, my Olympics were beautiful. I watched Cathy Freeman carry the nation to a gold medal in the 400m as Maurice Green's parents beside me cheered her on. Ben and I sang 'Waltzing Matilda' during half time at the Women's Hockey medal games, with a strangely patriotic man in the crowd leading us all in the chorus. He turned out to be John Williamson, which explained his gusto. I saw the vicious kicks and jabs of the water polo from below pool deck, and danced a celebration when the women won their gold. And when it all came to a close, Ben and I sat with four others on the roof of the Sydney International Aquatic Centre, watching the fireworks explode all around us, listening to the muffled hubbub coming from the luminous grand stadium. As the sparks rained over our heads, everything felt calm, everything felt good and I was sure we could finally move forward.

The Games were over. But so was the buzz.

I had been at home there, no matter how removed from the action I felt. Now it would be no more and I still had to find a new direction. I threw myself completely into studies and a new career in marketing, but I always, always, always kept a safety net close at hand because, behind my bravado, I was still afraid. I worked at the university where my mum and dad both worked and I knew most of the people there. I lived with Ben in my parents' house and I stayed close to home in every way.

There were more good days than bad, but always a cycle of manic activity was followed by a blinding crash that had me hopeless and helpless, unable to explain the darkness in my soul. I did all the things I wanted to do but I was never satisfied. I went wakeboarding every weekend on the boat Ben and I had bought with two other close friends. I loved the river, the sunshine, the thrill of going fast and risking injury just because I could, but still I berated myself for not being able to master the tricks as quickly as the boys. I excelled in my work and studies, but I was never proud of my achievements. I continued to give speeches, but I didn't feel the message anymore. I still cringed when people exclaimed, "You were sixth in the world! That's amazing!"

And all the photographs and memorabilia that Ben had so lovingly framed and labelled still lay, gathering cobwebs and filth under the bed. I couldn't bear to look at them and they became a symbol of my swimming life in its entirety: hidden under the bed, never to be looked at again. If I was going to lead a new life, it would be completely new; at least I'd pretend it was. And I'd never speak with black and white photographs again.

I smiled and laughed and drowned myself in Ben's life. His friends were my friends, his interests were mine, his joy was my joy and I liked that I could 'repay' the love and support he'd given me. The heaviness that lurked, always just below the surface, simply became part of my personality, not worthy of any more consideration than a fiery temper or the inexplicable workings of a female mind. Well, most of the time, anyway.

37.

"I'm pretending, see, to be strong and free from my dependency"

– *"Warped"*, Red Hot Chili Peppers

TRYING TO UNDO THE PROGRAMMING OF SO MANY YEARS is tough: the eternal search for perfection; the ultimate high; the leanest body; the most impeccable work ethic; the impenetrable force of self-discipline; the regimen; the self-analysis and criticism; the vision; the mission; the drive. It's hard to learn how to be kind to yourself when you've been a taskmaster with a whip and a reprimand all your life. It's hard to be satisfied and soft and average and happy with small pleasures – hard to be balanced. But I tried.

After we moved out of my parents' house and into our own little one-bedroom garden flat in East Ryde, Ben and I had a good life, but our relationship had changed when swimming left. We still laughed and smiled and enjoyed each other, but something had broken during my night. There was nothing I could define, nothing I could say was wrong, but something had shifted. We still talked, we still shared adventures, but a level of nearness had been erased, and I knew I was responsible. I had blocked him out, had crushed him with my sadness. But now it was his turn to find his passion and my turn to support him.

But I didn't realise I'd have to make a choice.

An opportunity arose for him to pursue a career he'd fantasised about in moments when he allowed himself to dream. I hadn't seen him sparkle that way since swimming left. He had found a black and white photograph of his own, and it whispered to him, challenging him to take a risk, give everything for a dream. He was hesitant, but I could see the sparks flying through his system. I recognised his frightened smile of knowing that this was his Olympics. I knew that power. And he was asking my opinion, my permission to throw himself in completely. Would I be okay if he followed his flame wherever it led?

I've never really understood what happened that night. He asked me if he should go for it, but his soul was already on the way. I said 'yes' with complete joy for him, and complete knowing that I could never go all the way down that road with him. We both knew, I think, but we both pretended that I would be the perfect support, as he had been for me.

He was made for his new career, but he never really talked much about it. I guess he couldn't. It was all top-secret. He came home late and sometimes didn't come home at all and I was afraid he'd been hurt. Eventually he'd call me and say, "I'm going to be away for a while…" but he'd never say where, for how long or why. When he did come home he was tired, and he still took calls in the middle of the night. The job never went away. But that he loved it and got a real sense of satisfaction from it was clear from the first day.

The cracks began to show. I was annoyed at how dependent on him I'd become. Now that his world revolved more around his career than it ever had, now that I was spending increasing periods alone, the silence returned and I needed him. I was weak on my own. My happiness depended on him, but I knew he would never forgive me if I asked him to be my crutch again. I lashed out more and more. I tried to be pleased that he'd found his passion and I truly did love the shine in his eyes when he had a success that he could talk about, but I still felt like a jilted lover. All I could do was watch as he strode in the direction of his dream, while I sat, again on the wrong side of a locked door, face pressed against the glass and whimpering like a new pup left outside for the night.

* * *

Another year passed and where I had once ached when he was away, I now quite enjoyed my time alone. Where I had once clung to him when he returned, I now bristled at the invasion of my space and the disruption to my routine. We had little to say to each other and I became increasingly aware that I had lost myself in him, and now with the time alone, I was being tempted to find me again, on my own. He had found his direction and it was time for me to find mine.

It was an awful day. We had both seen it coming, like cartoon characters who have run off a cliff and have that moment suspended midair, running in the realisation that they are about to fall. He had all his friends over for a barbecue and we had argued just before they arrived, but we both applied the smiles of welcoming hosts. And when the party was well underway, when the music was playing, barbecue eaten, and drinks flowing, we found a quiet space to say what had not yet been spoken.

We looked at each other in silence, for a long time, the love and pain I felt reflected in his eyes. I hadn't been so overwhelmingly in love with him for years, and I began to panic. Was it really too late? He spoke first.

"Is this what I think it is?"

"I think so," I said as tears filled my eyes in response to his trembling hand in mine.

"Yeah," he sighed, "I think so, too."

"I love you so much, but... I don't know..."

"I know. I love you, too. It's just..."

We nodded and held each other and cried for a long, long time.

It was October and the lorikeets that Ben had fed ever since we had moved into our little place in East Ryde three years before were squawking for food. We sat on the bed and divided our life – 'I want the couch, do you want the bed?' 'What about the sound system?' 'And the fish?' 'The TV and the washing machine?' 'What about the car loan? It's in both our names...'

It was surreal. We wept and laughed and cursed and ached and we knew it was the only way. We could not let 7½ years of togetherness disintegrate into bitter resentment. It had to be now, when there was enough love to know how to be selfless, to know that staying would be clipping each other's wings. But it made no sense.

Sometimes the heart speaks louder than the mind. 7½ years. Gone.

I went to Perth for a week with Jade. She was the beautiful, philosophic friend she'd always been and I was comforted that our friendship had sustained diverging paths. I wondered if it was the fact that she'd found a way to retire from the chlorine with a little joy in her heart. She'd had so much fun in the US and then made the deliberate choice to move on with her life, while I had reacted in despair and still suffered. She was also working too hard, but perhaps that was just a feature of being part of the corporate world. She had plenty of friends and parties to go to and projects that she was keenly pursuing and I wondered if, maybe, I had done the wrong thing by leaving my element so quickly. Maybe that's why I was leaving everything else in my life with equal speed and finality. She was such a comfortable friend to be around and she seemed so sure of her future that I could not help but believe her when she told me I would be okay.

I spent too much money on frivolous things while I was in Perth, I cried and wondered and bargained with God on the beaches of Rottnest Island. I listened to music and went to the beautician and bought a new bikini and a spray tan… And a week later, when I arrived back in Sydney at 11.45pm, in the rain, not a soul around, I wept for the joy that would never be mine again. He was everywhere, but I could never touch him again. I could smell him in my car, but I'd never be wrapped in that warmth again. The songs I heard were all his, every motorbike was him coming to take me back to a time when we were lost in the joy of each other. But he'd never be mine again.

I crept into my parents' spare room long after midnight and prayed that the morning would not come. I didn't want to have to stand on my own.

38.

"There's a darkness deep in my soul"

– *"Put Your Lights On"*, Santana

I LOST IT.

At 27 years old, I drank and partied like a rebellious teen by night, and I worked myself into a stupor by day.

I moved in with a colleague from Macquarie University and went out some more.

I smoked cigars and swore, had flings, broke hearts and had mine broken.

I went on fitness kicks that lasted two, maybe three weeks at a time, each time ending in self destruction and as the cycles got shorter and shorter, I'd work like a maniac and end up in a heap to which I responded by getting drunk. I was having fun and I didn't need anyone.

But the words of Emily Dickinson followed me wherever I went:

One need not be a chamber to be haunted;
one need not be a house;
the brain has corridors surpassing material place.

She knew.

I flew high and crashed to the depths of inexplicable despair, searching furtively for the next way to be up. My life became like a series of flashes, as though something out of my control kept turning the lights on and off and on and off and on and off...

* * *

Over those 18 months from October 2003, when my life with Ben ended and my world spun out of control, my aunt Marianne died of a brain tumour, my mother nursing her at home until her last day; Mutti died in the same room in my parents' house, also after four months of my mum nursing her; Rob Henderson, my first and truest sponsor, died in a plane crash with his daughter Jackie; and I remained stoic, a pillar for everybody to lean on as I ignored the pathetic little girl that resided in me, begging only for the kind of love and attention I lavished on everyone else.

I changed career, looking for a path that would make me feel as though I was doing something meaningful. I began teaching and found a world of students on whom to dote, in whom I could find joy and purpose.

I lost myself in working for them. My every moment revolved around them, my dedication as complete as it had been in the pool, but it was unsustainable. They were my priority and I relished feeling like the overworked, under-appreciated school mistress – it gave me an excuse to have bouts of misery and I no longer had to blame the swimming – an excuse that had long ago worn thin. I could run off the rails, I could lash out and I could piously cite my dedication to the future as the cause of my distress. But it didn't last, because, while I loved my students, was patient and gentle and nurturing with them, the neglected little girl in me began to scream.

I had managed to sustain my manic, fear-driven life for almost six years after my black and white photograph had been destroyed and it had to eventually stop – one way or another.

39.

"While I'm so afraid to fail so I won't even try, well how can I say I'm alive"
 – *"Life for Rent"*, Dido

LOOKING BACK, THE PATTERNS ARE SO CLEAR. I struggled with the manic cycle of depression for many years and it took a long time to wade though the mire. I think I've finally found a place where I can feel the sun, but I don't have that old, urgent need to stand on its surface. I can strive but I don't have to be perfect. I've finally hung my swimming pictures on the wall. It was Michael, my husband, who forced me to acknowledge that I was not coping on my own, that I needed help and that it was time to accept it. And it was the birth of our son, Leo, that finally put it all into perspective.

Michael met me at the peak of my craziness and for some reason, he was intrigued. A friend of my flatmate's, he visited from time to time for over 12 months before I really noticed him – his eyes as blue as the water I loved and framed with thick charcoal lashes; his tall, lean physique and strong, gnarled hands; his thick, prominent nose above a John Travolta smile that instantly transformed the snarl that appeared when he concentrated. He was intense in every way – energy, interest in people and the world around him, desire to know and understand – to me it was exhilarating; to others, exhausting.

When my flatmate and I moved to Manly, Mick came for a celebratory, post-move drink and we spent that one night drinking and dancing and talking... loudly. We took the long walk home along Manly Beach and his honesty disarmed me completely. I had never met anyone so at peace with themselves that they were unashamed to talk about things that really mattered. He cried about his father whose death still shook him, he told me about his kickboxing days and the friends he missed, he talked about his job at the Shell Oil refinery in Sydney and his moves around the country with his work – the good ones and the stuff-ups. He talked about his large family with the kind of warmth I felt for mine and his relaxed enthusiasm for life made me feel calmer, more myself than I had been for years. We talked until the dawn was heralded by a cool breeze, but I felt so very warm.

By April, only three months after that first night, I knew he was the man I would marry and his eyes said the same to me. In June, we moved in together and he began to see the crazed work-a-holic, the irrational, emotional roller-coaster, the highly-strung, self-destructive perfectionist I was, and it was too hard for him to simply watch the cycles.

As a tradesman, Mick sees something that doesn't work and fixes it. If it is a challenge to fix, there's a greater sense of satisfaction when he figures it out. I was a problem. I short-circuited at fairly random moments. While his instinct told him why I was snapping, he could not implement the fix for me and it drove him crazy. He wanted to talk me through my down times, he wanted to tell me what to do, but like a teenager lashing out at authority of any kind, I snarled at him and scorned his idea that I should see the psychologist who had given him so much help during his dark times. I didn't want his help because that would mean I was a failure on my own, and I never wanted to need anyone the way I had needed Ben, the way Sean had said I needed other people in my life. I wanted to be stronger than that.

But I underestimated his persistence. I underestimated his resilience and his absolute dedication to us. Mick was a talker, and when the message didn't get through the first time, he simply said it again, then again, then louder and louder again. Whenever I crashed, he talked and finally, after many months, I agreed to see his psychologist – partly to shut him up and partly for a whole new reason: I wanted to write, but I didn't want to write a bitter, angry sob story. I wanted to find the truth of my swimming experience, a truth I knew was there, but was having trouble finding on my own.

January 2006.
>A new year, a new project and a fresh approach.
>And it was with unattached, professional help, at long last, that the lights switched on, one tiny flickering bulb at a time.
>And this time they stayed on.

40.

"No longer is my cup half empty 'cause there you are"
 – *"Peaches and Cream"*, John Butler Trio

I WENT IN, GUNS A-BLAZING: "I've never had any luck with psychologists, so don't take it personally, but I'm not expecting much."

She laughed with warmth, "That's good."

"They all tell me I'm too self-aware already and I already know what the problems are. I know where all my destructive patterns come from. I can see them coming a mile off but I can't stop them and I just can't break out of the cycle and psychologists usually say they can't help because I'm already aware of the issues and..." I could have gone on forever with that defensive spiel. I was terrified that this last resort would prove that I was a permanently damaged relic from the swimming world and that I was doomed to a life of catastrophic ups and downs.

"Well, that's lucky, because I'm interested in fixing those destructive patterns. I don't really care where they came from."

That shut me up.

It started as eight sessions, developed to 'a few more' and ended up almost every week for 18 months. Coralie guided me though forests and mists and wild, raging seas; I have seen myself as a tiny child, hurt and scared; I have revisited people who hurt me and have let go of the pain; I have rejoiced in the freedom of forgiveness and understanding and I have cried with regret and anger; but none of it was as dark and lonely and hopelessly forlorn as I was for a week in March, 2007. I cried continuously for five days and I had nothing left. Helpless, I took three Panadine to knock out the pounding in my brain and crawled under the covers and prayed for the storm to pass.

Have you ever had a dream so real, so powerful that it changes your view of the world? In my fitful Panadine sleep, I dreamed:

A wretched, rotting creature shrieks. It's the sound of death. The creature's skeleton glows where its putrid claws have stripped the grey flesh away. Its eyes are fire and its rancid breath drowns me. It rushes at me, bringing its empty skull right to my face and I can see the other side of the room through its decomposing gullet. The sound pierces my core and I try to get away but at every turn it is there, pulling greasy clumps of hair from its half eaten scalp, waving them under my nose. I want to vomit, I want to run, but it dances around me, possessed and screaming the sorrows and pains of the whole world.

My only chance is to stand still and wait for this filthy demon to exhaust itself, and as I watch, breathlessly praying for it to go, I see something familiar in its shape, something haunting in its cries. I recognise that pain. I understand that torture and it lashes out at me with black claws in response to my thoughts. She knows I see her. I know her name and she cowers, whimpering and spent in the corner of that nondescript room; rocking her skeletal frame like a crazed inmate in hell's own prison.

I walk to her and she spits fire from her blazing eyes. I stoop to pick her up and she shrieks again, but I restrain her and she becomes weak – a reeking bundle of bones.

I carry her to a waterfall and as we sit under its spray a small Oriental man, with a pointed hat and beard white with wisdom, approaches with a lantern in his hand. He raises the lamp to the creature's face. She screeches and writhes with untameable fury and a thick black vapour pours from her mouth. It flies skyward where an angel, brilliant, with wings of steel and a sword of silver, slashes that devil from the sky and it dissolves into oblivion.

The creature's flesh returns and the wise old man repeats the ritual. Again she screams and again the angel cleaves the blackness with his faultless sword. She has regained her pallor, but the hatred still burns in her eyes. A third time the light shines on her, a third time she cries and a third time the angel destroys the darkness.

The fire leaves her face. She smiles, whole again.

In my own voice she says, "Thank you."

In my own voice I say, "I am sorry."

In my own voice she says, "I know."

And we embrace – young Wobbles and Nadine. We merge. She is me, no longer tortured, no longer fighting to be heard.

The wise man orders each part of my body to let go of the pain, he bathes me in his light and he places an amulet with three stones around my neck. "For courage," he says.

He holds his lantern high, revealing a path through the thick forest, a path leading to a brilliant light, and he says, "Now go, my warrior. Go and be free."

I wake and feel the weightlessness of freedom.

Breakthrough.

41.

"Flesh and blood and skin and bone, all you see is what you're shown"

– *"Flesh and Blood"*, The Waifs

MY FAMILY NEVER REALLY TALKED ABOUT IT, the awkward subject that cut too deep to discuss openly. I knew they hurt as much as I did after my Olympic dream died, and I felt guilty for dragging them through it. I didn't want to discuss it, so they never brought it up; but I knew they hurt, and they worried.

Then I started writing. And I started talking. And healing. Opening the doors on how I had experienced my swimming career allowed so much pain to dissolve into understanding. I wanted my family to feel the same kind of freedom I had found in releasing the bitterness, the sadness and anger over how it all ended. So I brought it up. I asked them to write to me; to tell me how they felt then, how they feel now.

They found it hard. I had to wait a few weeks before they had independently gathered their thoughts, but when the letters arrived, I knew they were the real thing: genuine, honest and more revealing than any conversation laden with the passion of the moment.

* * *

Mum wrote:

My mouse,

On that hectic Saturday morning, so many years ago, without warning, you planted yourself before me and the world stopped as you declared that you would compete for Australia. Your solemness was funny – nature hadn't blessed you with an athlete's body or great coordination. But, over time, your dedication to the tough regime convinced us that you would make it. Your resolve demanded absolute commitment from us and it was never questioned. That's what we did. Our little girl had a dream and parents do everything in their power to make it happen. You will understand that kind of commitment when your children want to chase dreams.

The rollercoaster of successes and mishaps kept us all on our toes and gradually sent us prematurely grey. We lived and breathed every part of your swimming journey with you, sometimes to the puzzlement of family and friends, but you already know that. Nothing could have prepared me for that night, that one breathless moment at the 2000 Olympic Trials when your dream turned to dust.

As a mother, what could I do to cushion the blow? You looked as though your purpose had been removed, your identity lost. What could I do to make you better? What could I say to remind you that what you had said all along – that 'the journey counts, not the destination' – still held truth? I was angry. To my mind, your years of dedication should have ended differently, with a 'thanks for playing' medal of any colour. It should have ended in any way other than that jarring exclusion! And yet, part of me sighed with a long-awaited 'Thank God it's over'. No more watching you hurt yourself. An unjust, dissatisfying release.

Standing by helplessly during the long aftermath did nothing to dispel the ball of bitterness in my gut; to know how close you had come to that pinnacle, to know that time and time again it had been foiled by mismanagement and lack of consideration by opinionated 'others'. You deeply resented us for wanting to, trying to help; you weren't a child anymore. For the longest time I felt that the swimming world had taken my cheeky daughter and left a shell I couldn't communicate with. I didn't know you anymore. You were reckless, defensive, aloof. Your eyes were lifeless. Had anyone asked me whether I would recommend elite sport for children of any age, I would have screamed, NO! NO! and NO! again!

It is since you started seeing your psychologist that you've gradually regained your sense of humour, your sparkle. Now that the swimming world is beginning to wake up to training methods that don't rely on masochistic abuse of young bodies for split-second gains; training methods that were considered ignorant and naive by so many of the establishment while you and Papa were using them, I feel vindicated. I still believe that your true potential was never reached through no fault of your own. At the same time, your pure childhood dream was reached and exceeded, the years of striving have paid handsome dividends in the end, and for that I am thankful.

Finally, I feel enormous gratitude for your resolve to unravel the internal chaotic tangle that following your dream had left within you, and that could have caused you lifelong depression. It is the one thing that brought true healing to me and for that, I thank you.

I love you.

Mum

I cried. I had never really grasped that the pain she felt was my pain. Somewhere in my mind I had always believed that she was hurt because I'd fallen short; upset for me, yes, but upset for my failure, not my pain. I finally understood her nagging, her worry and her bitter outbursts every time swimming had been brought up over the years after I retired. I finally knew that, in the end, all she ever cared about was my happiness, and it made me warm.

* * *

Dad wrote:

Naddi,

Watching you in the last couple days before your 200m Breaststroke final, we knew: a tired, aching body; a slow, disappointing heat swim; a sluggish warm-up; and then your farewell kiss to the camera… It was a sinking feeling. You had a jerk in your stroke. You know the one you always had when you were tired and forcing the rhythm. You were trying to be so brave, so strong. But we all knew what was coming, even though we didn't want to believe it would finish like that.

It's hard to remember what I thought straight away, but I know I still analysed the race... old habits... If it makes any difference, you were on target until the last 50 where the flu took hold of you. Still, going over the splits felt pointless at the time. My mind was full of 'What are we going to say to her? She will not go on with swimming (can't blame her!). How will she take it (stupid question!)? What will happen now?'

At the same time, though, we'd had enough of that rollercoaster ride. It's not easy to sit on the sidelines and get ready for damage-control. It was time to move on with all our lives, our 'normal' lives. We were tired, Naddi, all of us.

You can be so stubborn. For a long, long time you would not be convinced by me or anyone else that there was anything good about what you had achieved. But I honestly believed, and still do, that your swimming destiny was completely fulfilled. You were so dark that I eventually just stopped trying to say it. I couldn't get to the bottom of what was happening to you. I could understand that you'd be disappointed; of course there could have been Olympic gold medals, superstardom and financial rewards, but they never figured in your original dream, in your 'little girl dream'. Everything you achieved beyond becoming an Olympian, to me, was a bonus. So what could I say?

It strikes me even now, every time I catch a glimpse of a swimming carnival: all those children, hundreds of thousands of them across Australia alone. How many more around the globe? You were sixth in the world. You represented Australia for four years, captained the Australian team. I am so proud of you! And if I had to name any regrets, or frustrations rather, it would only be that we never found a way to make that Backstroke of yours more efficient. I think you had the potential to be the best in the world in the 400m IM, even with only a 'decent' Backstroke, and you know how much I love that event!

Remember always that you did what you set out to do, and that is all anyone can ever ask.

Your Papa

He always was positive, seeing the blessings rather than the injustice. I knew he and Mum had arguments over their different views. He thought she was being overly emotional even though he could see her point. She thought he was being cold, even though she could see his point. But each in their own way felt the effects of my sadness and each was proud of me and so grateful for what I had achieved. I knew I was truly loved and I thanked God for that.

* * *

Collie wrote:
It's funny you know, I thought I was over it, I would have sworn I was, but then you asked me to write this! At first, I guess I saw the swimming as your struggle. It was your choice, a goal you set for yourself. I didn't think of it as something that could affect me, but how wrong I was!

When I think of your career, the first thing I remember is the overwhelming moment in the stands, at the final of the Olympic Trials for Atlanta '96, where no one and nothing mattered to me but you in the pool. My sister. I knew if I just yelled and whistled that little bit louder, I could will you to win! I've never felt more connected to another soul than in that moment. For me, that was it. That was where your dream, my dream for you, came true. I think that's when I realised that, in truth, I had followed your dream all my life. You were the person I felt I should strive to be. You were so strong and disciplined, so brave and tough and I envied you for those traits. I had zero discipline, the toughness of a slug and strength enough only to rebel behind our parents' backs! I wished I could be like you, so it was natural that your dream was mine also.

But the sadness that came in 2000 made me realise how much you'd missed out on. A life like yours was not to be envied. Growing up is hard at the best of times, and judging from what you've been through, elite sport forces you to do it twice. Your life had been put off in the pursuit of something more, something bigger and better, and suddenly things changed. You became the weak, frightened, lost little girl and, suddenly, I seemed to know more about life than you did. And it felt all wrong.

While I enjoyed watching you grow up as an athlete, even if I did get sick of living in the shadow at times, I've enjoyed watching you grow up as an 'average' so much more! I'll never forget taking you out and getting drunk with you for the first time. You were 23 and so uncool! I think it was that night that I finally felt on par with the 'awesome goddess of the pool' for the first time!

I don't watch the swimming now. I still turn sour when I see those prepubescent stick figures gliding through the water. I know it's not their fault, and I know they too will grow (in all directions), and make it or not. I think the bitterness comes from discovering, in hindsight, the intense strain that being driven had on you. Elite sport has taken on a new meaning since our journey together. It's a strange world, that world of ultra-competition, and it's one I choose to not be a part of. I don't miss it, I don't mourn it, but I don't regret it either. I think your career taught all of us a great deal about ourselves and each other.

It was a good trip in the end. It got us to where we are today, so I wouldn't change it. I do know that I'd support a child in a pursuit of a dream just like Mum and Dad did for both of us, but as for pushing or recommending that anyone follow their chosen sport to an elite level: I could NEVER force that upon anyone.

Nad, I love you. I'm proud to call you my sister. You have become such a beautiful being and you've finally found a balance that could never have been there during your time as a water baby. You made it in my eyes, and that's all that should matter!

XXX
Collie

I smiled. I finally understood what lay beneath their dedication to my black and white visions, what fostered their strength. As Collie so eloquently wrote, 'I've never felt more connected to another soul than in that moment'. It was that connection between souls. Love.

I was home and I was me and I was happy.

42.

"Don't you remember the famous men who had to fall to rise again"

– *"Pick Yourself Up"*, Diana Krall

TELLING THE STORY HAS FELT LIKE WHEN YOU SING your favourite tune over and over and over again. At first you feel the emotion deeply, it brings tears to your eyes every time and the pain is delicious, the way the lyrics pluck and jab at every corner of your heart. You have to feel it again... and again... and again. But eventually the meaning fades, you get sick of the tune and you cast it aside for a while. But then one day you stumble upon it, dusty in the corner and as soon as the melody strikes up you are flooded with the trill again.

I have given countless motivational speeches to high school students across two states. Working with young people is where I come alive. But for many years I sat in my car after convincing those fiery young faces to be strong, courageous, to fight for their passion, and I felt like a fraud peddling false hopes and certain doom. I would sometimes cry because my mind knew that what I was telling them was the truth; that it is better to strive for a future you hope for than to rot away in your own stagnant listlessness, but I couldn't feel it in my heart. Somehow the absence of a black and white image of my own, a loss of passion had left me no real hope at all.

It was at one of these speeches, at a Youth Leadership Forum in Sydney, that a young woman looked me in the eye and asked the questions I had been too afraid to ask myself.

"Okay, first question... over here," I opened the Q&A segment.

"Um, do you know Ian Thorpe?" she said, sheepishly. I wondered what it was about Thorpy that had all the young girls swooning.

"Yes, I do."

"Um, is he gay?" And what was the obsession with his sexuality?

"Should I care?" I quipped, a bit annoyed that Q&A had been degraded to this.

Everyone laughed. First point to me.

"Next question... yes?" As I made eye contact with another girl, I hoped this question would have a little more meat to it.

"Yeah, um, hi. I was just wondering, do you ever feel bitter that people like Susie O'Neill and Ian Thorpe get all this success and medals and records and stuff, but you worked just as hard as them and you got nothing? Like, do you ever think you deserved it as much as them and does that make you angry that you didn't get it?" She was nervous.

I was stunned. The audience was, too, their gasps audible, but I was on the spot and I could sense that this was my moment to either grasp credibility or to fall into clichés. I took my time.

"Wow, that's a tough question. Thank you," I started slowly. "I have to be honest and say yes, sometimes I do feel bitter and angry, as though I've been cheated out of something I just know should have been mine, but I don't resent their success. They are amazing athletes and they deserve admiration for that. But, more often, I am grateful for what I've lived through. You see, while people like Thorpy are heroic figures that we put up on pedestals, I think they are so extraordinary that they can become something far removed from how we see ourselves. We admire them, but we don't ever really dare to believe we can be like them. On the other hand, I think I'm one of you. I'm no different to anyone who has tried and failed and wondered whether it's worth trying again. I've made bad mistakes and fallen short and I know what it takes to get up and fight again... and again... and again... and again..."

The audience chuckled and I knew they were with me.

"...and the very fact that I never quite got that shining prize I worked so hard for is the very reason I am able to stand here and feel like one of you. There are so few people who can become legends in their field and for every legend there are hundreds of people like me, who get there, who taste the brilliance but never quite become it. But it's people like me who can really come back and say to the average Joe, 'I know what it's like to hurt. I know what it's like to struggle. I know what it's like to feel as though you are lost, what it's like to fall short. I know what it's like to be an ordinary person striving for the extraordinary'. You and me, we're the same, so you can trust me when I say it's worth it. And you can trust me when I say you can do it. You can taste the brilliance you dream of, and maybe, if you've got that something special, you can even become it."

Silence in the auditorium. They were beginning to believe, to know that it may be treacherous, terrifying at times, but that it would also be beautiful and rewarding and precious. They were thinking big, I could feel it.

"So, if you had the chance, would you do it again?" The courageous young woman became the voice of the group. A few of the crowd nodded in unison.

I wondered and flicked through my catalogue of memories, an album of black and white moments smiling from the past. I could see the faces – the Bens, the Jades, the Kates, the Ursulas, the Pauls, the Gregs and Glenns; the Seans, the Jesses and Megans – and I finally realised: there are no heroes in my story, there are no villains, only people who were striving, just like I was, to create their own idea of perfection. Sometimes their vision was the same as mine and we shared wonderful moments of synergy, of harmony. Other times their visions were different to mine and we clashed, each of us fierce with belief in our version of perfection. None of us right, none of us wrong, all of us trying to find our own best way to the top. Without any of them I would not be who I am today, and I thank them all for their role in my adventure. I can finally smile without pain, without malice, anger or judgment.

I finally answered, "Would I do it again? If I could know what I know now, I would do it all very differently. Hindsight and reflection teach you so much. But do it, I certainly would."

The girl was sill standing and asked, "So what are you going to do now?"

It felt good to know. "I'm going to learn how to sing a new song on a whole new adventure. I'll find a new set of people, some with similar visions to mine and some with ideas of perfection that challenge me. I'll glimpse their worlds and learn from them, and I'll wobble and fall and get up and try again, until I find my own best way, because I reckon that's what life is all about. And maybe I'll meet you there, on that road – wobbling and falling, laughing and crying and getting up and trying again, who knows…"

In the quiet times, I remember that girl and I think:
"Long live living, if living can be this."
– *"Miserere" The Cat Empire*

The Weekly Times, 13/11/96.
Photo by Ray Wood.

Other Prose @ IP

A Beginner's Guide to Dying in India, by JM Donellan
ISBN 9781921479304, AU$32.95

Willow Farrington Bites Back, by Rebecca Bloomer
ISBN 9781921479366, AU$24.95

The Hitchers of Oz, by Tom and Simon Sykes
ISBN 9781921479199, AU$32.95

Sacrifice, LR Saul
ISBN 9781921479168, AU$32.95

The World Cup Baby, by Euan McCabe
ISBN 9781921479205, AU$32.95

The Voyage of the Shuckenoor, by Erica Bell
ISBN 9781921479045, AU$32.95

Primary Instinct, by David P Reiter
ISBN 9781921479021, AU$30

Blood and Guts, by Gloria Burley
ISBN 9781921479069, AU$30

As If!, by Barry Levy
ISBN 9781876819804, AU$32

The Umbilical Word, by Darren Groth
ISBN 9781876819798, AU$30

For the latest from IP, please visit us online at
http://ipoz.biz/Store/Store.htm
or contact us by **phone/fax** on 61 7 3324 9319
or sales@ipoz.biz

www.ingramcontent.com/pod-product-compliance
Lightning Source LLC
Chambersburg PA
CBHW071423150426
43191CB00008B/1019